MEANING, CREATIV
THE PARTIAL INSCRUTABILI
OF THE HUMAN MIND

CSLI LECTURE NOTES
NUMBER 79

MEANING, CREATIVITY, AND THE PARTIAL INSCRUTABILITY OF THE HUMAN MIND

JULIUS M. MORAVCSIK

CSLI PUBLICATIONS
CENTER FOR THE STUDY OF
LANGUAGE AND INFORMATION
STANFORD, CALIFORNIA

Center for the Study of Language and Information
Leland Stanford Junior University
02 01 00 99 98 5 4 3 2 1

Library of Congress Cataloging-in-Publication Data

Moravcsik, J. M. E.
Meaning, creativity, and the partial inscrutability of the human mind /
Julius M. Moravcsik.
p. cm.–(CSLI lecture notes ; no. 79)
Includes bibliographical references.

ISBN: 1-57586-127-5 (hardcover : alk. paper).
ISBN: 1-57586-126-7 (pbk : alk. paper)

1. Language and languages–Philosophy. 2. Philosophy of mind. 3. Semantics.
I. Title. II. Series.
P106.M587 1998
401–dc21 98-13456
CIP

∞ The acid-free paper used in this book meets the minimum requirements of the American National Standard for Information Sciences – Permanence of Paper for Printed Library Materials, ANSI Z39.48-1984.

This book was designed and set in type by Tony Gee in Minion, a typeface designed by Robert Slimbach, and Trajan, drawn by Carol Twombly and based on the lettering of the inscription at the base of Trajan's Column, Rome, carved at the beginning of the second century AD. The picture of the eighteenth green of the Stanford Golf Course that appears on the front cover of the paperback edition was photographed by Maureen Burke. The cover was also designed by Tony Gee. The book was printed and bound in the United States of America.

CONTENTS

PREFACE

This book evolved out of my continuing to think about the theory of lexical meaning that I sketched in *Thought and Language*, the proposal that humans are essentially explanation-seeking and -forming animals rather than information-processing creatures, and the consequences of these themes for understanding human understanding. Underlying my thoughts about these matters is the claim that I developed in the years following the publication of my earlier book, that a natural language is not and should not be represented as a formal language in the sense of Tarski. This is hardly an original insight, since Tarski himself said this about the impact of his own work. But because this has been denied so often in recent times, I felt compelled to present my case for what is basically Tarski's insight. I combined it, then, with my views about explanation and understanding. The result is the general theory of cognition and language sketched in this book. This general theory leaves plenty of room for a modular approach to explanation and understanding. Four general factors, namely constituency, structure, function, and agency will be introduced as fundamental to explanations of all sorts. But within these general factors there is much room for different structures dealing with, language, physics, and so on, respectively.

The introduction gives my analysis of why philosophers still use semantic notions inherited from quite different enterprises for the analysis of natural language. The first two chapters are designed to vindicate Tarski's interpretation of his own work. The third and fourth chapters expand the views of lexical meaning and humans as "HOMO EXPLANANS" given in the earlier book. The last two chapters compare Chomsky's recent views on language and the mind with mine, with stress on the common elements and only secondarily on the differences, and then explore the basis on which one could construct an argument showing that the human understanding of human understanding must remain always partial.

This book is intended for the type of interdisciplinary audience that constitutes the Center for the Study of Language and Information research group, and made up the majority of earlier workshops on meaning and grammar that were held at Stanford University. These groups typically included philosophers, linguists, psycholinguists, and AI researchers. Within such groups there will be researchers who do not know too much about some neighboring field. We solve the problem by introducing here and there material elementary for the expert in the given field but helpful for the researcher from a neighboring field, at least to get started on learning relevant matters from, for example, logic, philosophy, or linguistics. This same approach is taken in this book. Such strategy requires patience on all sides. Thus in the earlier chapters there is material that may seem elementary to the logician or philosopher, and in the later chapters some material that is elementary for a linguist or artificial intelligence expert. I hope that the needed tolerance will be shown by all sides.

Many people have helped me to clarify my thoughts on these matters. I owe a great deal to Noam Chomsky both for stimulation and encouragement. I am also very grateful to Tom Wasow for having read a draft of this book and having made many helpful suggestions. In recent months I had the benefit of comparing notes with James Pustejovsky. I found the interaction very rewarding, and his work on lexical meaning not only congenial, but also very insightful. I gave much of the material of this book in a seminar at the University of Geneva. I wish to acknowledge gratefully Professor Kevin Mulligan's help.

The last two chapters benefited also from comments by my colleagues, Solomon Feferman and Grigori Mints. They are not responsible for any errors that remained in the book.

I presented this material in two seminars at Stanford, and I wish to acknowledge my indebtedness to the participants. In particular I owe a lot to Michael Fehling, Ron Textor, Peter Bauman, Tim Haeg, David Grover, Tony Pfaff, Stacy Friend, Brian Eppstein, and Ann Copestake.

These researchers clarified much of what I wanted to say. I am afraid that I have not always modified my views as much as some of them would have liked it, in this or that context.

Some of the material was also read by the groups of linguists in Wuppertal, and I want to thank Professor Gabriel Falkenberg for his help and useful comments.

Finally, I wish to thank Trudy Vizmanos for manuscript preparation. Without her help this work would never have seen completion.

INTRODUCTION

WHERE HAS THE PHILOSOPHY OF LANGUAGE GONE WRONG?

On a late fall afternoon I walked up to the eighteenth tee of the Stanford golf course, where at that time of the day one can see clearly across the Bay into San Francisco. As the sun set and the fog rolled in over the hills, I could hear players calling to each other, communicating with shortcuts acquired after years of companionship. I also saw a tablet in memory of a club member who died years ago who had loved that spot. In the distance I could see the library, containing thousands of written sentences, addressed to no particular audience or time. For a Martian the sound and written symbols would have presented simply a variety of sensory phenomena with no common perceptual denominator. To me this variety presented different uses of language. Such an interpretation required construing the phenomena as different manifestations of underlying abstract elements. This underlying abstract unity, giving sense to the surface chaos, is the miracle of language. It is so much a part of our everyday life that we have difficulty keeping in mind its miraculous nature. We also have difficulties ordering the abstract and concrete so as to have it present an appropriate subject of theoretical and empirical understanding. We use a variety of verbs to characterize the functioning of language. Language expresses, contains, transmits, is used, understood, and so on. Likewise, the speaker-hearer says, asserts, understands, uses to communicate. It is questionable whether one could relate all of these expressions and reconstruct on the basis of their uses a commonsense theory of language. It is more plausible to suppose that commonsense has no theory but rather a mere plethora of claims, intuitions, about language.

When we attempt to step back and gain some perspective of these phenomena we see that, just as in other sciences like physics or chemistry, the subject matter contains layers of abstraction. Particular actually occurring sounds are gathered under the concept of a sound in the phonetic alphabet of a language, certain sound combinations are construed as making up words and certain words as sentences. Thus in addition to the hierarchy of sound, word, sentence, we have the abstract dimensions of phonetic, syntactic, and semantic elements and organizations. Theories of language ought to deal with all of these items.

It is difficult to see this complexity and the level of abstraction at which language and language understanding must function, because language is so "close to us." This metaphor needs to be unpacked. Physical distance is not at issue. Our skin is "close to us," but we have no problems conceptualizing it, and make it the object of science. Nor is it enough to say that language is a "part of us." After all, so are our arms, legs, and lungs, and fortunately medicine has succeeded in interpreting these as objects of scientific theory. The closeness of language is best interpreted with reference to its relation to thought. We need not be committed either to the thesis that there can be no thought without language or to the thesis that languages mark great differences between modes of thinking, to maintain that there is an intricate interrelationship between thought and language. The developments of these are typically interrelated, and both are constituents of human cognitive functioning.

This account differs from claims that we must have difficulty conceptualizing language because we use language in studying language. After all, it is also true that we use physical objects to study physical objects, and this led to no mystery.

Language being close to us in the way suggested leads to our having difficulties establishing what needs to be explained, and what should count as explanatory structures. We never simply study a range of phenomena. With respect to our approach to any range of phenomena we must ask: What is to be taken for granted? What is problematic? and What should count as explanation? Different points of view will suggest different specifications of these ingredients. For example, some philosophers find the context-independent aspects of semantics most puzzling and in need of explanation, while others take the context-dependent as characteristic, or basic in some sense. Again, some find physicalistic causal explanations the clearest explanatory structures, while others find the mathematical structure of function and argument explanatory in accounting for semantic structure, and take for granted that such structures can be represented in the human mind in some fashion. We need to consider the different assumptions about data, explicans, and explicandum carefully in order to make sense of the variety of theories of language in this century, and not end up seeing these as a mere jumble of fashions. In this chapter a sketch of modern theories will be presented with the differences just listed as scaffolding. This will serve as the background for the general outline of a theory.

What is it to have theories about languages? Some might think that any such attempt is in principle a mistake. After all, the word 'language' has an ordinary, heavily function-laden use. One could compare it to the meanings of words like 'table'. It would make no sense to try to construct a theory about tables. Tables are defined functionally, in connection with human use. A number of sciences, such as physics, geometry, chemistry, study in abstraction various aspects of tables. But neither the sum of these, nor some overarching theory will yield "the table theory."

Parallel with these considerations, one could say that 'language' is a term of common teleological use and does not denote an object for scientific work. One could then claim that there is a separate technical use of this word that does denote a legitimate domain for a science. The burden of proof to delineate this technical use rests on those who believe in such a science.

But is it really fair to think of 'language' as semantically analogous to terms like 'chair' or 'table'? Other analogies suggest themselves as well.

Let us consider numbers. The term 'number' has important technical and ordinary uses. The ordinary use does not cover irrationals or negative numbers. Nevertheless, there must be an important link between the ordinary and technical use. For, among other things, mathematics is to account for intuitions that we have in everyday life about numbers and numerosity. These intuitions are about numbers in the everyday sense. The science of mathematics accounts for these intuitions, and hence must account among other things for numbers in the ordinary sense. The situation is not analogous to that of tables. The ordinary notion of table does not require a science of tables, and above all, does not require accounting for intuitions about tables, whatever this might mean. The case of mathematics is different.

As we shall see, sciences concerned with language must account, among other things, for intuitions about sentences, words, and so on in the ordinary sense of these expressions. Hence one expects a tight conceptual link between the everyday uses and the technical notions of linguistics.

Thus to say that 'language' and related expressions have everyday uses is not enough to exclude there being a science or sciences with such entities in their domain. Likewise, pointing to analogies between the uses of 'number' and 'language' is not sufficient for denying that a number of different sciences could be concerned with these objects. As we shall see, these considerations play important roles in assessing recent proposals by Chomsky and others concerning the nature of what is considered today linguistics. This, in turn, also affects one's conception of the nature of the philosophy of language. The various sciences have to account for intuitions and observations couched in ordinary language. But the explanatory framework need not include these commonsense notions expressed in ordinary language.

In the twentieth century we encounter many conceptions of what is called philosophy of language, and also different proposals, both in linguistics and in philosophy, concerning what a theory of natural language should be. Using the distinctions drawn so far, I will show how to organize a coherent picture of the variety of proposals, and will indicate the conceptually important differences between different proposals, so that moving from one proposal to another should neither seem to be merely changing fashions, nor seem to be collecting attempts to answer the same questions about language.

For example, in the early part of this century some philosophers were interested in the structure of language as a possible guide to the basic structure of reality. Within such an investigation basic and superficial structures of language are distinguished, but the criteria for what counts as basic are motivated by metaphysical quests.

In addition to the interest in language serving metaphysical quests, we see also a concern with how language can mirror what was taken to be the basic structure of a science. Both of these interests were motivated partly by the rise of symbolic logic in this century and the resulting problems concerning how the structures unearthed by symbolic logic are or can be embedded in natural languages.

It is fair to say, then, that most of the philosophical interest in language in the first half of this century construed language as having–within philosophical investigations–instrumental value. The resulting theories were partly normative, since these viewed language from the point of view of how good an instrument it was for the assumed philosophical purposes. Thus in comparing and relating the development of philosophical theories of language with developments in the sciences, especially linguistics, our main question should not be why there are no closer connections between the two, but why there should be any relationship at all, given the widely different motivations.

A key issue that emerged both in philosophy and in linguistics concerned the variety of uses to which language can be put. In the philosophical literature in the early stages it was assumed that some use or uses were primary, and others derivative. This view arose naturally, since the whole enterprise focused on antecedent speculations concerning basic structures of language and basic structures of reality. Investigations about multiplicity of use become less arbitrary and more constructive when pure normative assumptions about what must be basic are replaced by considerations of semantic and syntactic interdependence. For example, what level of complexity could be achieved by commands if we lacked the kind of complex syntactic and semantic structures that we find in natural languages?

The following survey is meant to raise in the minds of the readers the following questions. We started from work on the foundations of mathematics and metaphysically necessary links between language and reality (logical atomism) and ended up considering the semantics of adverbials in ordinary language. What shifts in aims, problems, types of solutions took us here? Is it like a development of a unitary science, like physics, or more like moving from one conception of a discipline to the conception of another, without explicit reflection on whether the conceptual tools adequate for tackling one set of problems in a discipline proposed should be seen as also adequate for another set of problems and field? How did philosophers come to see ordinary language as a watered down version of scientific language? Should a reaction to positivists' view of science and common sense be a refusal to formalize or to explore a variety of different formalisms? The historical sketch shows that there are shifts in subject matter: science, everyday language use, the study of grammar as an isolated phenomenon. How should these topics be related? Pondering these questions can help us to see, for example, that while in a language designed to encode the result of a scientific theory polysemy would be a flaw, the same phenomenon might be serving a vital function in the ordinary use and learning of natural languages.

I. HISTORICAL OVERVIEW OF MODERN PHILOSOPHICAL THEORIES OF LANGUAGE

This section gives a brief overview of dominant twentieth-century philosophical theories of language. The purpose is not to give a detailed account of the variety of claims made, but to summarize enough of these theories to show that different theories attempt to answer radically different kinds of questions, and hence use different purported explanatory structures. Within these theories language is viewed from different points of view; for example, as an instrument for coming to understand at a deep level the fundamental categories of reality, or as in need of reconstruction in order to understand the linguistic structures required for the expression of scientific theories.

The value of looking at these theories in historical sequence is to see the continuity in terms of how a theory is a reaction to another, either in terms of influence or in terms of what was thought as opposition. Frege stimulates Russell and Wittgenstein, and these, in turn have an influence on the positivists against whom the so-called philosophers of ordinary language like Austin and Ryle react. But looking at this kind of continuity can obscure the fact that these philosophers set themselves different questions, and what is a useful technical device for answering one question need not have that role at all in answering another.

FREGE

The main purpose of this admittedly sketchy review is to provide material supporting the claim that philosophers often lapse into the tacit assumption according to which tools useful for some earlier philosophical projects will be useful also for other projects with quite different aims that surface later. For example, a tool of logic that helps explain how some formal languages have parts that relate to parts of reality might not be very useful for the task of characterizing that part of human competence which involves rather indirect ways to link descriptive vocabulary and sentences to what is construed as reality.

We shall start with seeking some of Gottlob Frege's key insights, not only because historically he precedes the other philosophers with whom we shall deal, but also because his way of thinking about language contributes much to the theoretical structure of the proposals of this essay. For Frege a key fact about natural human languages was that these could express propositions that required no relating to specific time, place, speaker, hearer, or other context, and that what was thus expressed could be understood by speakers not related in any necessary way to the source of the thoughts the sentences express.[1] Since Frege was a mathematician and logician, it is natural to suppose that his paradigm cases would have been statements of mathematics or geometry. We understand that $2 + 2 = 4$, without knowing anything about who said this first, where, when, and why, and without our needing to have any causal link to the origin of sentences expressing this proposition.

There are, however, also theoretical considerations why this feature of natural languages should be one of the central explananda in a theory of the semantics of natural languages. For it is reasonable to assume that this property of human languages is not shared by animal communication systems. Indicating where food is, signaling danger, expressing need, are typically context-de-

1. G. Frege 1892, *Philosophical Writings*, ed. M. Black and P. Geach (New York: Humanities Press, 1952), pp. 56 ff.

pendent communications; for example, that is what they are for animals. Frege's choice of key facts to be explained can be thus justified, since if we can explain this fact, we have explained a key way in which human languages differ from other communication system, including animal communication. Frege's solution to this problem was not meant to be an a priori claim. It seemed to Frege to be the most plausible empirical hypothesis that also fitted well with other hypotheses that he regarded confirmed by general experience. As we shall see, one alternative would be to take context-dependent, indexical statements as fundamental, and regard Frege's noncontextual examples as somehow extensions of these. As to lexical items, someone might claim that these do derive their semantic content from being parts of long causal-intentional chains, leading us back to the source of the items in question. We shall see later why these alternatives are less attractive than the Fregean one.

In order to account for the internal structure of the propositions in question, Frege relied on refined versions of the notions of truth value, reference, and meaning. What the sentences with "Fregean content" express is true or false, and their structure includes reference to certain elements of reality as well as sense or meaning – that is, criteria of application of the expressions involved, under idealized conditions.[2] The thesis that meanings are instructions to perform certain operations would be an alternative to Frege's view. This suggestion has been raised in this century, and has been found wanting.[3]

Another key feature of the Fregean proposal is that the key semantic notions of truth, reference, and meaning are not reducible to causally definable relationships. Frege would not even accept the claim that the subject and the object referred to must be in some kind of causal relationship. Again, mathematics supplies the key evidence for this view.

Frege takes as the most fundamental structure for descriptive units that of function and argument.[4] All complexes are built out of such units. Here again the paradigm is mathematics. Function-argument structures are among the most general ways of representing something in mathematics and logic. These representations of semantic units of natural language are the most general and

2. "Whatever may be the speaker's intention and motives for saying just this and not that, our concern is not with these at all, but solely with what he says." Gottlob Frege, "Compound Thoughts," 1923, reprinted in *Essays on Frege*, ed. E. Klemke (Urbana: 1968), p. 547.

3. On operationalism, see P. W. Bridgeman, *The Nature of Some of Our Physical Concepts* (New York, 1952)

4. See the second and third essays reprinted in Frege, *Philosophical Writing*. For more detailed interpretation see J. Moravcsik, "Frege and Chomsky on Thought and Language," in P. French, T. Uehling, and H. Wettstein, eds. *Midwest Studies in Philosophy* (1981), 105–23.

abstract levels of capturing something that is descriptive of reality. We shall consider later what if anything that is essential to the semantics of natural languages is left out of such representations.

Why does Frege think that representing the meanings of simple sentences of subject–predicate form by these structures is explanatory? For the answer we go back once more to mathematics. Frege assumes that if there is anything fundamental in mathematics and logic that we understand, it is function and argument. Therefore he sets out to explain one thing that is problematic–the semantics of natural language including the unity of subject and predicate–in terms of something well known and familiar. He then takes for granted that such structures can be represented in the human mind. From the working mathematician or logician's point of view this is quite natural. We know that people understand mathematics, and hence we conclude that they can represent such structures. Can we say more specifically how the mind or brain does this? Will such explanations ever be physicalistic? Will we ever be able to say something specific about these cognitive operations? Frege regards these as psychological questions, to be answered by research quite different from his. Furthermore, he does not think that this other kind of research can overthrow his general abstract characterization.

These points are important to keep in mind when we look at subsequent critical reactions to Frege. Meanings become suspect because these are abstract entities. Why should that make something suspect? As we saw, already in the specification of a language as words and sentences we are knee deep in abstract entities. Furthermore, the discipline needed by all others, mathematics, deals with myriads of abstract entities. Why and which way are physical observable elements clearer than the abstract? My theory claims that the Fregean point of view is correct and that the questions just raised have never been satisfactorily answered by Frege's critics.

Frege's theory accounts for the semantics of explicit definite descriptions of the sort we find in mathematics and the natural sciences. It will not account for specifications as in "Give me the screwdriver over there." It is not merely a matter of incompleteness. Merely filling in spatiotemporal specifications for the desired screwdriver will not settle the matter. The screwdriver referred to might be the one that from the point of view of speaker and hearer is most easily within reach. This involves knowing the minds and orientational schemes of speaker and hearer. We should note at least two ways open to us. We can say that these everyday specifications are incomplete approximations to genuine definite descriptions and should be represented as such. Alternatively, we could develop a separate formalism for the colloquial specifications and similar other semantic structures involved in everyday practical discourse. We could then regard a natural language as the result of interactions among different systems of semantic representations. The second alternative has not been discussed in the recent literature. It will be dealt with later in this essay.

Frege's semantic explorations left a deep imprint on subsequent work in theories of meaning. Its formal rigor set a standard for subsequent theories, and its positing of the function–argument structure as basic served for others as the proposal to be dealt with in working out possible alternatives. Its treatment of the relation between the context-free and the indexical or context-dependent posed a challenge for all who thought they could do better. We will find these themes recurrent in our review of more recent work. But first we will look at the theories of those who used their linguistic analyses for metaphysical purposes and in the course of this made interesting claims about the way logic was embodied or was covered up by the structure of natural languages.

Within symbolic logic we interpret the reality to which logic in a particular context is applied as a totality of distinct elements. If the domain is finite, we can assume that in principle each individual can be designated by a distinct individual constant. Such distribution of names is possible also for certain well-defined infinite domains and accompanying recursive modes of name generating (e.g., series of positive integers). We construe the variables as ranging over this well-characterized domain. Individuals make up collections, and these in turn larger complexes. The tools for the constructions–or the opposite, reductions–are the logical connectors and quantifiers. Projecting this framework unto reality gives us an atomistic conception of the world. The world is made up–within such a conception–of logical atoms, and with the help of logical connectors and quantifiers we construct out of these all of the larger elements of reality. The process can go both ways. If the domain admits such a logically well-behaved structure, then we should be able to reduce the larger complexes to atoms.

RUSSELL AND WITTGENSTEIN

This picture of logic and the world captured the imagination of two brilliant metaphysicians, Bertrand Russell and Ludwig Wittgenstein. Russell took the logical atoms to be sense data, the minimal perceptual units of each sentient being. He then undertook to define on this basis material objects, and out of these larger units. He thought this "real" world to be underlying the world of common sense, and analogously, a purified logical language as underlying the language of everyday discourse.[5] This led to a philosophical critique of ordi-

5. B. Russell, *The Philosophy of Logical Atomism* (Minneapolis: Department of Philosophy of the University of Minnesota, 1918).

nary language. But at the same time, it also starts a view of two kinds of linguistic structures: a superficial one, carrying with it the accretions of common sense and everyday use, and a "deeper" one purified so as to capture only those aspects that help us in discovering what is fundamental in reality.[6]

Russell's atoms were both logically and epistemologically fundamental, since they fitted his empiricist theory of knowledge. Wittgenstein was no empiricist. His atoms were not empirically accessible, nor were these entities particulars, as in Russell's system. Wittgenstein's atoms are facts, entities that are on such a deep level that no example can be given, and yet their existence can be shown to be necessary.[7]

These metaphysical constructions would have been impossible without seeing symbolic logic as at the heart of what language ideally can be. Even if subsequent generations of philosophers were much more cautious in their approach to metaphysics, the questions Russell and Wittgenstein raised about the relation between logic and natural language became a part of the twentieth-century philosophic tradition.

Some of the key criticisms of natural language from the point of view of logic centered on quantification and the referential apparatus. In a language like English quantified noun phrases like 'all humans' constitute a syntactic and semantic unit. Not so in logic, where, for instance, the universal quantifier is a separate syntactic unit, and its joining with variables and predicate letters does not provide a subject for propositions, except in the trivial sense that the subject becomes all of reality. The logician's analysis facilitates the representation of negation, compatibility, and incompatibility involving quantifiers.

Perhaps the key criticism centered on definite descriptions. In natural languages these are taken as syntactic and semantic units, as in 'the wisest woman in Europe'. In symbolic logic this unit is broken up into separate parts, occurring not even adjacently in a sentence, representing distinct entailments that the use of such an expression brings with it. Thus, with regard to our example, the logical analysis shows the content to be the conjunction of the claim that there exists such a woman, and that there is only one such entity. The syntactic representation of such entailments becomes a matter of logical perspicuity rather than attempts to capture our intuitions about what is and is not a unit in a natural language. Later a second generation of formal semanticists tried to

---

6. Later on Chomsky developed a two-level view of linguistic structure, but it would be a major mistake to identify what is seen as surface and deep in these two traditions, though philosophers of language up to this day tend to be guilty of such confusion.

7. L. Wittgenstein, *Tractatus Logico-philosophicus* (London: Routledge & Kegan Paul, 1922).

combine logical perspicuity in their analyses with preserving what we feel intuitively are units in everyday discourse. (See the later section on Montague.)

POSITIVISTS

Many philosophers drew the conclusion from the works of Russell and Wittgenstein that even if we are less sanguine metaphysically, we should see that natural language is not an ideal tool for doing philosophy. An emerging group, the so-called positivists, went further and claimed that natural language was not an adequate tool for doing science either. This view led to the rise of manufacturing ideal languages, suited to capture the truths of this or that science. These efforts gained inspiration also from the success of axiomatization and logical rigor in defining terms for science. For only this rigorous presentation could show that of the four basic axioms in geometry about parallel lines one was logically independent of the others, and hence provided the conceptual foundation for non-Euclidean geometry. Thus it became assumed by many philosophers of science that if we constructed languages that had the structure of quantificational logic we could present sciences in their most perspicuous form. Furthermore, the application of logic would facilitate reducing one science to another. Such reductionistic programs helped the rise of the unity-of-science thesis that all sciences have the same logical form, and that eventually we could reduce all sciences to one "basic" science.

In assessing these claims we should distinguish two different questions: What is an ideal form for presenting the results of a science? and What is the form of a language or languages that scientists use while investigating and doing research? My teacher, Gilbert Ryle, said that in relation to science, he is interested in knowing how "scientists talk to each other across the bench." The language presenting what we know need only reflect the structure of a part of reality. There is, then, a fundamental difference between the language in which the current theories of science are presented as already established, and the language which we use (including questions, speculations, proposals for what to investigate next, etc.) to conduct ongoing search. The language of research and investigation presumably includes expressions of doubt, inquiry, expressions of belief, mere conjecture, and so forth. While explicitness may be a virtue in a language of presentation, a certain amount of vagueness and ambiguity might be helpful in a language within which we only try to reach knowledge. But such questions and issues were not raised until later, at a stage in which philosophers no longer wondered what the main function of natural language was, or what it had to approximate, but considered language as having structures that made possible its having a variety of very different purposes.

It is fair to say then that in the metaphysical and positivistic stages philosophers had only an extrinsic interest in natural language. They did not see language of intrinsic philosophic interest, but considered it for whatever instrumental value it might have as a tool of metaphysical or scientific investigation.

When we consider this, it becomes surprising how much influence this work had subsequently even during the period in which natural language was investigated as an object worthy of interest on its own. What I said at the outset of this chapter about the miracle of language motivates in the later period ascribing intrinsic interest to language. The reason the work of this earlier period left a considerable impact is that it focused to a large extent on the relation between logic and natural language, and elicited in the minds of many the question of whether we should view the purpose and function of natural language in a monolithic or a pluralistic way.

ORDINARY LANGUAGE PHILOSOPHY

Positivism was antitheoretical in its rejection of metaphysics but as we saw quite dogmatic with regard to various assumptions about natural language. A group of British philosophers who worked in Oxford and Cambridge already before World War II, and really came into their own after the war, adopted an antitheoretical approach toward natural language itself. They took an intrinsic interest in natural language but felt that one should first come to describe and thus appreciate the variety of complex semantic and syntactic structures in a natural language, before venturing grandiose hypotheses. This work was fueled also by a conviction shared by Wittgenstein in his later period that detailed attention to how natural language works can rid us of many philosophic puzzles and problems. But there was also another motivation, even for those who did not think that attention to linguistic detail could have this therapeutic effect. In the study of living things we can distinguish, as Chomsky reminded us, between the interests of the biologist and those of the naturalist. The biologist focuses on what seems essential or at least necessary in biological structure, while the naturalist is interested in collecting any kind of data about animals, not only data on their anatomy, for instance but also on their fur color, usual habitat at a certain point in history, and so forth. It is a mistake to think that the biologist wants eventually to account for all of this data. John Muir was a great naturalist and gave superb descriptions of parts of the Sierras, but not every detail of these descriptions became an object of scientific interest.

The important philosophic figures of this time, such as John L. Austin, Ryle, and J. O. Urmson, had the attitude and interest of the naturalist. They assumed that a natural language has a large variety of different functions, and that minute differences between similar terms may be relevant to this or that function. Some of the semantic differences such as between 'pleasant', 'pleasurable', and 'pleasing' were investigated in order to bring out the amazingly subtle expressive power of the English language. Other differences such as that between "I presume that this is Livingston" and "Mr. Livingston, I presume" were examined to bring out uses of natural language other than merely that of assertion and stating facts. Symbolic logic was no longer seen as providing the backbone of the semantics for natural languages, and varieties of ways of using quantifiers were not seen as feeble approximations to the "canonical uses" of such expressions in symbolic logic.

Looking at this period, we see three key issues emerging. First, the value of looking at natural language for its own sake, a marvelous net of structures that rewards investigations without ulterior purpose. Second, the amazing richness of semantic data from languages like English, calling at least for description, but in the minds of many also a new kind of theory. Third, the rather indirect way in which language and logic worked together, and seeing this as not a flaw in natural languages. Could one become quite precise about natural languages and account for this newly unearthed plethora of data? The first generation of philosophers practicing this way of investigating natural language was skeptical, but new schools of language theory arose that took up the challenge. Strawson concludes a famous article of his on referring with the claim that "ordinary language has no logic."[8]

MONTAGUE

A few decades later a generation of semanticists, led by Richard Montague, rose to refute this claim. Can one get precise about natural language? This question needs to be answered both on the semantic and on the syntactic level. On the syntactic level the question was whether a formal approach could accommodate the large variety of syntactic categories that linguists traditionally deemed necessary for representing, such as the grammar of English. Could one work categories like noun phrase, verb phrase, adverbial phrase, and so forth into a formal grammar of English? The problem was different for Montague than it would be for a linguist, for given the constraints of a formal language within which Montague worked, it was necessary to provide a semantic characterization of each syntactic category as well. Furthermore, could one recreate the way syntactic complexes are built up in natural languages within the constraint of compositionality that Montague had to set for himself?

8. P. F. Strawson, "On Referring," *Mind* 59 (1950): 320–44.

Montague's project was not simply to find some formalism that would represent the semantics of English. He thought that the appropriate formalism would be that of a "formal language" as defined by his teacher Alfred Tarski. This choice seems strange in retrospect, since Tarski himself thought that natural languages cannot be represented as formal languages. We shall return to this point later.

Tarski's concept of a formal language was introduced as a technical tool that would mirror adequately the kind of semantics and syntax that is ideal for the encoding of scientific theories.[9] Such a language has the following ingredients:

1. There must be a way to enumerate the class of simple well-formed formulas of the language.
2. There must be rules generating all of the complex well-formed formulas out of the set of simple ones.
3. There must be semantic interpretation for the semantically simple expressions.
4. There must be rules generating the semantics of complex expressions out of the semantics of simple ones.
5. There must be a way of specifying the class of all sentences.
6. The rules of inference must be stated.
7. Conditions of assertability must be given.
8. The language must be such that for the relevant parts conditions of truth and satisfaction can be given.

The last condition entails that the language cannot contain ambiguities, vagueness, or context dependence. Furthermore all rules must be explicit.

The last condition points to what is the interpretation of formal language in Tarski's sense. This involves assigning to each predicate expression the elements that satisfy–in the technical sense–the predicate. For example the class of horses, or sequences containing these, would be assigned to the predicate 'is a horse'. For the sentences of the language the interpretation specifies what it is for the sentence to be "true" in a technical sense. This truth is relativized to a language, and the interpretation says, roughly, that the sentence 's' is true iff and only s; that is, we can attach 'is true' to the name of the sentence if and only if what the sentence asserts obtains. This complicated structure is at times not understood by those who look merely at examples like

9. A. Tarski, 1936, "The Concept of Truth in Formalized Languages," reprinted in *Logic, Semantics, and Meta-mathematics* (Oxford: Oxford University Press), pp. 152–278.

'snow is white' is true if and only if snow is white.

The ingenuity of this construction lies in having a biconditional in which the name of an entity appears in subject position on one side and the very entity named appears on the other.

Tarski's theory was misunderstood by many philosophers, and because the theory spread to some parts of the social sciences, misunderstandings continue to flourish. First, the theory should not be confused with the trivial observations that some sentences are true and some false. To deny–as I will–that sentences of a natural language like English lack truth conditions in Tarski's technical sense is not to deny that some sentences are true. Furthermore a sentence having truth conditions in Tarski's sense has no consequences as to whether the sentence can be verified, and if so how.

Accepting for some range of applications Tarski's theory of truth leaves it quite open what if any philosophical theory of truth one accepts. Tarski's scheme does not adjudicate between rival claims of the correspondence, coherence, or pragmatic theories of truth. Tarski's proposal is metaphysically neutral, and has no connection with the so-called verificationist theory of meaning.

Tarski felt that his work was not adequately understood by philosophers, and wrote a paper in 1944 that was designed as a more popular introduction to his notion of truth than the earlier long technical paper referred to in this book already. Since the appearance of that article, misunderstandings multiplied; hence the need to distinguish Tarski's theory from other approaches to truth.[10]

First, some philosophers have attempted to describe the meaning of 'truth' as used in ordinary discourse. Strawson's view, that "p is true" simply means "p" as asserted, is an illustration on such work.[11] Such attempts are independent of Tarski's project. To be sure, Tarski wants of capture for formal languages a notion that is intuitively related to what we usually mean by 'true' and 'false', but no strict correspondence is presupposed. One could not deduce from Tarski's work a definition of the ordinary use of 'true', either Strawson's or any rival account. Likewise, none of the accounts or ordinary uses of 'true' can be used to judge Tarski's theory that is designed for other purposes.

Second, there are philosophical theories about what the ground for truth is, such as the correspondence, coherence, and pragmatic theories. According to

10. A. Tarski, "The Semantic Conception of Truth," *Philosophical and Phenomenological Research* 4 (1944), pp. 341–375.

11. P. F. Strawson, "Truth" *Analysis* 9, no. 6 (1949).

the first, what makes a sentence or proposition true is its corresponding to some configuration in reality. According to the second, the justification for regarding some claim as true is that it is a part of the maximally coherent set of our beliefs that one could articulate. The third theory says that a sentence or claim is true if and only if it "works"–that is, fits in practical terms into the conceptual web with which we interpret reality successfully.

These theories do not answer Tarski's question, and his does not answer theirs. One can accept Tarski's way of rigorously defining how veracity is to be expressed in a formal language (rigorously so defined) and then accept any, or none, of the philosophical theories that try to ground truth in correspondence or veracity or pragmatic success.

Tarski's theory says that within a special kind of language with rigorous constraints on syntax and semantics–called a "formal language"–a sentence like "snow is white" could be represented as true by the equation: "'snow is white' is true if and only if snow is white". What makes the sentence true? That is a separate question. Some say correspondence to facts or other configurations, some coherence, and some have other answers. Finally these conditionals say nothing about whether Strawson's or any other semantic analysis of ordinary language is the best available as of now.

Applying the Tarski conception of a formal language and its scheme of truth conditions to natural languages has far-reaching consequences for how to conceptualize a language. First, in this scheme, there is no point for syntactic rules except to facilitate the semantics. Syntax in this scheme is the slave of semantics. Within Tarski's scheme, it is slave to a semantics in which only truth and satisfaction conditions are specified. As Quine put it: "Grammar is designed with no other thought than to facilitate the tracing of truth conditions."[12] From more simple to the more complex, "Logic chases truth up the tree of grammar."[13] There are no independent (i.e., from semantics) motivations for syntactic rules. We shall see if this is plausible for natural languages.

Within Montague's presentation of English as a formal language the earlier criticisms of Russell and others against natural languages disappear, but at a price. Should we really regard ambiguity, vagueness, and context-dependent specification of meaning as disadvantages in natural languages? Before we answer these questions, we should look deeper into the analogies that the imposition of the Tarski scheme posits between logic and natural languages. In a formal language interpretations are given over well-defined domains. Thus 'ev-

12. W. V. O. Quine, *Philosophy of Logic* (Englewood Cliffs, NJ: Prentice-Hall, 1970), p. 65.
13. Ibid p. 30.

erything', 'something', and other quantifiers have clear meaning. Is this true of natural languages? Here the domains over which we quantify are not well defined, and are not separable as domains for a given science. Natural languages are forged to express many different theories and act as link between these. Perhaps considerations like these moved Tarski when he denied that natural language can be interpreted as formal languages.[14] He thought that natural languages are distinguished by their universality. But universality and totality of entities outside of given theories are not well-defined notions.

There are also problems in attempts to relate the individual constants of formal languages to the names or pronouns of languages like English. In a formal language assigning individuals to constants is a part of what we called interpretation. Without it, the semantics has not been specified completely. Since these assignments are matters of legislation, they are independent of context and do not lend themselves to problems of misunderstanding. In sharp contrast, natural languages contain a variety of different types of names. Some of these, such as names for positive integers, are systematic, and given their domain, their referents are guaranteed by the nature of the language and its interpretation. Others, however, are dependent on contingent unpredictable baptismal customs, varying from group to group within the same linguistic community. One could make a good case for claiming that family names are only syntactically parts of natural languages. There are also names of famous entities (cities, person, buildings) that have definite qualitative content. In short, in a formal language the semantics of individual constants must be a part of the semantics of the language, and it has to be complete–that is, cover all constants. In natural languages these conditions do not hold, and there are good grounds for regarding it a mistake to posit a uniform semantic interpretation for all kind of names.

We see then important differences between logic and the interpreted formal languages on the one hand, and the semantics of the variety of items called names in natural languages on the other. This raises larger issues: Given that natural languages have a variety of functions apart from encoding theories, might it not be the case that what are objects of taboo in formal languages are definite advantages in a natural language? Formal languages are not built to capture the semantics of shifts of denotation or even parts of meaning, while such phenomena are crucial for natural languages that are dynamic diachronic phenomena.

Before we consider alternative interpretation of semantics for natural languages, we should point out that while Montague's semantics contains many

14. A. Tarski, "Semantic Conception of Truth."

types of intensional constructions and commitments to intensional entities, other attempts to construe Tarski's truth conditions as forming the backbone of semantics for natural languages such as the proposal made by Donald Davidson, try to avoid such commitments.[15] We cannot judge such an enterprise however, until we have seen detailed proposals for large segments of the semantics of English as we have in the works of Montague and his followers.

A natural way to turn from the work just surveyed to that of Chomsky is to consider what other conditions besides semantic and logical convenience might constrain and motivate the syntax and semantics of natural languages. It is significant that Montague never talks about the human mind, and the possibility that the structures of our languages might be molded by the demands and needs of cognitive and perceptual organization. Montague sees natural languages as parts of a larger set, namely that of the set of all languages. Chomsky's interest is in what is unique to human languages. He thinks that if we can give at least partial answers to that question, then we will also be giving a partial characterization of human essence.

Chomsky's reformulation of the task and scope of linguistics has implications for the methodology of the social sciences in general, and for the nature of philosophizing. Hence the emergence of a bitter feud between Chomsky and analytic philosophy on the one hand, and Chomsky and the social scientists on the other. After a brief characterization of Chomsky's conception of linguistics and its lessons for philosophy, we shall turn to the larger issues that separate his views from those of almost everyone else.[16]

Chomsky's conception of grammar unites the formal and the empirical, without bowing to empiricist epistemology. His early work was devoted to the question of why expressions mean what they do. But the published work was widely interpreted in the following way. One considers the class of simple well-formed formulas of a language and then the set made up of all possible combinations of these. Syntax is to provide a function that ranges over this domain and separates the complex well-formed formulas from the not well-formed ones. Since we can assume that a natural language contains an infinite number of expressions, the function and its delineation by our syntactic theory must have enough recursive plasticity so as to cover sets of that magnitude. The function will be formally defined. At the same time the notion of well-formed formulas of language L is empirical, and thus the proposed function posited by

15. D. Davidson, "Truth and Meaning," *Synthese* 17 (1967): 304–3.

16. J. Moravcsik, "La Radicale Rottura di Chomsky nei Confronti della Tradizione Moderna," in N. Chomsky, *Regole e Rappresentazioni* (Milan: il Saggiatore,) 1981 pp. 233–37.

the theory is subject to empirical verification and disconfirmation. Well-formedness and intuitions about grammaticality need not be an all-or-nothing affair. Indeed, in the ensuing literature there are plenty of uses of degrees of grammaticality. As we saw earlier, sentences and words are abstract entities. The competent and idealized speaker-hearer is to judge these. Such activities, given the object of the judgment, cannot be merely behavioral. Chomsky combines formal rigor in his theory with an attack on behaviorism in particular and empiricist epistemology in general. His conception follows the line from Plato and Aristotle down to the latest version of advanced sciences such as physics, chemistry, and geometry that take the empirically observable to be merely evidence (and not all of the evidence) for the nature of facts to be explained, where these facts themselves are not subject to observation by the senses. The explanations, such as the function representing the grammar of a language, are then on an even higher level of the abstract. If the explanations concern the most fundamental elements of a science, then we can say that the empirically observable is twice removed from the (ultimately) real.

Before we go any further, let us define what a natural language is. The definition I propose leaves it a contingent empirical issue whether various computer languages or Esperanto could be natural languages. According to the definition, a natural language is a language that can be learned by human or device sufficiently resembling a human as his or her first language under normal circumstances. Expressions like 'normal', and 'sufficiently' cry out for further specification, but for our purposes this is irrelevant. The definition is adequate to capture Chomsky's conception of the kind of languages the grammars of which he wants to determine. At the same time we see how this definition leads us from the consideration of languages and linguistic structures to the consideration of the human mind. Learning, a key phrase in our definition, is a psychological process. So is then the resulting mastery of at least the syntactic part of the language. It is easy to see how Chomsky's account also covers phonology. The empirical verification procedures do not constitute a monolithic set. For these include behavioral evidence, introspective evidence, and whatever indirect evidence we can gather concerning the competent speaker-hearer's intuitions about grammaticality. The grammar is supposed to account for the set of well-formed formulas. But obviously there will be more than one function generating the same set. Chomsky sets as the task of a linguistic theory with genuine explanatory power the delineation of the mastery or competence over a language of an idealized speaker-hearer; not only generating the right set, but approximating the way of generating that set that is reflected in human cognitive operations.

Chomsky's conjectures about these cognitive operations have two important aspects. First, he concludes that given the data about human language acquisition and the formal complexity of the rules to be mastered and applied, there must be a rich innate structure in the human mind that we share and apply in conjunction with the rule systems that are added by specific languages. Hence as in syntax a universal core and a language variant structure and analogous distinctions can be drawn also in phonology and presumably also semantics.[17]

This methodology and outlook on language are designed to mirror standard procedures in the other natural sciences. In these too, we regard the observable as merely evidence, state the facts to be accounted for on the first level of abstraction, and the explanatory structures on a still higher level of abstraction. The development of Western science is characterized by the assumption that what is most "real" that is, explanatory, lies beneath the surface; we account for the observable with reference to it, and not the other way around.[18]

Second, Chomsky formulates the hypothesis that the mental is modular in nature, meaning that our linguistic competence has as its foundation in the human mind not merely an all-purpose organizing and rule-generating mechanism, but also a faculty of language that has represented in it rule schemata specific to human language.

Except for keeping in mind the seductive power of empiricism and behaviorism in particular at the time of the rise of Chomsky's conception of human languages and their masteries by humans, it is difficult to understand why the methodology and conception aroused so much opposition. The framework follows standard scientific frameworks as in physics or chemistry or biology. It was felt by the opponents that the proposal was antimaterialist. This is a strange objection for two reasons. First, as we just sketched the Chomskyan framework, it is clearly neutral between various ontologies for cognitive operations. These could turn out to be materialistic, or dualistic (mental in some special sense), or something different, not yet articulated, not fitting into the mental-material straitjacket dominating the social sciences since Descartes. Worry about materialism seems especially strange at a time such as ours, after the notion of matter has been falling apart. For many of the entities of physics posited in modern times resist the material–immaterial categorization.[19]

---

17. N. Chomsky, *Aspects of the Theory of Syntax* (Cambridge) MA: MIT Press, 1965.
18. On behaviorism, see J. Moravcsik *Thought and Language* (London: Routledge, 1990), pp. 184–87.
19. N. Chomsky, "Language and Nature," *Mind* 104 (1994): 1–61.

To understand the developments of ideas at this stage it is useful to draw an analogy between linguistics and anthropology. In anthropology under the influence of authors like Ruth Benedict and Margaret Mead research concentrated on variety and differences in customs and habits, and with this came the fashionableness of relativism. Subsequently we saw the reaction to this in works such as those by Harvard researchers led by Clyde Kluckhohn, who showed that underlying variety and pluralism on the surface we could find often deep common elements that are not directly related to the observable.[20]

A simple and simplified example can make this clear. Let us suppose that humans in general have a tendency to dress in such a way that their clothing facilitates comfort and maintaining health. Clearly in different parts of the world under different circumstances this tendency will manifest itself in different behavior patterns. Furthermore, the physical environment by itself does not determine the behavior patterns. These will be also the function of what beliefs, traditions, and so forth the agents in question carry with them. Unearthing a prudential maxim that agents embrace from underneath behavioral variations and collateral information about beliefs, history, and so forth is often just as difficult as uncovering beneath a variety of symptoms in different contexts the underlying illness or bacteria that are the genuine sources.

With ethical relativism came also linguistic relativism, on the basis of similar methodological moves. In this context one can see what Chomsky proposed as the analogue to the reaction of some anthropologists to cultural relativism. He assumed that language mastery is a biological phenomenon and hence must have a basis in human nature. He went on to assume that this basis is highly specific to language and mastery. Finally, he thought that the best way to get at the underlying faculty is to specify as rigorously and formally as possible the structures of complexes of rules the mastery of which is called for. Such presentations constitute indirect data for ascriptions of certain properties to the human mind.

Within this conception language is seen as an object of intrinsic interest, and having a varieties of functions. Hence neither logic nor any other–metaphysical?–organization should be viewed as the "basis" of linguistic organization. This had far-reaching consequences for philosophy of language. One could now raise questions about what kinds of constraints the human needs to communicate under normal circumstances, and our perceptual and cognitive structures and so on place on the shape our phonology, grammar, and semantics. The legitimacy of such questions about phonology has been always ac-

20. C. Kluckhohn, *Mirror for Man* (Tucson: University of Arizona Press, 1985).

knowledged, but it took the reflections briefly sketched to see that the same should apply also to the other components of a language.

These reflections not only show how Chomsky's views differed from those of twentieth-century philosophy of language, but also illuminate the uproar it caused. It forced the social scientist to reconsider the relation between observable, fact, and explanatory structure so as to see what it would be like to construe a social science in these respects as analogous to the natural sciences. It forced philosophers to take natural language seriously not only in the "naturalist" way in which the Oxford dons did this, but also as an object worthy of theoretical and empirical study in its own right. Above all, it presented philosophers with an interesting challenge to approaches in the study of human essence. In the humanistic disciplines the emphasis was on discovering human essence–on what makes humans allegedly unique individuals. In contrast with this Chomsky, like Plato, Aristotle, and others before him, sought human essence in what we share as a species. Such studies did not–and do not–distinguish sharply between the purely conceptual and the empirical. Salient facts are proposed to be accounted for, such as the creative aspects of human language use, and the explanations have both empirical and theoretical impact. This approach moves discussions about human essence beyond studies restricted to behavior and also bypasses debates about the analytic and the synthetic empirical, a distinction with respect to which Chomsky's approach can afford to remain neutral. The view of human languages as biologically grounded helps also in bypassing debates about how to distinguish rules from habits, a problem for the dogmatic behaviorist. Nobody ever suggested that biological mechanisms exhibit mere tendencies or dispositions. We assume that they work according to principles or, one could also say in this context, according to "rules." When Chomsky talks about the internal rule-system that governs the learning and utilization of a language he means to talk about the same things as biologists would refer to as the principles of certain biological mechanisms. There may be differences in terms of what we can bring to consciousness, but for Chomsky's purposes that is not relevant.[21]

Thus the rise of generative grammar helped to rehabilitate rationalist epistemology, shook philosophers out of their dogmatic slumber with respect to possible relationships of syntax and semantics, and helped linguists to construe their subject so as to combine empirical relevance with formal rigor.

As we saw, Chomsky's proposals are neutral with regard to debates about dualism, materialism, and alternatives to both. This is also true of the formal

21. N. Chomsky, "Language and Nature."

representations of Montague. One of Chomsky's main reasons for being skeptical about the various views listed is his justified complaint that the key terms involved in the formulations of these "isms" are unclear. Some philosophers, however, want to impose further restrictions on frameworks within which we are to explain phenomena like the mastery of language. According to this view we should seek to give "naturalistic" theories of knowledge, reference, and in general language understanding.[22] Naturalistic theories, as recent philosophers use this term, include materialist and physicalist theories. In general the category includes whatever theory presents a causal analysis involving elements that the natural sciences of the day would regard as legitimate, and attempts to explain semantic phenomena and language processing within this frame. We should, however, raise the question of whether such demands place arbitrary restrictions on linguistics and philosophy of language. For example, some people believed, and a few still believe, that biology will be reduced eventually to physics. But be that as it may, would it be reasonable to regard such a reduction as a necessary condition for the adequacy of a theory of language and language mastery? Whether the sciences will converge on a single basis on some fundamental level or end up in distinct but internally well-ordered units is a purely empirical matter. A priori speculations on topics like these are about as useful as in an earlier age continental philosophers theses about the number of planets of tomorrow. During the past decades it was fashionable among philosophers to try to reinterpret biology so as to construe teleological elements as not fundamental. But much as we know, maybe the physics of tomorrow will contain teleological elements. Why should we regard mechanistic explanations as yielding more insight than nonmechanistic ones? Furthermore, there is nothing fundamental or conceptually clear about the notion of matter. It is certainly not needed for the understanding of the physics of today, and it is only a hindrance to the understanding of the past. For example, there is controversy about the nature of Democritus's "indivisibles" (atoms). Were these purely mathematical-geometrical entities? Or did they have in some unique sense mass? Or were there two kinds of indivisibles in the Democritean system? It is of no help to the unraveling of these matters to ask if Democritus was a materialist.

I conclude then that the philosophical predilections for what is called naturalism or–more narrowly–physicalism is arbitrary. It lacks serious philosophic justification, and comes at a time when pluralism–though confined–seems a better strategy in the sciences than is a hankering for the "good old days" of

22. P. Churchland, *Matter and Consciousness*, rev. ed. (Cambridge, MA: MIT 1988).

the unity of science movement. The flowering of reductionistic schemes seems anachronistic. For the purposes of this book we shall concentrate on abstract representations of linguistic and logical structures, leaving the relation between these and an account of actual cognitive processes an open issue. This issue raises a number of questions; perhaps some are beyond the limits of human understanding.

II. WHAT IS TO BE DONE?

Frege is concerned both with the foundation of arithmetic and some very general features of natural languages, in particular those that come into play in that part of language–the "Fregean core"–that can be understood without knowing who said when, where, and how. There is a link between these endeavors since Frege thought that mathematics is a part of the core. We must understand his explanatory structures, such as function and argument, sense and denotation, in their roles as helping to solve the main problems Frege set for himself. Initially there is no reason to suppose that these notions would be helpful in explaining the variety of other uses to which natural languages can be put.

The rise of symbolic logic and Frege's very abstract and hence general way of characterizing semantic structures influenced both Russell and Wittgenstein, whose aim was to use logic and language to uncover the deepest categories of reality. It is not surprising that within such an enterprise the everyday use of natural languages should be seen as a hindrance rather than an aid. Everyday use was seen as an impure version of linguistic structures that in their purity mirror reality. It seems reasonable to suppose that the technical notions and their employment in this kind of work would be of only very limited use in the general study of natural languages with their varieties of uses.

Similar considerations hold for the work of the positivists. If one views natural languages as in need of reform in order to understand the language within which scientific theories are to be couched, it is unlikely that either the methodology employed or the technical notions used would be of great help when we try to understand natural languages in their own right.

One can appreciate the rise of ordinary language philosophy as a reaction against views within which natural language is an impure manifestation of some ideal language that we use either for metaphysical or scientific purposes. Once one views natural languages as objects worthy of study in their own right, the kind of fine distinctions and variety of semantic configurations that the Oxford philosophers patiently unearthed become relevant as data to be accounted for. At that point one can also compare profitably the equally detailed semantic work of linguists like Jespersen with the work of Austin, Urmson, and others. As we saw, the Oxford philosophers were data oriented. But their discoveries may well require for systematization tools not found in the works of their philosophic predecessors.

The contrast between the positivists and the Oxford philosophers led to the unfortunate dichotomizing of philosophers of language as the formalists and the informal philosophizers. This is unfortunate because it covers up the deep distinction between those who ask what the key semantic structures of a natural language are and those who ask what the key semantic structures of the language (or languages) of science are.

Other differences among these schools of philosophy of language concern the question of how philosophical work can dissolve philosophical puzzles and problems. Dealing with this separate issue would require another volume.

There is, however, an important methodological issue that needs airing, for it affects both the methodology of this book, and the way the recent history of philosophy of language is presented in this book.

Positivists tried to reduce human knowledge to two categories. One of these is the apriori analytic, the category containing only those objects of knowledge the truths of which depend solely on the meaning of the descriptive words these contain. The other is a posteriori synthetic knowledge, which, roughly, corresponds to the ordinary conception of empirical knowledge. This scheme assumed the highly controversial assumption that mathematics could be defined within the framework of modern symbolic logic. But even apart from that problem, a quite different challenge met the positivists' scheme. In a very influential paper, in 1951, Quine attacked the analytic–synthetic, and by implication the a priori–empirical distinction.[23] In place of the claim that there is a separate domain of knowledge, the analytic, that is immune to revision in the face of experience, and another, the empirical, that is not immune to such revision, Quine–in the spirit of work by Duhem and Poincaré–substituted the picture in which the conceptual and empirical form a continuum, with the "empirical" closer to the periphery of our conceptual framework, and the "conceptual" constituting material at the core or close to the core of our way of interpreting experience, with no sentence immune from possible revision in the face of experience.

23. W. V. O. Quine, "Two Dogmas of Empiricism" *From a Logical Point of View* (Cambridge, MA: Harvard University Press, 1953), pp. 20–46.

Quine's view was attached to other claims of his. These include behaviorism, the holistic interpretation of how theories relate to experience, and attempts to limit the commitment to abstract entities in one's philosophy or science to a minimum. We can bypass these additional claims and concentrate on the first one.

The acceptance of the Quinean view about the conceptual and empirical enables one to look at work in the philosophy of language not as a series of attempts at establishing analytic propositions, but as proposing explanatory schemes that are empirical in a very broad sense, designed to be linked to other hypotheses, theories, all of which eventually help to explain human experience. This is, in fact, the approach adopted in this book. I am not trying to produce allegedly analytic truth about the meanings of 'explain', 'meaning', 'linguistic competence', and other notions. The aim of this book is, rather, to present an articulation of some aspects of human linguistic competence, within which more specific hypotheses about semantics and human understanding can be formulated.

The alternative of attempting to produce analytic accounts of, say, 'meaning' have been attempted by others.[24]

Whatever one may think of the achievements of such efforts, the results, if any, do not affect my project. The relation between my views on meaning and understanding may be only very indirectly related to the ordinary uses of these expressions. As for technical meanings of the related expressions, I see not much use in trying to elucidate these apart from looking at empirical theories in which these expressions play important roles. I would not try to define 'atom' or 'energy' apart from looking at the use of these words in physics; why should one not adopt the same strategy toward words like 'meaning'?

What is empirical is often not closely related to experimentation. In a wide sense statements like "I have a head on my shoulders" are also empirical, though we hardly go about verifying such claims via experiments. Verifications are often very indirect affairs. This should be kept in mind when viewing theories of language, or any other sufficiently abstract domain.

Adopting Quine's views about analyticity allows one also to view the proposals of Carnap, Montague, Tarski, and others not as a series of analytic claims, but as broadly empirical proposals and hypotheses. Indeed, how could a claim like natural languages being representable as formal languages be anything but empirical? Hence the approach to the history of philosophy of lan-

24. H. P. Grice, "Meaning," *Philosophical Review* 66 (1957), and S. Schiffer, *Meaning* (Oxford: Clarendon Press, 1972).

guage adopted in this introduction. And hence viewing the differences between Montague and Chomsky as empirical in a wide sense.

Richard Montague's reaction to Chomsky's work and that of the Oxford philosophers was the attempt to enlarge the syntactic and semantic structures employed by the positivists and thereby to represent natural languages like English as formal languages in Tarski's sense. As we shall see, if this approach were to be successful, it would place very strict constraints on analyses of semantics and syntax.

Both Chomsky and Montague regard natural languages as objects worthy of scientific and logical study. But while Montague is interested in presenting a semantics for natural languages that can be used to formulate the semantics of many other kinds of artificial languages as well, Chomsky's interest is in what is true uniquely, or at least primarily, of natural languages. Furthermore, in presenting adequate systems of phonology, syntax, and semantics for languages like English or German, Chomsky is also concerned to represent the linguistic competence of human language users. This was not a part of the prescribed task of any of the philosophers mentioned here, except to some extent for Frege.

This survey shows that philosophical theories of language developed in this century have a variety of different concerns, answer different questions, and carry different methodological assumptions. This by itself is not a bad thing. Language can be viewed from different points of view. So where has the philosophy of language gone wrong?

One of the main claims of this book is that the philosophy of language has gone wrong in not seeing the drastic differences in purpose underlying the surface continuity, and hence not keeping in mind that technical tools useful for some of these projects may not be appropriate to others, and questions, for example about learnability, that may be irrelevant to the metaphysical quests mentioned above are highly relevant to the consideration of natural languages as the objects of human linguistic competence.

The contrast between the formalists and the informal investigations of the semantics of natural language (in the words of a former secretary of the UCLA Philosophy Department: logicians vs. lotus eaters) is superficial. Among the formalists there may be drastic disagreements on whether a natural language like English can be represented as what Tarski calls a formal language. There are many formalisms outside Tarski's. Again among the "informalists" there may be important disagreements on the feasibility of investigating detailed small semantic differences among English expressions without paying attention to the syntax.

From the general point of view of Frege, and the special tasks of the metaphysicians and the positivists, there may be no point in articulating the internal structure of word meanings, or lexical semantics from here on, while this may be imperative in order to reach an adequate characterization of human linguistic competence.

In this book I adopt various stances and projects of the previous theories, but eclectically, with awareness of the initial conceptual contexts of these theoretical arsenals. From Frege I adopt the assumption that linguistic competence should be studied, and characterized under idealization. This view is also accepted by Chomsky. It is merely an application of the practice of most empirical sciences. I concentrate for the purposes of formulating a lexical semantics on the Fregean core, ignoring indexicality. In my work I assume that just as in current formalizations the purely qualitative component is a basic and noneliminable ingredient, so in our theories indexicality, a very important phenomenon, is a separate layer from what I am investigating, namely qualitative word meaning. In this respect I follow Frege.

From the philosophers of ordinary language I take over the data that they unearth, and regard it as the kind of thing my theory should account for. I distinguish the semantic puzzles that they posed for us from their work on the pragmatic dimensions of language use–an important field but beyond the scope of this essay.

Finally my theory is meant to be within the broad outlines of how Chomsky sees linguistic competence. Hence I see natural languages as an object of study of intrinsic worth. I see it as necessarily linked with human understanding, as any rational competence is, and thus as requiring concern for learnability, as one of the studies that should cast light on human essence.

Since the positive parts of the book argue for lexical representations that allow for polysemy, partial meaning specifications, and other features ascribed to natural languages as needed ingredients for the mastery, learning, and use of them, in the first part two chapters argue against the claim that natural languages should have their semantics represented as if these languages were formal languages in Tarski's sense. Tarski's specifications rule out polysemy, partial meaning specifications, and so on as acceptable within formal languages as he defines this.

In the second part we turn to constructive suggestions. A theory of lexical meaning is sketched that contains three rather than just the traditional two levels of semantics, thus allowing much of semantic content to be determined by context. The core elements of meaning are portrayed as explanatory structures with four key ingredients that are assumed to be given innately to the human mind.

My lexical theory focuses on mental representations and not on denotation. In Chapter 4 we see that in this respect the theory is similar to the one developed by Chomsky in his recent writings. The chapter explains the relevant parts of Chomsky's theory and attempts to keep Chomsky's basic insights and still assign some, though not fundamental, role to denotation on the lexical level.

The conception of meanings as explanatory schemes raises the question of how basic explanations and the corresponding mental state of understanding are for human cognition. Chapter 5 sketches a view of human cognition in which explanatory schemes are basic, and beliefs, pieces of information make full sense only when embedded in these.

In the last chapter a speculative and nonformal argument is formulated that relies on what the previous chapters said about understanding and lexical meaning. The argument points in the direction of the human mind being partially inscrutable to human understanding at any stage of historical and conceptual context.

PART I

WHY NATURAL LANGUAGES ARE NOT AND SHOULD NOT BE REPRESENTED AS FORMAL LANGUAGES

CHAPTER I

NATURAL LANGUAGES CANNOT BE FORMAL LANGUAGES: THE LEXICON

Representing languages like English or Chinese as formal languages and representing these natural languages as having structures of their own but different from those of Tarski's formal languages, are two radically different conceptions with far-reaching theoretical consequences. Thus, for example, if someone could give a unique delineation of natural languages as a subset of formal languages, that would not satisfy those who think that natural languages have quite different relationships between their grammars and semantic systems, and that the factors shaping syntax and semantics in natural languages are quite different from the ones shaping these respective systems in formal languages. Hence it is not merely a technical issue, but an important philosophic task to show that natural languages cannot be formal languages. It is a necessary first step in the direction of the kind of conception of natural languages that this book presents. The demonstration is contained in two chapters. One of these concerns the lexicon. It will be shown that most, if not all, lexical items of a natural language are affected by a kind of multiplicity of senses that cannot be eradicated by construing the phenomenon as ambiguity and thus merely adding a number of separate lexical items. Nor is this to be treatable as another type of indexicality, on par with those of temporal, spatial, or speaker-hearer relational nature. The second chapter concerns not lexical items in separation, but sentences that in symbolic logic exhibit what is called a "logical form." I claim that these have in natural languages semantic features that, while relevant to semantic interpretation, cannot be assimilated to the class of semantic phenomena constituting logical form.

The notion of natural language defined earlier is conceptually dependent on certain conceptions of the human mind, since the notion of learnability and that of a human agent play essential roles in the account. Such characterization does not rule out the possibility that there is a formal characterization in Montague semantics of the class of natural languages–under my definition –but this would be merely a case of logical equivalence, and from my point of view one without any theoretical significance. The work done so far within Montague semantics leaves this question open, along with the question of whether within a set-theoretic semantic framework the class of natural languages would form a theoretically important and interesting class.

The conception for which I will argue–both by criticizing the most prevalent alternative and by presenting a constructive lexical theory–leaves a number of questions open as either empirical, or as in principle decidable by purely technical means. For example, the definition of a natural language assumed leaves it open as an empirical question whether Esperanto or an invented language like Algol or Lisp, are natural languages. This seems to me a great improvement over definitions of what a natural language is that are based on crude intuitions such as ones that construe as a natural language anything that –as far as we know–emerged "naturally," and as a nonnatural language anything that was born in a laboratory or seminar room.

For the purposes of our first demonstration involving the lexicon, it is very important to understand why ambiguity cannot be tolerated in a language answering Tarski's notion of a formal language. A key element of Tarski's semantics is the set of truth conditions characterizing the declarative sentences of the language. These constitute biconditionals that must be true. But let us consider

'snow is white' is true if and only if snow is white

If all is well with our semantic interpretation, the biconditional must be true. But if we give 'snow' on the right side a different meaning, hence interpretation, than the meaning/interpretation we give to the token on the left side, then the sentence on one side can be true while the sentence on the other is false. Maybe 'white' on the left side has a meaning roughly corresponding to "the color of flakes coming down in winter from the cloudy sky, under completely unpolluted conditions," while the meaning on the right side has the meaning roughly corresponding to "the color of the laundry after Mrs. Smith washed it," where Mrs. Smith is less then a conscientious washing lady. Then the statement on the right side is false, while the statement on the left side is true. Students learning this material at times suggest: Why can you not add a rule stating that you must assign the same meaning to the occurrences of a word on both sides of the biconditional? Such a rule would be unacceptable within Tarski's scheme, because it would leave semantic interpretation as partly no longer a strictly formal, general, matter. The question we must raise now, is: Can we, within the constraints of the principles of formal set-theoretic semantics achieve acceptable interpretations of 'snow' and 'white' in English that leaves these expressions meanings that are completely explicit and without any plurality of sense?[1]

We shall use Tarski's rigorous definition of a formal language which was summarized in the introduction. We shall now distinguish between ambiguity, polysemy—or difference in senses, in contrast with meanings—and index relative truth. It will be argued that polysemy is a key element in the semantics of natural languages in their ordinary uses but cannot be accommodated within Tarski's semantics. These considerations also support the thesis that the aims of semantics for formal languages and those for natural languages should be different. As Tarski designed these, the semantics of formal languages are supposed to embody the content of specific theories. Hence, the semantics for one theory should be as explicit as possible, in order that we should see clearly all implications and independence. (The ability to see such things clearly led, among other things, to the discovery of the independence of the parallel postulate, and hence to the articulation of non-Euclidean geometries.) The semantics for a natural language deals with fluid usages, developments, and abilities to formulate discourse within which we can look at different theories without being committed to any of them. It also has to take into consideration that a basic use of natural language is person-to-person communication. Given these considerations, one would want to construe the semantics of natural languages as leaving as much as possible to factors of nonlinguistic context.

A formal language must be disambiguated. Ambiguity can be illustrated by the meanings of the word 'bank'. One meaning is that of something being a certain financial institution, another that of being the containing element of a river like the Ohio. Two definitions, two meanings. Such disambiguation can be achieved easily within a formal language that is typically designed by a language user or by a group of such. Polysemy does not lend itself to the same treatment. Let us take two examples. The verb 'walk' admits of polysemy. On the one hand, there is a common meaning core, locomotion with the legs in appropriate position. But one has to add: "appropriate distance, covered in an

1. Effort to represent English within the Tarski scheme: R. Montague "English as a Formal Language," in R. Thomason, ed., *Formal Philosophy* (New Haven, CT: Yale University Press, 1974), pp. 188–221.

appropriate time." For what counts as a walk for a toddler's first attempts does not count as a walk for a normal, healthy adult, and the walk of a recovering patient in a hospital is still a different matter. What counts as a walk depends on different *senses* of the word. There is a common conceptual core, and yet an indefinite variety of ranges of application, with different criteria of what counts as a walk, and thus different entailments. We see the same phenomena in connection with what linguists call "underspecified" words like 'use'. There is a common core, roughly, "employ for a purpose," but different senses. We use a car to get the work. This is an instrumental sense. But when we use our imagination, we are not using some external element as an instrument. Still different is the case in which we use a treaty in the defense of our territory. In this context use is linked to relying on some document. In Chapter 3 it will be argued that polysemy in a natural language is much more common than usually supposed, but for our immediate purposes, my own lexical theory will not be presupposed.

Why not treat polysemy as ambiguity, and handle it in that way in formal languages? There are two possibilities; either there is a finite number of cases of polysemy in a language, or there is an infinite number of cases. If an infinite number, then either these can be surveyed conceptually the way we survey the series of positive integers, or there is no way to "generate" in some formal sense all of the cases.

If the number of cases is finite, one might want to simply list these with separate definitions, but we face two disadvantages of such a move. First, we miss important generalizations among some of the different meanings, such as the different senses of 'use' or 'walk'. For in a formal language all of these count as distinct meanings, without closer or less close relations. Furthermore, we place an enormous burden on learnability conditions for such a semantics. Is it really plausible that humans learn all of these separate meanings, or is it more plausible to suppose that they learn what was called above "conceptual cores," and acquire the ability to understand denotations in context in which one would intuitively discern different senses.

If there are infinitely many cases of polysemy, and we cannot survey or generate these in a systematic fashion, then their incorporation into the semantics of a formal language is impossible. In Chapter 3 a lexical theory will be proposed in which such creative aspects of language development are accounted for. But even at this preliminary stage, evidence can be given to show the indefinite variety of polysemy in languages like English or German, and hence a creative aspect in lexical semantics of natural languages. The key point is not that we never know what contexts will emerge in the future that will require multiplying senses, but that we do not know *in the present* which senses are required to explicate our use of most terms in English. We do not know what the different senses of 'emergency' are that are needed to cover all that we want to talk about now, never mind the future.

Why is this kind of infinite/indefinite polysemy a key feature of the semantics of natural languages? It is because natural languages need to have a dynamic semantics; one in which core meanings are linked to potentialities of sense multiplication, thus facilitating the gradual evolution of meaning complexity, so sharply in contrast with the rigid and explicit meaning specifications and meaning postulates of the structures of formal languages.

The meaning structures of natural languages are developed so that these can deal with a constant barrage of small semantic emergencies. A formal language is interpreted over a domain that is assumed to be static and totally surveyable.

This leaves us with the alternative of relegating polysemy to pragmatics. Pragmatics deals with phenomena that involve some specification of meaning which depends on intentions, state of knowledge, or social context of specific speakers or hearers. For example, it is a matter of pragmatics that when talking to the sister of a bank director we refer to him as "your brother," since this is the more apt reference, while this reference may be quite useless when talking about the same person to people who do not know anything about his family status. Or again, the success of locutions like "Give me that thing!" depend on shared tasks or knowledge between speaker and hearer that are not matters of communal linguistic knowledge.

There may even be reference fixing on a most concrete level that depends on pragmatic factors. For example, an executive and his secretary may agree on what they will call emergency during the two weeks of the executive's vacation. Such an agreement is strictly local; that is, it is between two persons, it is designed to cover only a certain time period, and knowledge of this reference fixing is not a part of what the speakers of the relevant language are to know.

These examples show that polysemy of interest here is not a matter of pragmatics. The different senses of a given word bring with them different entailments, and mastery of the various cases of polysemy is a part of knowing the language. Not understanding the different senses of 'use' limits a person's mastery of English, and the same can be said about the senses of 'walk', 'snow', and so forth.

If polysemy is not a matter of ambiguity or pragmatics, could it be assimilated to indexes that relativize truth, like "indexical expressions" and personal pronouns? Indexical expressions like 'now' or 'here', require relativizing the truth assessment of what the sentence they are in contains, to a given temporal or spatial point. The expressions themselves do not indicate a given point for a given utterance; the determination is a matter of relating a sentence inscription or utterance to an externally given point in time and space. The same holds for personal pronouns like 'I' or 'she'.

Such indexing of truth can be accomplished formally by introducing index that require truth assignments relative to what the given index specifies. Why not introduce an additional index for the kinds of denotation fixings that we saw lies at the bottom of polysemy?

There is, however, a huge difference between these semantic phenomena. The different senses contribute to the content of what a given sentence expresses. This is the Fregean core – that is, the qualitative contributions of descriptive expressions in a sentence, that constitute the descriptive power of a sentence– that which is expressed, regardless of when, where, and by whom it is uttered. The "when," "where," "who" are not affecting the descriptive content; these notions only locate in the world the external conditions under which the sentence needs be interpreted. But polysemy does affect the descriptive, qualitative core. Furthermore, polysemy and its interpretation depend in many cases on linguistic context. In this respect too, difference in senses differs from indexicality.

Finally, a key difference is that we can generate indefinitely spatiotemporal or speaker-relative points for interpretation. We can start with a temporal point and order an infinite number of additional ones with the use of 'before' and 'after'. We can take a spatial point and generate an indefinitely large collection of these by adjacency conditions. The same holds for a collection of speakers of a language. But this conceptual survey cannot be carried out with multiplication of senses for a given expression. We have no way of enumerating or surveying all of the senses of 'use', or 'walk', or 'emergency'. This limitation holds not only for future uses, but also the present. I don't know what nonindexically and hence purely qualitatively describable conditions face humans right now for which a multiplication of senses in needed.

Thus the two facts, first that polysemy affects the *Fregean core* of what sentences express, and second, that there is no conceptual way of generating all of the polysemy demanding contexts, makes polysemy unsuitable for truth relativizing, if we are to take seriously Tarski's scheme, explained in the introduction, as having explanatory power.

Of course, if we construe formal languages as a mere device for sentence segmentation and truth assignment, we can always introduce additional indexes as primitives. But such a move–unlike Tarski's specifications–is a completely ad hoc move, and has all of the virtues that theft has over honest toil.

I. BETWEEN AMBIGUITY AND SYNONYMY

Let us return to the sentence cited above. Is snow white? Even brief reflection will tell us that obviously not all snow is white. Much of it is gray, or even black, and still other parts are colored in a variety of other ways. Yet, there seems to be something intuitively right about the sentence. In "some sense" snow is white. How are we to sort out these conflicting intuitions? 'Snow' is a mass–term, that is, one without a principle of individuation, or divided reference. How should we, then, interpret its occurrence in this sentence? Does it have the force of "all snow"? Tarski, when he used this example, must have interpreted it this way.[2] But another interpretation is open to us. We can read the sentence as having the same semantic force as so-called generic sentences like "beavers build dams". In that sentence what is expressed is not that every beaver builds dams, but that a healthy beaver will build dams under natural conditions. Can we apply an analogous reading to our sentence about snow? It seems to work well with a sentence that is grammatically like the one about snow, but whose content is more like the one about beaver, since it deals with something organic; namely the sentence "grass is green". Here too, something seems right, but if taken to mean all grass, then the sentence is false. Some grass is brown, other parts are yellow, and so on. The healthy grass–if one can speak that way–or rather grass when it is "healthy," that is, growing, getting enough water, sunshine, and so forth, is green under normal conditions.

This brief excursion into generics will help us later in dissecting senses of various common nouns. But for the time being let us stick to the interpretation that construes the sentence to be about "all snow." Such a reading is given either if we interpret 'snow', like any mass term, mereologically as denoting the sum of all entities that are parts of the one scattered particular, snow,[3] or we can attempt set-theoretic interpretations and come up with something like "all portions of snow," where "portion" is introduced as a technical term, defined as by Parsons and Montague.[4]

For our purposes it is also irrelevant whether we take the sentence to have modal impact or not. One could take it to be asserting a necessary truth, but one can also construe it as a simple universal generalization. We shall consider

2. A. Tarski, "The Concept of Truth in Formalized Languages," in *Logic Semantics and Metamathematics* (Oxford: Oxford University Press, 1936, reprint 1956,), pp. 152–278.

3. J. Moravcsik, "Mass Terms in English," in J. Hintikka, J. Moravcsik, P. Suppes, eds., *Approaches to Natural Language*, (Dordrecht: Reidel, 1973), pp. 263–285, 301–8.

4. R. Montague, "The Proper Treatment of Mass Terms in English," reprinted in F. Pelletier, ed., *Mass Terms: Some Philosophical Problems*, (Dordrecht: Reidel, 1979), pp. 173–78.

it in the second way, since this is the simplest, and additional complications do not affect the points made here about the lexicon.

We shall start now with considering the semantics of 'snow'.[5] We need to raise three questions: What is the nature of snow? What is it to be snow according to everyday conceptions? What is it for something to count as snow, in this or that context? Answers to these questions are interlocking. Answers to the first bring in whatever scientific accounts of the subject we have, and call for us to see what if any connection this has with everyday use or uses. Finally, we have to investigate to what extent the combination of scientific and everyday use determines extension, or denotation, in specific contexts. Initial speculation suggests that there should be links among the three factors. For the scientific account presumably gives us not only ways of recognizing what is snow, and guidelines for using it or reacting to it, but an explanation, or explanatory sketch, of its origin and constituency. This, in turn, is likely to influence the everyday use, since within that we want to distinguish the real from the merely apparent or fake subject–gold from fool's gold. Finally, the everyday use should determine or at least should provide guidelines for what will count as snow in various contexts. It is instructive to look at the entry in the Oxford English Dictionary, because it can be seen as an attempted compromise to meet these different considerations. It says: "the congealed vapour of the atmosphere falling in flakes characterized by their lightness and whiteness." The first part of this links with science, and the idea that some explanatory information should be a part of the meaning. But we must ask whether it is really true that a person who does not know the account of origin listed here (congealment…) is really missing a part of the meaning of 'snow'. A more realistic characterization of linguistic lexical competence in this case would be: knowledge that there is an explanation grounded in accounts of nature, and that this explanation would account for the fact that normally snow comes "from above," and its constituency, flakes. Furthermore it is different from other stuff that "comes from above." It is also interesting to note that whiteness is included in the Oxford account, even though as I noted not all snow is white. Intuition says that snow is white if "nothing nonnatural interferes" in some hard-to-define sense. Even then it is questionable whether we could say that snow–before it hits polluting factors in the sky or hits the ground–must be, analytically white. These reflections show that lexical definitions should be construed not as analytic in the logical sense, but as functioning within somewhat vague and

5. This section owes much to J. Moravcsik, "Is Snow White?" In Patrick Suppes, *Scientific Philosopher*, vol. 3, (Amsterdam: Kluwer, 1994), pp. 71–87.

very general presuppositions, such as the uniformity of nature, general but still contingent assumptions about the atmosphere, laws of gravity, and so on. These limit the application of the definition to a subset of all logical possibilities (or possible worlds, as some say). The Oxford entry suggests also recognitional features. There are, however, at least two different dimensions along which snow must be distinguished from other stuff. First, it has to be distinguished from other items that "fall from above" such as rain and mist. Mere perceptual distinguishing is insufficient in many contexts. For example, it might be very difficult to tell just by looking whether what we see is the result of snowfall or heavy frost. (I am indebted to an anonymous referee for the example.) Second, it must be distinguished from stuff on the ground such as slush, ice, or dust. This last consideration shows that the extension of 'snow' is not only a set of flakes, but also items that consist of fallen flakes, such as snow fields or patches. Throughout this we assumed that snow has "natural" origin, but we must allow also for snow machines and their products. One could say, however, that we have here a case that parallels the relation between legs and artificial legs, and other miracles of modern medical technology. Even if the artificial product could be in substance the same as the natural one, one would draw a distinction without changing the definition of 'snow' that includes its not being an artifact but primarily a natural phenomenon.

So clearly we cannot restrict the extension of 'snow' just to falling flakes. There is the snow field, snow cover, and so on but also the snow turning into slush, and the melting snow. How far are we to go? And is this merely a case of what is ordinarily called vagueness? The negative answer suggests itself when we try–unsuccessfully–to restrict 'snow' to cover only "dry" snow. For here we see that this is no longer an issue of vagueness. The question "How dry?" leads into questions about different criteria, depending on the context at issue, and this is a function of the nature of the interaction between humans and nature. Some snow might be dry enough–and wet enough–for making snowballs, but the same snow would not have the required dry constituency for skiing. Then within snow appropriate for skiing, we distinguish between more dry and more wet snow. We hear ski reports about wet snow on the slopes, and this is not a contradiction. Still different criteria come into play when we talk about a snow fields. The constituency can be even closer to slush than either that of the snow good for skiing or the snow used for snowballs. These examples show that what counts as snow is not a matter of mere vagueness, but rather a matter of different items counting as snow within different contexts of human interaction and use of nature.

Some might try to rescue the situation and still stick to a unitarian account by bringing in purity. Should we say that snow is white when it is pure snow? For example, one might think of snow in the Alps or of the Himalayas as having pure snow, not affected by pollution and other forms of human intervention. But even in these cases, the question of how dry or wet can be raised, and this will change with the seasons. Furthermore, questions and answers about these things will still depend on human interest. Finally, we should not think of snow in the Alps as substance under idealized conditions. For example, one could say that water is H_2O under idealized conditions. But that would not be reflected in the meaning of 'water', as we shall see. H_2O may be pure water for a scientist, but for the layperson pure water is really good drinking water. Thus purity is use dependent. The case of the snow in the Alps as "ideally white" is not. Furthermore, we do not call only good potable water 'water', as we shall see shortly. Our notion of snow is not derivative from whatever we call snow in the Alps and other mountains of high elevation. Many humans know how to use 'snow' without ever having heard of the Alps and other such ranges.

It might be suggested that what has been described here as various uses could be reinterpreted as varieties of species. Maybe we need to specify more exactly each time whether we speak of snow for snowball, skiing snow, snow for painting, or some other snow. But there are two reasons why such an approach does not work. First, what is to count as snow is often a matter of negotiation among language users in a concrete context. Maybe for uniformity among weather forecasters at a certain station exact specifications for what should count as snow need be determined. This cannot be built into a linguistic specification as demarcating a kind. Most important, dividing a genus into species does not lead to describing the same entity in contradictory terms. But in the case of denotation-fixing contexts this situation does obtain. The same patch of white stuff will be described as snow from one point of view (e.g., children playing outside) and not snow (e.g., by the snow removal people, for whom the substance referred to is only wet, partly icy, stuff for which their equipment is not appropriate). A duck correctly described is always a duck, though it may be a certain kind of duck such as a mallard. But the same bit of stuff can be correctly described as snow and not snow from different points of view, and it makes no sense of ask: "What is it really?"

The last point brings us also to the important observation that 'snow' is not a part of scientific vocabulary. We need not define snow in scientific terms. In this respect it is unlike water. This is turn leads to having different relations to scientific explanations than 'water'.

An adequate definition of 'snow' can be given within the lexical theory to which we will turn in Chapter 3. Here we need only point to this indefinite plurality of uses to which 'snow', and as we shall see, most other lexical items in natural languages, is subject. This is not a case of ambiguity. There is one everyday meaning for 'snow'. But it generates an indefinite variety of denotational uses (how dry? how light? how much of it in flakes?). These are the function of human interactions with nature. We cannot predict or give a qualitative exact specification of all past and future human interactions with nature that have or will affect our use of 'snow'. Hence this kind of multiplicity of senses or uses remains an uneliminable aspect of the meaning of 'snow'. But if this is so, then the truth condition proposed initially breaks down. For now we take "'snow is white' is true if and only if snow is white", and assign one use to the first occurrence of 'snow', another to the second, and we can obtain a situation in which one half of the biconditional is true while the other is false.

Let us assign to the first occurrence of 'snow' the use fixing denotation as the snow falling at high elevations throughout the world apart from any human intervention and use, and to the second occurrence the material regarded as snow at a certain time in the winter in all the main cities of the world. Then the left half of the biconditional can be true, while the right half false. Furthermore, as we saw, the situation cannot be remedied by regarding this as a case of ambiguity, since the semantic phenomenon pointed to does not fit any formal definition of ambiguity.

Now let us turn to the other general term of the original sentence, namely 'white'. Intuitively we construe this also as a mass term, just like 'snow', but some have attempted for terms like this also set-theoretical interpretations. We shall bypass this issue, as we have in the case of 'snow', since it does not affect the key points to be made about natural languages not being formal languages.

The word 'white' is a perceptual word; in the everyday phenomenal sense its meaning is simple and undefinable. It is the primitive, irreducible quality of whiteness. At the same time, science has provided an explanation of how this color emerges. Thus, the Oxford English Dictionary's "of the color of snow and milk... produced by reflection, transmission, or emission of all kinds of light... devoid of any distinctive hue." The full account refers also to the color spectrum. Obviously, here again, we have an attempt to state some of the scientific conditions for the emergence of whiteness, and some fairly crude examples that, under suitable conditions, exemplify the quality that is the meaning of this adjective. Since in the everyday phenomenal sense we cannot define 'white', we explain its meaning by contrasts. White contrasts with off-white, yellow, light pink, light brown, and other shades. The boundaries will not be sharp, and hence the term suffers from vagueness. I shall leave this aside, however, since our main aim is to show that 'white' is affected by the same multiplicity of denotational uses as 'snow'. Furthermore, there seems to be no good reason to confuse the ordinary phenomenal sense of 'white' and the meaning of this word in the context of scientific explanations. The lengthy sketch the OED adds to the examples is not a part of the competence of a competent user of English. We can use 'white' in everyday contexts without knowing anything about reflection, color spectrum, or other technicalities. The phenomenal notion of white is a data that science accounts for within a theory. The theory, or even its existence, need not be a part of the semantics of English. One can take the existence of the directly experienced color white as given, without any views as to whether science can explain it or not.

The fact that we explain whiteness by contrasts does not say anything against formalizability. As long as the contrasts stay fixed across all contexts, truth-conditional accounts can be given for the colors. As we shall see, however, contrasts and demarcations of required shades vary depending on different human interactions with nature, artifacts, and the connected differences of interest.

In different contexts we invoke different criteria for what should count as white. For example, a white shirt is white even if it has spots on it. This is true even if the spots were made intentionally in the factory. Another context is provided by our gazing at a landscape. How much white snow must be covering the ground for us to say that the fields are white? Many patches of brown are permissible. Other contexts open up when we consider artifacts. When is what we call a white suit white? It seems to be a matter of contrast peculiar to clothing. So it is a white suit as long as it is not a yellow (lemon colored) or light brown one. In other contexts, however, even minute differences of shade can be very important. This is exemplified by the cartoon that appeared in the *New Yorker* many years ago in which a painter is confronting the lady of the house, and–obviously after quite a bit of conversation–declares: "I know what you mean Madam; there is no such shade."

These examples illustrate points we made in connection with 'snow'. The variations in the extension of 'white' are not random. They depend on human interactions with nature and artifacts, and relate to human interests. These factors are orderly, and can be projected up to a point. At the same time, there is no way of predicting all of the human interactions and developments of interests, past, present, and future. Who could have predicted the highway markings that developed in the United States? On many roads we have now white and yellow lines. A white line counts as white even if it is worn out or dirty. A white line that has become yellowed because of accumulated dirt is still a white line, though misleading, in need of repair. So with different uses and artifacts the extension of 'white' varies. But once we fix denotation in a context like the ones we illustrated, the denotation remains fixed; it is not open to subjective variation.

What about the meaning of 'white'? The nature of whiteness is construed differently in science and in everyday contexts. Furthermore, the everyday conception is independent of the scientific one. Unlike the case of gold and fool's gold, we do not change our views about extension in view of what science says. The meaning of 'white' rests on a firm phenomenal, intersubjective basis. The meaning, however, allows for lack of hue, brightness, and so on to be interpreted within appropriate limits. And this, in turn opens up the possibilities of contextual denotation fixing. The denotations fixed contextually are influenced also by such factors indicating human interest as the pragmatic link between whiteness and cleanliness. Many things are such that if they are clean, they should be white. But "how clean?" "how white?" are questions receiving different answers in different interactional contexts. Many other examples illustrate the same point. We speak of white skin (humans), white gold, and white wine. In each case different contrasts and different practical considerations are involved.

These observations apply not only to nouns and verbs, but also to words like 'in'. Someone can be in the river, a piece of wood is stuck in a rock, a foot is in a shoe, and many of us are–all too often–in trouble. This is not ambiguity, but neither is it a matter of applying one rigid set of criteria.

Returning to the original sentence illustrating Tarski's truth conditions, we see now how complicated the semantic situation is once we consider the full richness of the meaning structures of the descriptive terms 'snow' and 'white'. To the different uses of 'snow' we must now add the different uses of 'white'; thus getting an enormous variety of readings. If we assign different uses to the first and second occurrences of 'white' in the sentence, we might easily obtain occurrences with different extensions, thus falsifying the bi-conditional. Maybe in one occurrence 'white' receives the relatively narrow interpretation of what is used by the interior decorator, while the other occurrence is assigned a relatively wide interpretation as, for example the one we obtain when applying 'white' to landscape.

We should, however, consider a reply to our demonstrations by a defender of the view exemplified by Montague. This reply relies on the extension of formal semantics to include index relativizing truth and suggests that the phenomenon we unearthed requires only the addition of another index so as to save the applicability of the truth conditions to sentences of natural languages.

Assessing this reply requires a look at what indexicality really is. In its initial

Fregean modern use, indexicality means restricting the application of truth and assigning of denotation to particular times and spatial points. The sentence "2 is an even number" is simply true, whereas "Joe is eating apples" can be judged as true or false at different times. Similar conditions apply to spatial indicators in sentences such as "It is raining here". In the cases of space and time, we can delineate the class of all indexes as correlated to the class of all temporal or spatial points. Just as we can order the infinite series of positive integers with the successor relation, we can order temporal points with the earlier/later relation, and spatial points with contiguity. Furthermore, in both cases we take interpretations of descriptive terms that apply to all of reality, and at times also to all possibilities. Then we restrict the applications to a part of reality, carved out by spatial or temporal restrictions. When giving a semantics of natural languages it was necessary to introduce also indexes to account for personal pronouns like 'I' or 'you', and their respective possessive forms ('my', etc.) This can be seen as a speaker or hearer (or intended hearer) relativization of truth, still maintaining the characteristics of the spatiotemporal indexes – that is, surveying conceptually the class of all speaker-hearers. We should note also that these indexing procedures are tied to specific parts of vocabularies of natural languages. Other indexes might also be formed. For example, we might want to restrict truth to perceptual situations.[6] These too have the characteristics of being conceptually surveyable like positive integers, time, space, and speakers (hearers). Would it make sense to introduce a further index, making the interpretation of truth relative to one of the contextual denotation fixings just discussed? We have already seen that we are not dealing with ambiguity; why not try to assimilate this multireferentiality to indexicality?

There are a number of ways in which the phenomenon we point to differs from the legitimate ways, where introducing indexicals makes sense. Specification of meaning is purely qualitative within the original Fregean framework. Hence we label words whose meaning can be given purely qualitative construal parts of the Fregean core. When a word also requires elements outside of the qualitative external items, such as spatiotemporal location, bringing in speaker and addressee, then we regard the word as being outside the Fregean core. The distinction turned out to be very useful in work on semantics. Several of the recent suggestions about the semantics of ordinary proper names can be interpreted as claiming, among other things, that proper names are outside the Fregean core. Recent suggestions that many items such as natural kind terms, and other types of general terms, are semantically like proper names can also

6. J. Barwise and J. Perry, *Situations and Attitudes* (Cambridge, MA: MIT Press, 1983).

be seen as having the implication that these terms are outside the Fregean core. The issue of where to draw the line between what is and what is not in natural languages a part of the Fregean core is a key question of semantics and will be addressed in Chapter 3. Here simply note that the multiple senses or uses that we detected and assigned to just about any descriptive term in a natural language are still within the Fregean core. For these are still purely qualitative supplementations of meaning. Reference to human interest and functioning are references to qualitative aspects of reality.

Second, unlike the case of legitimate indexing, in these cases we cannot tie the indexes to a subclass of the vocabulary of the language. It affects all descriptive terms with empirical implication. Finally, and perhaps most important, the class of possible denotation-fixing contexts is an infinite and indefinite class that we cannot give overall characterization as we can with successor notion for positive integers, and spatiotemporal ordering predicates with space and time. In all of the legitimate cases the indexes restrict application of truth to parts of the totality of what there is, even if in an extended sense. But denotational multiplicity does not do that. One might say, it ascribes values to contexts and states of affair that are created by the undefinable plurality of potential human use and interest increases. As we shall see, in this and other ways the lexicon is productive; its meaning specifications are guidelines for creating what are at any given time unforeseeable new uses, interests, and practical applications.

Introducing an index for our multidenotationality would be a completely ad hoc device without any serious conceptual or explanatory force. If would violate what we saw as the intuitive motivations and justifications of the indexes that are already parts of our semantic systems. The new index would not refer to a well-ordered class but to an "I know not what" that develops in unpredictable ways through history, and unlike the other indexes, remains within the Fregean core.

Our conclusion, then, should be that though there is room for a rigorous semantics for natural languages, this will not be within the Tarskian framework, as Tarski himself said, and will not center on truth conditions. One can only speculate that this is what Tarski had in mind—apart from the paradoxes of truth—when he said that natural languages are distinguished by their universality.[7] Indexing should be not a mere ad hoc mechanical device, but a conceptually constrained mechanism, and hence a rigorous concept, not merely expressing something vague that we want to force arbitrarily into a conception

7. A. Tarski, "The Concept of Truth in Formalized Language."

of semantics that by any nonarbitrary criterion does not work here if rigorously applied. As my colleague, Patrick Suppes, often enunciated in seminars: "It is better to be clearly wrong than to be vaguely right."

II. FORM, FUNCTION, INTERPRETATION

In this section we shall consider further relevant details concerning the ways in which certain contexts fix denotation, and consider also, both in detail and in general terms, the relationship between meaning and denotation. Let us consider as our initial example a question encountered often in everyday conversation:

> Is there water in the refrigerator?

On the surface this is a simple question.[8] But even brief reflection, concerned with possible answers that make good sense in this or that context, shows us that there are many different factors building different contexts, underlying the surface simplicity.

One can imagine a thirsty child coming into the house after play, asking this question of the parents in the kitchen. But one can also imagine two people engaged in defrosting the refrigerator in order to start repair work, and one of them asking the same question, expecting an answer that will inform him whether every drop of water and melted ice has been removed from the refrigerator. A less stringent criterion is imposed if the task is simply to defrost the refrigerator so that the next couple renting the apartment can start clean. Examples of this sort, bringing in different human interests and hence uses, and different social contexts, can be multiplied indefinitely.

Normally, we do not go through dozens of possible scenarios in our mind. We understand the question and the context that gives it a certain specific appropriateness, and we respond correctly. Given the nature of the question and the likely responses, the conversation should result in some action. An adequate semantics, however, has to make allowances for the fact that action need not result in all cases. Hence ensuing action cannot be a part of the semantic structure that we build up to account for the conversation; only the possible

8. An earlier version of this section was presented in 1992 to the UCLA Philosophy Department. I owe good criticisms to Tyler Burge, Kit Fine, and David Kaplan.

request implicit in what is said, and the potentiality for action is to be acknowledged.

In what follows we shall concentrate on the kind of contexts we treated already in the previous section. Thus we shall ignore elements involved in what is usually called indexicality, that is spatiotemporal or speaker-hearer relativity. Our context is constituted by intersubjective presuppositions, aims, and constraints, independent of indexicality. The contexts do sort out pure water as H_2O from pure drinking water, polluted water, and simple water not designed to be potable that we find in the pipes of heating systems. These are qualitative distinctions, thus leaving the types carved out within the Fregean core.

The semantics to be sketched should account for the following facts:

i. We understand the sample sentences but not always in the same way. In normal circumstances we have no trouble understanding how the sentence is to be interpreted and what would count as an adequate answer, often linked to some search-and-find activity.

ii. The varieties of ways in which we can understand the sentences have underlying them qualitative core meaning constituents that we ascribe to parts of the sentences prior to the consideration of contexts. These ascriptions must help in seeing along what dimensions series of contexts can be generated.

iii. The adequate semantics should bring out why some explanatory element is needed as parts of the meanings of the key descriptive words of answers to our initial question.

iv. An adequate semantics should clarify the conceptual and empirical relationships between meaning and denotation. That is, are meaning structures and reference quite distinct, or does meaning place constraints on what counts as the domain of reference; or does meaning completely determine reference?

Let us look now at the meaning structures of the key descriptive terms and phrases of the sentence that is the affirmative answer to the question with which we started:

> There is water in the refrigerator

For ‘water’ the OED gives, roughly: “in pure form a colorless transparent tasteless liquid without smell; of which lakes and oceans are made, and which comes as rain or in springs.” Once more we see the attempt to give recognitional features and–this time in common sense terms–some explanation as to origin, and suitable location. In fact, the situation of giving a semantics for 'water' is far more complicated than the OED entry would have one believe, though we can learn things from this entry as well. Unlike 'snow', 'water' has an exact scientific meaning. Hence it also has a scientific use. Thus we need to look at three factors: (i) the nature of water according to science, (ii) what water is according to everyday use, and (iii) how these factors constrain as well as give guidelines for denotation.

As most of us know, water is H_2O. Is this fact completely irrelevant to the determination of everyday use and meaning? Could it be that what the scientists and the ordinary speaker mean by 'water' are totally different entities? Such a hypothesis is contradicted by the fact that among the phenomena that the H_2O definition is supposed to explain are our singling out in everyday use a certain substance and ascribing reliably properties to it. Science is not just trying to explain why humans formed a concept of water and found this useful. It wants to give an account of what is in some rough way the same thing as what the everyday use acknowledges. This raises interesting questions about the relations between scientific use and everyday use of language, which will be discussed later. For our purposes it is sufficient to note that there is a scientific use, a characterization of nature, and that this meaning and denotation has some relation to everyday use. For example, what the scientist takes to be water has some relation–not exact identity–to what we take to be water in everyday use, and of the properties the scientist assigns to water cannot be in straightforward contradiction to the basic properties everyday use assigns. At the same time, we should not think of the meaning of 'water' in science as defining this notion across all possible worlds. The definition is given within the theory of the table of chemical elements. It could happen that we discard this theory some day, and replace it with a better one. At that point we will need a new scientific definition for water. So the scientific account we have now holds for all those possible worlds only in which the table of chemical elements holds.

As we turn to the everyday account, the most striking feature of this is the dominance of functional characterization. Water is what we drink; water is what can be used for washing; water gives humans, animals, plants nourishment. It seems to me that it is within this functional context that we ordinarily interpret the notion of "pure water". Pure water is what we can drink, what nourishes organic things in general, what we wash with. Only rarely do we mean by "pure water" the H_2O of the scientist. The functionally pure can even conflict with the scientifically pure.

These functional characterizations are accompanied by some, rather vague, structural specifications and also some of constituency. But only a small segment of the class of competent users know that there is a scientific use, and would be willing to say, as an act of faith, that the nature of what they use is whatever scientists happen to be saying it is at a given time. Likewise, the constituency requirement is that water in its "natural form" is a liquid, but beyond this only a few will venture some condition in terms of molecules. The recognitional features are roughly the ones the OED lists, but even here qualifications are needed; for depending on the functional use, different kinds and degrees of colorlessness, tastelessness, and other properties will be invoked. This leads us to the key point in the context of this chapter. Purity in the everyday use turns out not to be simply a matter of degrees, but also depends on functional specifications.

Water is construed by us in a way in which functional specifications are dominant; that is, determine partly, and thus constrain, structural, distinguishing, and constitutive specifications. In this way the everyday conception differs sharply from the scientific one. Unlike Putnam and others, I do not believe that we would let our concept be guided or governed by the scientific notion. Within the account given in Chapter 3, scientific use is merely one of the many uses that the lexicon must account for; it has in general no privileged status. Philosophers sometimes give the case of gold versus fool's gold as an example of science correcting common sense, introducing different rules for denotation. But that is an unusual example. Gold has for us strong functional structure. It is something valuable and also rare. Hence the discovery that there are things indistinguishable in ordinary ways from gold, but in terms of their nature different, shows that something alien can and has diluted what we conceive of as the real supply of gold. Hence change in meaning and denotation was dictated in order to preserve the functional assumptions. But this is most unlikely to happen in the case of water. If we discovered that science distinguishes two substantial kinds among the things that for purposes of potability, nourishment in general, and so on we regard as water, we most likely would not change meaning and denotation, but simply note that what we conceive of as water in functional terms has for the purposes of science two distinct subspecies.

Turning to denotation fixing, we see that functional contexts prescribe different denotational contexts and corresponding ranges on the basis of at least the following considerations: How pure must water be in order to count in a context as water, and how much of it must there be in order to be counted as being present in a context?

How pure must water be, and what besides H_2O must it contain in order to count as drinking water? Furthermore, are not the criteria for drinking water changing dependent on contexts related to what we can put up with in order to save our lives or those of others?

Criteria for drinking water are quite different from those determining the kind of water we regard as needed in order to put out a fire in the Oakland hills. What about criteria for water accepted for use in a laboratory? As for quantity, how much must be present in order to say that there is drinking water in the refrigerator? And how does this differ from the quantity that must be excluded in the case of a check prior to starting a repair job on the refrigerator?

Some will say, as in the case of snow, that we are talking about different kinds, or species, of water, and ordinary use is merely incomplete, leaving it up the speaker's knowledge of the nonlinguistic context to figure out which species are we talking about. But this will not do for the same reason that this suggestion fails in the case of snow. For the same thing can be judged as water from one point of view, and as not water from another. For example, a thirsty crew comes in the desert upon a hole with some dark brown stinking liquid in it. If they have plenty of drinking water with them, they will say that the liquid in the hole is not water. It is some kind of disgusting muddy stuff, and they will pass it by. But if they have been for days under the hot tropical sun, and are on the brink of dehydration, they will drink it as long as there are good reasons to suppose that it will not poison them.

One might say that though the liquid in question is not treated as water, it could still be believed to be "really water." But further reflection should convince us that there is no absolute, unambiguous sense to saying that something is "really water." Do we mean by this that it is H_2O? Or do we mean that it is still the right kind of potable liquid, but not what we would like to consume ordinarily? Purity is one aspect of assessing something as counting for water, and the functional specification for us is another. These need not go together, and have equal weight in ordinary use. Neither our functional needs, nor the table of chemical elements, which might change tomorrow, leads us to some absolute sense of "really." In many cases desert travelers will note in their diaries that finally they found water. How many purists–in more than one sense–will write in the diary: "We found some more or less potable water?" To be sure, in some cases we say–in a context–"that water is not good enough", but this is not always the way we describe our situation. There can be borderline cases in terms of what additives are present in the water, where one group says: "No, this is not water anymore", and another group disagrees. Such disagreements may have serious legal and medical consequences!

The entry in the OED does have some sound underlying intuitions. There should be some explanatory factors in the meaning of a term denoting a solid or liquid substance, even if in some cases this is quite primitive, namely a condition about typical origin. (Such a condition is hardly analytic.) There must be also a list of some salient distinguishing or recognitional features. But in addition we do need a strong functional specificatory structure, and the first two parts of the meaning structure need be contextualized along the lines of the third. This is how we generate an indefinite number of denotational contexts in which it must be decided what counts, or should count, as water. Water for drinking, for the fire department, the golf course ("untreated" is the euphemism we use to cover up the semantic subtleties), and even within these kinds of contexts emergencies and various vicissitudes can influence not only practical use, but also semantic legislation and use.

In turning now to the other main descriptive term, 'refrigerator' we should note the feature that makes it radically different from the items considered so far, namely that it denotes an artifact. This is caught by the OED which gives as its entry: "apparatus for cooling and freezing, and maintaining such cool temperatures involving a container (chamber or vessel of some short)". Interestingly, unlike in the case of snow or water, here the OED features the functional specification. Some might think that the notion of artifact is necessarily connected to functional features, but this need not be so. The play instinct can stimulate humans to produce also strictly nonfunctional entities. Still, in most cases artifacts are related to human need and interest. But more important, specifying refrigerators as artifacts also contributes an explanatory layer of meaning, since with this we also indicate origin and mode of coming into being. Refrigerators have also scientific explanations, but unlike in the other cases surveyed so far, here the link is to the applied sciences, and not the theoretical ones. This does make a difference, since even if someone insisted that scientific accounts of snow or water are quite independent of functional considerations, this can hardly be said of the applied sciences. Whatever separates the scientific understanding of refrigerators from the everyday conception, it is not lack of functional consideration. It is more likely that the difference lies in the applied sciences accounting for modes of production and maintenance, while the everyday use focuses on what we want the refrigerator for, and how this interest places some constraints on constituency, structure, and distinguishing characteristics.

Let us lay aside concerns about detail in the OED entry. Even if we accepted the entry in terms of qualitative specifications, we should see that it gives at most necessary but not sufficient conditions. For we must add the riders that the cooling must be to the appropriate level of cold temperature, and that the same holds for maintenance. Furthermore, the container must meet specifications in terms of size, depending on the need and use that the apparatus to be called a refrigerator is to meet. A refrigerator used for keeping food must cool and maintain temperature in such a way that the food does not spoil. In Texas on some ranches giant refrigerators contain the semen of exemplary bulls; this material is then shipped to various parts of the world for breeding. How cold must this apparatus be? What must be its structure? Then there are all sorts of other cooling devices used for cars or for space travel, and refrigerators need be distinguished from these too. Thus what we call a refrigerator will depend on contexts in which it is specified what is to be cooled, and to what temperature, and for what use.

This is, once more, not just a matter of "different kinds, or species." A refrigerator that is designed to preserve food for humans in kitchens that fails to function in this way, is not just another kind of refrigerator, but no refrigerator at all. Furthermore, given that we cannot see ahead all of the ways in which things will be needed to be kept cool for human use, we cannot specify once and for all the denotation of 'refrigerator'. (This can be seen on brief reflection to apply to all sorts of artifacts, such as vehicles, clothing, etc.)

In view of these considerations it is also important not to confuse the meaning of a word like 'refrigerator' with typicality, because the meaning must have the conceptual structure to provide conditions for the engendering of future contexts, some of which may be at present even unimaginable to us.

We shall now turn to the phrase "there is... in...". First, a few comments on the existential claim. One might take its presence in everyday English as evidence that language at times connects us with a reality independent of us. But the presence of these locutions and their successful use by itself does not lead to such conclusions. What we can conclude is that such successful uses show that language can help to coordinate action among members of a linguistic community. But this only proves intersubjectivity. The jump from that to a mind-independent reality is huge, and is beyond the scope of this essay. Still, even the assumption of intersubjectivity is relevant to consider different views on the relation between language and reality, and this between different conceptions of language, as we shall see in Chapter 4.

What about 'in'? At first glance this might seem a simple notion of containment, but as we saw already this is not so. Clearly being 'in' something entails spatial containment of some sort, but in different contexts different containment is appropriate. For example for someone to be in the house means that the person is in one of the rooms, or other areas inside the walls. But for a gold ring to be inside the house could mean that it is hidden, built into one of the walls. In what ways is a house a container? Is it the outermost "skin"? In some contexts yes, in others no. Again, what does it mean that there are fish in the ocean? Here containment can be measured from the surface. But in other contexts this will not do. What does it mean that the information is in someone's head (or mind)? Are there precise boundaries involved in this sort of containment? Does one have to know neurophysiology, or an alternative dualistic account in order to understand the sentence? Further complications arise when we try to specify outside of practical contexts what is meant by something being in a country. This interesting kind of polysemy is illustrated as well by the following two deductive schemes. (I am indebted for these to Tom Wasow.)

(A) My foot is in my sock
My sock is in my shoe

My foot is in my shoe

So far so good. But contrast (A) with

(B) A hole is in my sock
My sock is in my shoe

A hole is in my shoe

(B) is clearly not a legitimate inference. So once more we see that functional considerations affect what is in some general sense spatial containment ("in her eyes"?) but must be taken in different ways in different contexts. Hence this locution too would present problems for construing natural languages as formal languages in Tarski's sense. For this is yet another case of polysemy. We saw already that Tarski's definition of a formal language allows disambiguation and relativizing truth to indexes, but not polysemy. There is nothing indexical about the different, qualitatively distinguishable, sense of 'in' that we unearthed. The sample sentence about water in the refrigerator presents the same lexical problems for truth conditions as the previous sentence about snow.

III. THEORETICAL REFLECTIONS

The examples investigated bring out questions about the relation between scientific use and everyday use. This issue has been the subject of debate for some time in the philosophy of science, and–as we have seen–also in the earlier history of twentieth-century philosophy of language. But as we shall see in Chapter 4, this issue becomes central also to the debates and differences among most recent proposals about language, and affects conceptions of the relations between meaning and denotation. The examples show that no simple dichotomy, such as science versus commonsense thinking, can capture the variety of semantic structures and interrelations that we find in these different uses of a natural language. Some terms, like molybdenum, had until recently a scientific use–accompanied perhaps by a very limited and derivative use among a few speakers of the language. Other words like 'water' have both a definition in science, and one in everyday language. Furthermore, there is a presupposition that in extension the two uses and applications are roughly covering the same ground. In other cases, like 'snow', there is no scientific definition, since the term does not figure in any of the sciences except meteorology. At the same time, there is the assumption that science can explain snow, and if we can trust the OED there is an explanatory component also in the everyday meaning. Still other words, like 'refrigerator', have underlying their meanings scientific explanations, but these are from the applied sciences, and hence contain a functional element. The comparison between the words just listed and other of our examples, like 'white' and 'in' shows that the meanings of some words contain a rich explanatory layer while that of others is only thin. In some cases, like 'white', there is a scientific account correlated with the everyday phenomenon, while in other cases, like 'in', there is no need for that. As we shall see later, we also need to consider words that have one meaning for the expert and another for the layperson, where the expert, or specialist, need not be a scientist.

This variety of types of meanings and interrelations show that we need a more complex and subtle semantic theory for the lexicon to represent conceptual relations among uses adequately. We can see already that an example like 'molybdenum'–used by Putnam in explaining his theory of meaning and reference[9] – is not at all typical of the kind of interrelations we find between scientific and everyday uses, such as with words like 'water', 'air'. The situation changes when our interests and practical uses involve in terms of functional values molybdenum. Some words have a double life in science and everyday use, others do not. Is this a sharp dichotomy or a matter of degree? We shall return to this question in subsequent chapters. The second sample sentence rais-

9. H. Putnam, "The Meaning of 'Meaning'," reprinted in *Mind, Language, Reality,* vol. 2 (Cambridge: Cambridge University Press, 1975), pp. 215–71.

es the question of how certain language uses are related to pointing at items in the external world. Can we have a theory of meaning in which meaning and reference are completely separated, and still account for the force of the existential sentence quoted, and its implications for accompanying search-and-find procedures?

Putnam has in recent times proposed a theory of meaning in which meaning and reference are separated at least for natural kind terms.[10] Though Chapter 3 will take up these matters in more detail, let us consider here three points that emerge out of this chapter and raise questions about a total separation.

First, as we saw, some uses of some sentences call for relationships between thought and action. Could we perform the required actions suggested by the linguistic context if we left the extensions of 'water' and 'refrigerator' up to scientists or other experts? Within the account emerging in these chapters, meaning partially explains and partially guides denotation-fixing contexts, and within these denotation is specified. So denotation is neither totally determined by meaning, as in theories by Frege and Carnap, nor is it independent, as in Putnam's conception. It sketches the outlines of a conception of a unified but many-layered system, unlike conceptions within which we treat meanings as objects of "pure linguistic competence" unrelated to practical concerns, and posit another conceptual system that relates our understanding of language to practical, action-oriented projects.

In preparation for more detailed comparison to follow later, we should raise questions about the conceivability of sheer conceptual competence, unrelated to activities. In a recent critical article of my lexical theory Mark Richard discusses this notion sympathetically.[11] Cognitive competence is apparently restricted to understanding language, and this, in turn, consists of tracing conceptual connections among linguistic items. But if we take away orientation toward what is taken intersubjectively as nonlinguistic parts of reality, abstracted not only from action, but also from reference, what are we left with? Mere manipulation of symbols? Are there any primitives in such a system, or is everything interdefinable? If there are primitives, then their meanings will have to be related to something extralinguistic. If there is total indefinability, then what kind of a plausible learning pattern can be linked with this conception? The only proposal made in this century by analytic philosophers that has no direct relations to truth and denotation are so-called verification theories of meaning. According to these the meaning of a sentence is specifiable in

10. Ibid.

11. M. Richard, Review of *Thought and Language, Dialogue* 32 (1993): 555–63.

terms in which what the sentence says can be verified or disconfirmed. These theories, first proposed by the positivists discussed in the previous chapter, have failed for various reasons, both within science and in accounting for ordinary everyday uses. Nothing in recent years suggests that such a theory could be revived.[12]

Richard's comments can be used to clarify the relation of the theory of this essay to those of Frege and Putnam. Frege is interpreted by many as holding that denotation is necessarily determined by meaning. Putnam's theory is interpreted as claiming that reference need not be linked to meaning. My theory is a viable alternative to the extent to which one admits semantic proposals as not analytic, but empirical proposals. (I am not convinced that Frege regarded his sense and reference theory as analytic. He seems to have thought that it explains general facts better than any other.) I do not claim that the connection between meaning and reference that I propose is analytic. I think that it is the best conceptual framework to explain general linguistic competence. If Putnam claims merely that meaning is not necessarily linked to reference, there is no disagreement. But if he assimilates natural kind terms to proper names and gives a "rigid designator" account of those, then there is indeed an important and nontrivial difference that is linked, even if indirectly, to empirical conditions. The multidenotational structures we uncovered allow both for differences in interpretation on the most specific level, and enable the competent speaker-hearer to select the appropriate context partly on the basis of guidelines provided in the core meanings of lexical items. The core meanings that are parts of this lexical theory give an underlying unity to the referential plurality. We saw that both science and OED type entries on the everyday level of semantics leave room for and indeed suggest an explanatory part in the core meanings. Finally, though the core meanings do not completely determine denotation, by supplying salient necessary conditions of application they delineate the wider conceptual space within which a multiplicity of denotations can be articulated.

If we step back and consider some salient features of natural languages, we can see why it is to the advantage of these languages that they do not have the structure of formal languages in Tarski's sense. For one thing, natural languages are diachronic processes. Hence the flexibility of the kind of semantics suggested in this essay can accommodate gradual change and development more easily than the rigid structure of the Tarskian languages, where every addition

---

12. For more on the verification theory of meaning, see C. Hempel, "Problems and Changes in the Empiricist Criterion of Meaning," *Revue Internationale de Philosophie* 11 (1950).

of an individual constant and every change of denotation in general terms introduces a new language.[13] Someone might say at this point that Tarski's scheme was never meant to explicate the meanings involved in diachronic phenomena. It applies to languages with certain logical structures, "frozen at a spatiotemporal location." But this raises the question: Is this not a bad idealization for the understanding of natural languages? These languages are always to some extent in flux, and one should look for semantic devices that facilitate this condition. Semantic change is a vital aspect of the meaning structure of a natural language. It is not an accidental imperfection. The reasonable course of action, in the face of these conditions, is either to try to modify the Tarskian scheme to accommodate diachronic phenomena, or to abandon it as a good idealization for the semantics of natural languages. Second, while complete explicitness of rules and semantic structure is a necessary feature of formal languages, in the everyday uses of natural languages – which often involve person-to-person communication–much can be, and should be left to contextual interpretation, hence placing also less of a burden on our memory and attention span. Finally, natural languages are learned gradually, in stages. Hence, having many layers of meaning and gradation of specificity within these facilitates the kind of language learning humans typically engage in. The semantics suggested here–unlike the structure of formal languages–makes room for this kind of learning, and meets the conditions listed in Section II.

So far I have restricted discussion to the lexicon. One might think that at least the notion of logical form, which plays such an important role not only in formal languages but also in other philosophic speculations about the relation between logic and natural language, can be applied to English, and other such languages. In the next chapter I will show that this condition does not obtain either and that the relation between natural languages and the structure of symbolic logic is much more indirect than one would have guessed from the writings of Russell and the positivists or, more recently, Montague.

13. For more details, see J. Moravcsik, *Thought and Language* (London: Routledge, 1990).

CHAPTER 2

NATURAL LANGUAGES CANNOT BE FORMAL LANGUAGES: THE LOGICAL STRUCTURE

So far we have dealt with lexical items that have descriptive content, and I have shown that their meanings cannot be fitted into the rigid format required by formal languages. We have not dealt with the vocabulary that specifies the logical power of various types of sentences. In a formal language quantifiers, brackets, variables, and individual as well as logical constants, connectives, and operators specify this structure. The so-called logical form of a sentence is that part of the meaning structure that is given by the meanings and syntax of the logical vocabulary, listed above, regardless of how we fill in the remainder of the meanings of descriptive elements.[1] Presumably we can reason with natural languages, not only with formal languages. Hence we need to look for the parts of natural languages that represent analogues to the logical vocabulary of formal sentences. Some of these are not difficult to find. 'All', and 'every' correspond roughly to the universal quantifier, while 'there is' or 'there are… some…' correspond to the existential quantifier with a variable. Natural language also has other quantifiers, as well as analogues to logical connectives and operators, but we shall bypass whatever problems there might be concerning their translatability between formal and natural languages, since much work has been done on that already, and the key issue I wish to raise does not depend on the interpretation of those items. We shall concentrate of sentences with the structure: "all A's…are B's," where 'A' and 'B' are replaced by appropriate descriptive words. What meaning does this structure contribute to sentences of the appropriate kind? Unlike in the case of descriptive terms, we do

1. More on logical form in J. Moravcsik *Thought and Language* (London: Routledge, 1990), pp. 103–04.

not ask for sense and denotation. Most philosophers view these items syncategorematically, that is, not as having denotation, but as contributing to the entailment structure into which the sentence is enmeshed. For example, if a sentence of the form: "All A's are B's" is true, then this entails that there is no counterexample to it; there are no A's that are not also B's. Its negation entails that there are some A's that are not B's (not that no A's are B's).

We call sentences of this form universally quantified sentences. There has been controversy about their interpretation on one specific point, to which we shall now turn. If we say something of the form: "all A's are B's", does this entail that there are A's? In more technical terms, do sentences of this form have existential import? Three interpretations have been offered. According to one of these, existential import is indeed attached to universally quantified sentences so that in case there are no A's, the sentence is false.[2] According to another interpretation, due at least in its recent version to P. F. Strawson, sentences of this form do not entail, but presuppose existential import, so that if there are no A's, then the question of their truth value does not arise.[3] Finally there is the interpretation adopted by modern symbolic logic, according to which there is no existential import, nor presupposition. According to this interpretation, the universally quantified sentence is true if there are no A's. The sentence does assert, however, that if there were A's, these would be B's; or at least this is what these sentences express if they are taken to cover not only the actual world as it happens to be, but also possibilities.[4]

All three of these interpretations assume that universally quantified sentences have one uniform logical meaning. This assumption is taken over from reflections on formal languages, and from the hypothesis that even if natural languages are not formal languages, at least they have logical form; that is, the logical vocabulary does specify uniform logical entailment structures across the language. If this is not the case, then presumably we need to ascribe to some members of the logical vocabulary ambiguity, and represent these items in that manner in the lexicon.

I. UNIVERSALLY QUANTIFIED SENTENCES

In this chapter a proposal will be sketched according to which there is more

2. Aristotle attached existential import also to lawlike sentences. But his reasons had nothing to do with analytic consequences of this form. Rather, he thought that all genuine sciences were about genera with members. This, then, guaranteed existential import.

3. P. F. Strawson, *Introduction to Logical Theory* (London: Methuen, 1963).

4. On modalities, see *Thought and Language*, pp. 21–6.

than one way to interpret universally quantified sentences in natural languages, but the interpretive options cannot be characterized adequately as cases of ambiguity, rather more like the multiplicity of senses we explored in the previous chapter. Furthermore, we shall encounter considerations showing why this is not a defect but a positive feature of natural languages.

Let us consider an example.[5] A salesman is selling toys door to door in a neighborhood. Encountering a reluctant customer at the front door of one of the houses, and he argues: "But all the other children in this neighborhood have some of these toys."[6] The woman responds: "You are a liar. There are no other children in this neighborhood. Our son is the only one." This is a reasonable sample of a conversation within such contexts, and if so, it would indicate that universally quantified sentences do indeed have existential import. Support for such a construal comes from at least two sources. One, by no means decisive, is the way we would ordinarily verify or disconfirm a claim like the salesman's, made in this context. We would resort ordinarily to empirical procedures; that is, look around, look for children in the neighborhood, and see what if any toys they have. The second consideration is stronger, for it raises not an epistemological issue, but a semantic one. It asks: What configuration in reality would make the salesman's claim true? We have two options. On one the configuration must include children with the appropriate toys. According to the other it is enough if in reality there is no child without the toys in question, and this state of affairs obtains even if the neighborhood has been devastated by bombing, and only one couple with a child survived. The first option is more appropriate, for it singles out a configuration that is relevant primarily to what the sentence expresses and its logically related network. The second one has a much wider and less determinate range of application. To reply that a universally quantified sentence is true as long as there is no counterexample is to suggest a partly epistemological consideration. Presumably we need a search procedure–at least an idealized one–to find out that there is no counterexample. But in cases like our example, the end of the procedure does not leave us with much. I can climb to a tower, look around the neighborhood, see no children, come down, and announce that the salesman is not lying, since there are no children in the neighborhood. As we shall see shortly, there are other examples the analysis of which makes the absence of counterexamples as a key consideration much more plausible.

---

5. The earliest version of my thoughts on universal generalization was presented at the *First Logic Congress*, Tehran, 1990, pp. 89–105. For further development of my thoughts I am indebted to Edgar Morscher.

6. A version of this story was given by Manley Thompson in class. His excellent presentations got me to think about this matter.

So far we have considered one interpretation of the example, and according to that universally quantified sentences do have existential import. What can one say with regard to this example on the other views? The presupposition view seems to me the weakest, for the question must be raised: Why is no truth value assignment emerging, according to this view? Is it that we do not understand the sentence, or more specifically what the salesman means by the sentence? This seems implausible, for the woman at the door, and we the analysts, understand perfectly well what is being said. To say that we do not know what is being meant sounds much more plausible in contexts in which we have a domain under consideration, but the predicate supposedly directing the search cannot apply on conceptual grounds to anything within that domain. We have then what used to be called a category mistake. For example let us consider the sentence: "All of the positive integers are smiling." We look into that domain, that of positive integers, and there is no rational procedure with which one could search there for smiling entities and those that do not smile. So there may be cases where we could not start a search on conceptual grounds, and in such cases the presupposition view might have some merit. But in the case of the salesman and the toys we *can* look for what might or might not make the claim true. Hence truth value should attach itself to whatever claim emerges as the correct one.

The modern views about universal quantification seem quite implausible in connection with this sentence. To point out that there is no counterexample to the salesman's claim is to give a very weak reason for accepting as true what is said *in that context*. Of course, it is not always the case that not finding a counterexample is a weak reason for accepting something as true. For there are many universally quantified sentences that express laws or principles. These are meant to be true across possibilities (be these logical or causal). Thus we might be able to prove that there can be no counterexamples, and this is indeed a good reason to consider a putative principle as prime candidate. This, however, leads us to consider now a wider range of examples; examples that may not fit the various interpretations in the same way in which the one given does, and the reason for this might be that not all universally quantified sentences in all uses have the same status in our conceptual framework.

A very different class is that of normative injunctions. "Trespassers will be prosecuted!"–if backed up by authority and enforcement possibilities–is true even if there will be no trespassers. So this and similar rules and laws seem to have a different logical form. One might say, however, that such rules are not empirical principles, and that the controversy about the nature of quantified universal sentences should be restricted to cases with empirical content.

Let us then take another example: "All pure water is H_2O." As we saw in the previous chapter, both 'water' and 'pure' admit of more than one interpretation. Let us consider what is expressed by this sentence here as the empirical law that water without additional ingredients is H_2O, as interpreted by common sense–not as true by a scientific definition, with which most users of English are not acquainted, but as a generalization about the nature of a substance familiar to us in many ways. Taken this way, we see this as a law that is a part of a network of other laws explaining the natures of various substances. The law explains the nature of a substance, regardless of whether it happens to exist in pure form or not. Here what I said earlier about the difference between epistemology and semantic questions is crucial. What makes the example a true sentence on the interpretation proposed is not simply that we found no counterexample to it, but its relation to lawlike contingent correlation between two properties: the property of being water and the property of being H_2O. Maybe some people come to accept the sentence on the basis of their not having found a counterexample to it, but this is not what makes it true. On the other hand, once we see what makes it true, we also see why it should be the case that on that interpretation there should be no counterexample to it, and existential generalization should not be attached to it. Laws and principles govern the universe of science or common sense under abstractions, hence the irrelevance of whether there are instances of what is signified by the subject of the generalization. Lawlikeness is not restricted to scientific discourse. Shared experience within a community can justify theorizing yielding a number of commonsense laws. For example, consider: "The most altruistic people do not receive rewards that they deserve." For many people this is not an empirical generalization, but a law based on the nature of altruism, on the effect that this has most of the time on human interaction, including the unfortunate human propensity to take advantage of those whose concerns are not wholly selfish, and including the typical laws and judicial systems of most societies. Let us suppose that a new theory capable of leading to diagnosis and prediction about human motivation on a much deeper level than what was supposed to be possible so far, becomes accepted by commonsense. Let us also suppose that with the use of this theory it is shown that the denotation of 'the most altruistic' as interpreted so far, is in fact empty. The commonsense law cited previously would still be valid.

These examples contrast sharply with the example of the salesman and the lady at the door. Given what we know today about toys, neighborhoods, and human nature, there is no good reason to suppose that there is any lawlike connection between being a child in that neighborhood and having the toys in question. But if it is not a law, then the sentence should express simply a truth that reveals a contingent relationship between the particular children that happen to live in that neighborhood at a particular time and a collection of toys. Questions about what kinds of toys a particular group of children have or do not have is–as far as we know in ordinary circumstances–a matter of enumeration, or if the group is too large, inductive generalization.

It seems then that different kinds of examples of universally quantified sentences leave us with different intuitions about existential import, and hence about logical form of sentences with the allegedly same structure. This would cause a great deal of consternation for those who believe that sentences of natural language have logical form. It does not bother those of us who reject that thesis, while agreeing of course with the claim that humans reason while using natural languages. From the fact that we cannot infer from the form of true sentences that are universally quantified that they do or do not have existential import does not mean that in suitable context with supplementary material such inferences cannot be drawn.

Let us stay with the hypothesis that in some cases universally quantified sentences do have existential import while in others they do not, and see if we can find a philosophically legitimate conceptual tool that will help us in drawing an adequate distinction between the two types of cases. Such a tool is indeed provided by Nelson Goodman in his book, *Fact, Fiction, Forecast*[7] in which he explores the nature of counterfactuals. In the course of this investigation he draws a distinction between lawlike and nonlawlike sentences. Goodman's analysis is within the frame of the technical notion of projectability, since his ultimate aim is to deal adequately with induction. We can, however, lay aside that larger issue, and utilize Goodman's distinction for our own purpose. Goodman's example of a universally quantified nonlawlike sentence is:

> All coins in my pocket on V-day are made of copper.

It is clear intuitively that in its current use this sentence does not express a lawlike proposition. We must present, however, an explanation for this intuition. As a first try, we can say simply that there is no law connecting the property of being a coin in Goodman's pocket on V-day with being made of cooper. Qualifications, however, are needed. We can hardly say that in no possible world could the sentence under consideration express a lawlike proposition.

7. Cambridge, MA: Harvard University Press, 1954.

One can only say that given the structure of the world as understood by our current linguistic community using English, there is no lawlike connection. This statement, in turn, needs be distinguished from the purely epistemological claim that we do not know any law that links the two properties mentioned. Our claim is that there is a conception of the empirical world that is adopted by qualified speakers of English today, and that it is incompatible with that conception that there should be a law connecting being a coin in Goodman's pocket on V-day with being made of copper. The emergence of such a law would raise havoc with many of our assumptions about the natural world and the principles that we take to be governing it.

Given, then, that there is no such law, what will make the sentence true will be a link between the particular coins that happened to be in Goodman's pocket on V-day with the property of being made of copper. If other coins would have been placed in Goodman's pocket on that fateful day, then our sentence might be false.

This illustration and explanation should make clear the notion of nonlawlikeness, at least to the extent to which we need this in our current project. In contrast, then, a lawlike sentence expresses in that use a generalization that does not just happen to be true of a collection of entities that happen to be actual beings, but extends also (or perhaps only) to possibilities. Thus, for example, in the case of water, as interpreted above, we not only maintain that all actual pure water is H_2O, but also that if there were any water that did not in fact materialize in the world's history, this too would be H_2O. Or again, even if humans would emerge who in fact did not enter our history but who would have earned the label of being most altruistic, these too would not have earned the rewards they would have deserved. Laws may or may not deal in all cases with actualities, but must–if they are to be laws–deal with projected possibilities. The distinction in terms of existential import that I wish to draw applies to all kinds of lawlike sentences, regardless of their epistemic grounding. Hence the class that I call here lawlike, and about which I claim that existential import does not hold include:

a. Definitions, generalizations, and their universally quantified logical consequences such as 'all brothers are siblings'.
b. Explicit normative rules and injunctions, like the one about trespassers already quoted.
c. All universally quantified necessary truths of mathematics. Of course, to the extent to which we interpret parts of mathematics as being about necessary existents, we obtain existential claims about the subjects of the relevant

sentences, but from a different source, not from the lawlikeness of the propositions expressed.

d. The laws and principles of the various empirical sciences.

e. The laws and principles embedded in common sense.

In light of the distinction drawn we can formulate the proposal of this essay concerning the semantics of universally quantified sentences. If the sentence expresses a nonlawlike proposition, then it has existential import. If the sentence expresses a lawlike proposition, then it lacks existential import. Hence there is no one logical form–in terms of entailments that follow–for all universally quantified sentences in a natural language, since sentences of the form: "all A's are B's" in natural languages can be used to express either what is lawlike or what is nonlawlike. Furthermore, the status of the use of any universally quantified sentence in a natural language at any given time is not a matter of the individual and private–that is, individually given use and privately held evidence. The states of a general claim as lawlike or nonlawlike is a public matter and reflects what is accepted in the relevant community. If I understand the given sentence as used correctly in the community, then I will give it the appropriate interpretation. Needless to say, the division here between public and individual is not sharp, and especially in cases of changes of communal understanding shifts may be initiated by individuals and a few people may have more impact on communal understanding than others. Still, not anything goes. An individual cannot just stand up and say that he means "all of the children in this neighborhood have this toy" in a lawlike manner if the communal interpretation of the elements of the sentence as well as its logical structure conflicts with such an announcement.

The semantic situation with regard to universal quantification is made complicated by the fact that many of our laws, in science or common sense, are formulated under idealizations. Idealizations are articulated explicitly in science, not so explicitly in common sense. As an illustration let us consider a sentence discussed many years ago by John Austin in one of his "informal instruction" classes in Oxford.

All snow-geese migrate to Labrador.

Austin asked–somewhat dramatically–"Suppose one flew off to Kentucky?" Austin's view was that we would not regard the generalization as simply false. We would keep it, with a "footnote" noting that in such and such a year one was observed as flying off to Kentucky. The ensuing discussion showed cultural differences. All of the American graduate students immediately came up with "psychological" explanations, and regarded the truth of one of these a natural necessity. "Maybe it was a neurotic goose," "Maybe the goose had been hurt by some of the others and developed an aversion to the flock," "The goose clearly had an attitude problem," And so on. Austin insisted: "No, no, I don't mean any of that. I mean, it just flew off to Kentucky." The British students in attendance had no difficulty envisaging such a situation. The conceptual background is vital to the understanding of the example. We take migratory patterns by species to be not mere statistical generalizations, but lawlike tendencies, the explanation of which (how do they do it? What tells them where to go or fly?) is an intriguing problem for zoology. Following the pattern is somehow in the nature of the species. Things, however, can go wrong with such "natural" tendencies, as we shall see even more clearly in the next section on "generics." If there are too many "footnotes," it is time to reconsider the law. Even then, such reconsideration is more likely to occur if a plausible alternative can be formulated. One can look at the exceptions as necessarily having some explanation lurking in the background, but this view is hardly compulsory. The denial of pure randomness in nature is not a law of logic.

The point of Austin's example for our purposes is that we are not always clear about the semantic impact of a universal generalization. If there can be a counterexample, does this show that it was lawlike but false? Or that it was nonlawlike all along, but strong enough so that we will abandon it because of one counterexample? Again, the flexibility of a natural language like English helps to ensure continuity of communication, and does not require always rigid explicit semantic distinctions.

We found, then, a principled basis for explaining conflicting intuitions, and a way of distinguishing those cases in which there is existential import from those in which such import is absent. What is the nature of the distinction that we now formulated? It is certainly not a matter of ambiguity, such as we have with lexical items like 'bank' or 'slip'. In these cases different definitions are ascribed to the same lexical item. This is not the case with the universal quantifier. Nor is this an epistemological distinction. For example, Kant thought that mathematical truths are known a priori, while J. S. Mill thought that they are empirical laws. Still, we would not say that the two interpretations require for us to ascribe possible ambiguity to a given mathematical truth. If some truths might be knowable in more than one way, this does not mean that we have to posit more than one truth as the epistemic object.

So the distinction is not a matter of pure logic, nor a matter of semantic definitions and ambiguity, nor pure epistemology. The felicitous description of the distinction is that it is based on a communal understanding and interpretation of the world, both in science and common sense. This understanding can change in time without changes in the meanings of lexical items. Hence it is the kind of understanding that surfaces also when we consider the kind of multi-denotationality of lexical items that we saw in Chapter 1. The opening of a new denotational context for a lexical item whose basic meaning structure remains the same is also not a matter of analytic changes nor of mere empirical increase in factual knowledge. This basis for multiple senses of lexical descriptive items and for quantifiers is linked to general conditions under which natural languages emerge and are used by human communities.[8]

Before we conclude this part, we should look at alternative attempts that have been or could be made to account for the phenomena under investigation. Johnson-Laird and Bara think that there is a syntactic mark indicating existential import, namely the presence of, or possible presence of, the phrase 'all of the'.[9] They think, for example, that what the sentence

all of the boxers are clerks

expresses does have existential import. The proposition entails the existence of boxers. This intuition, however, can be explained in a number of ways. The authors' favored explanation is that 'all of the' always introduces existential import. Another way is to say that in the case under consideration there is a coincidence of the favored grammatical form and existential import, but that this is due to other factors in the semantic structure of the sentence, and that in various other cases the presence of 'all of the' by itself does not guarantee existential import.

Phrases like 'all of the clerks' are semantically incomplete. One wants to know: Which clerks? Further specification is expected either by the addition of a relative clause, or implicitly by context. Let us consider a similar but semantically more complete sentence like

All of the students in Tel Aviv University are hard working

Competent language users today will give this sentence a nonlawlike interpretation. For there is no law in our understanding that would connect being en-

---

8. *Thought and Language*, ch. 6.

9. P. Johnson-Laird and B. Bara, "Logical Expertise as a Cause of Error: A Reply to Boolos," *Cognition* 17 (1984), pp. 183–84.

rolled as a student in Tel Aviv University with being hard working. It is consistent with all that we know about human nature and universities that a bright student enrolled at Tel Aviv University, while maintaining acceptable grades, eschews hard work and devotes himself to the "dolce far niente" life-style.

We can see that in this example the phrase "all of the" is not the crucial factor in licensing existential import. That import remains even without the phrase 'all of the'. Johnson-Laird and Bara would not doubt say that their theory requires only that the 'all of the' phrase should be a possible meaningful addition; this shows existential import. But to show that this need not be so, let us consider

All of the officeholders can claim perquisites.

This has in it the syntactic phrase Johnson-Laird and Bara require, and yet it is lawlike, without existential import. We can know this to be true even if there are no actual officeholders or we do not know of any. Rules of this sort are forged in constructing and maintaining institutions, prior to an investigation of the empirical facts as these happen to obtain. The crucial facts are that in the case of the boxers there are no laws linking the properties of being a boxer and that of being a clerk, while in the case of the officeholders there may well be laws or rules adopted linking offices with certain duties.

Someone might suggest solving the problem by adding to the normal modern logical interpretation an epistemic condition saying that whenever the speaker knows that the subject slot is nonempty she should say so. But this and other similar epistemic conditions will not do the job. For in the cases in which what we assert is lawlike, adding that in this particular instance there are elements in the subject slot may be quite irrelevant. We may say for example that under current conditions all sick people in condition C are beyond cure. It may be quite irrelevant to add that there are such people right now, as research on condition C is likely to persist regardless of such contingencies.

One might want to use Paul Grice's theory of conversational implicaturs to solve the problem. Within that theory we retain for all logical items the interpretation of symbolic logic, and add implicatures that are desirable for pragmatics of human interactions. For example, we can retain the technical definition for conjunction and add that in everyday use when temporal order between the conjuncts is relevant, indicate this by ordering them. This helps to distinguish "they had a baby and got married" from "they got married and had a baby." Could one not keep the technical interpretation of universally quantified sentences and add implicitur generating maxims like "be specific," "be maximally informational"? This approach does not work in this case, however. In the other cases one accepts a "minimal" interpretation of some aspect of logical form from symbolic logic (connectives, implication,...) and then adds further conditions for successful communications. But in the case of the universally quantified sentences the problem is not that we need at times more than the modern interpretation offers. The point is that in some cases, namely where the nonlawlike interpretation is required, the interpretation of the modern logician makes no sense. In the case of many lawlike sentences, however, the existence of subjects is simply irrelevant.

One might suggest formulating a maxim that says, roughly, that we should indicate existential import where this is useful, and indicate pure lawlikeness where that is of great relevance (idealized conditions etc.). But this would ruin the explanatory value of Grice's theory. To say that we keep logic and then add whatever and wherever something is needed to get successful communication is vacuous.

There are many approaches to pragmatics. Grice's is one; so-called speech-act theory is another. The latter focuses on what we can do, or accomplish, when using sentences or subsentential phrases. Of course, this is trivial in the cases of linguistic activities tied to syntax and semantics, like describing or inferring. But some speech-acts do not have this characteristic. For instances, we could use, in a suitable context determined by the state of mind and character of the hearer, the sentence "there are infinities of infinities" to scare or frighten people. Success in that case is not a matter of either the denotation or meanings of the relevant phrases, nor of the syntax, but of the causal effect that the utterance of this sentence has in this specific case on a certain audience. Promising is another case, where we do something with words and the action goes beyond mere communication of purported truths or complexes of such.

But the distinction between the lawlike and the nonlawlike is different from these effects that the uses of language can have. First, the lawlike versus nonlawlike distinction does affect content, in a sense rigidly definable, namely in terms of entailments. One has existential import; the other does not. This has always been counted as part of the core of what we mean by logical form and content. Second, these uses and their significance do not depend on the intentions of the speaker. If someone says: "all swans are white; and I mean this in a lawlike way", he is simply mistaken about current English use. It is up to us to use this or that sentence to scare someone, or to draw up agreements with specific people about a specific topic in our own unique way; but we cannot treat lawlikeness in that manner.

Lawlikeness depends on the state of knowledge of the scientific community, or in the ordinary cases on the state of knowledge of the linguistic community at large. The cases specific to a given science are judged by a subgroup of the linguistic community. So for this purpose we must talk about language uses restricted to subgroups. This is a common phenomenon. We must do the same when discussing scientific vocabulary. It would be a mistake to treat what is shared by subgroups as different languages. There is a great deal of overlap between these and ordinary usage. Indeed, without overlap, how would we be able to communicate across disciplines, and to tie the mastery of disciplines to the ordinary reasoning and language use from which they must take their origin?

Our account seems, then, to explain the facts better than other available alternatives. It also has the advantage of relating the mathematical use of the universal quantifier, without existential import, to the empirical use of this quantifier by showing that there is a correct uniform interpretation for all of the lawlike cases, regardless of whether they apply to the apriori or the empirical.[10] Still, some may lament the loss of logical form. According to the solution presented the biconditional

'all beavers are clever' is true if and only if all beavers are clever

is not true; for one can take an interpretation–such as lawlike–for the occurrence on the left-hand side, and there will be no mechanical way to single out one configuration in the domain (model) that makes what is on the left-hand side true.

Given the needs of a natural language, however, this is a gain rather than a loss. In everyday uses of natural language distinctions like the one between lawlike and nonlawlike are best left implicit, to be separated by context, since our understanding of the world is not rigidly uniform for everyone and undergoes gradual changes often not noticed immediately. It is more like the language of scientific research and less like the language of presenting firmly established results of science. It is very useful to leave some semantic flexibility in various parts of the language, rather than introducing the mechanism of meaning change for every new contingency.

II. GENERICS AND GENERALITY

In the previous section we saw that in ordinary use universally quantified sentences have two interpretations. One is in terms of lawlikeness and the other

10. I am indebted here to conversation with Jonathan Stavi.

nonlawlikeness, with existential import. We also saw that the ground for this distinction is neither logic nor semantic legislation, but a communal understanding that does not fit into the conventional straitjacket of semantics versus pragmatics. We shall now turn to yet another way of expressing something general, and see that while it is needed both in everyday and scientific use, it too defies logical form. We considered the general so far in two forms:

lawlike and no existential import
nonlawlike and existential import

This leaves us other possibilities:

lawlike and existential import
nonlawlike and no existential import

We can eliminate the second of these. For if the generalization is not lawlike, then it must be about particular entities that as a collection possess a certain property. Hence there must be existential import. But the first possibility is open to natural language, and indeed we find a form of expression called 'generics' that exemplifies this conceptual pattern. Linguists have looked at this construction for some time, but its semantics has not been discussed in the philosophy of language.[11] Let us consider the examples:

The beaver builds dams
Beavers build dams

Syntactically, genericity resides in these cases in "the F" indicating a subject that is not a particular instance of a character. This same subject can designated also by the bare plural. A brief survey should convince us that what is expressed by such constructions cannot be reduced to a standard logical expression. By 'standard logical expression' I mean any expression within the sentential calculus and set theory, with individual constants ranging both over particulars and sets. Species cannot be sets, since they can change their members and historical connections are needed linking the members together. Nor can they be individuals in the logical sense of this term, since they admit of def-

11. For an earlier version see J. Moravcsik, "Genericity and Linguistic Competence," *Theorie des Lexicons Arbeiten des Sonderforschungsbereich* 282, no. 54, (1994). I am indebted for helpful comments to Gabriel Falkenberg and Henriëtte de Swart.

initions, as general predicates do, and have elements related to them that are analogous but strictly speaking not the same as the elements of a set. In particular, the sentences above do not say that all beavers build dams. There may be some injured or sick ones that do not. Thus by implication the sentences cannot say something necessarily about being a beaver and dam building, since not all instances are involved in whatever the link is. The truth is that the sentence asserts something about the normal, healthy, well-functioning beaver. These animals build dams under natural circumstances. Exploring the subject further, it becomes clear that the sentence does not say that many or most beavers build dams. Illness, natural disaster, human intervention can create conditions under which only a minority of members of the beaver species retain their health and normality. Hence such quantifiers as 'many', or probabilistic statements cannot express what the generic expresses either.

We arrived thus at the conclusion that these sentences say something about the species, whatever that may be. But of course generics are not the only sentences that deal with species. Consider

> The beaver is an animal

This sentence is about the species, but it is also about all members. It asserts something that is necessarily true of specimens, as well as the species. Furthermore, though lawlike, it has existential import. We shall account for that shortly as we take up the analysis of what a species is.

Let us consider now:

> in the summer cows come up to these Alps

This sentence does not say anything necessary about all cows, nor anything about what a healthy normal cow would do. Rather, it expresses a frequency. It says that at a certain time of the year many cows move up to the Alps to their summer pasture. In other sentences of similar types the frequency affects the predicate rather than the subject. The example

> these children eat tomatoes at suppertime

could be made more explicit by adding 'frequently', or 'usually' to modify the predicate.

In both cases we can talk of a "frequency interpretation" of the sentence, and even if in some forms these correspond to what could be used also as semantic generics, there is no need to interpret these as being about the species. Rather, these sentences are about a collection of particulars, in some cases about a large collection, and in some cases about frequently occurring events.

We have reached, then, two conclusions so far. First, that generic statements about the species are not equivalent to standard logical forms of sentences that we find in formal languages. Secondly, that sentences in the same grammatical form in a natural language can express either genuine generics or statements about collections of specimens, involved in frequent or usual activities. This shows that in natural language syntax and semantics are not isomorphic. Unlike in formal languages, in natural languages the same syntactic form can correspond to two quite different semantic configurations. As we shall see later, this is an advantage rather than a disadvantage for natural languages.

The lack of sharp syntactic criteria for generics helps us to gather under the label of generics not only sentences with count terms as subjects but also those with mass terms as subjects. Thus, for example

grass is green

is also a generic. It cannot be translated into a universally quantified sentence, since clearly not all grass is green. Some grass is brown, some yellow, and so on, depending on the season and climate. Yet there is truth in what our sample sentence says. We need to interpret it, however, as being about grass when it "is at its best," or "functions at its best," namely when its nourishment, liquid and other, is what it requires under normal circumstances. The same also holds obviously of much of what we say about trees, flowers, and other such things. There are generic statements about flowers, to be understood as flowers in bloom, not when withering, and trees when their leaves are out and not in the winter. As we shall see shortly, generics surface also in connection with what we say about human institutions, not just about nature.

First, however, let us look at what our generics assign to the dam-building beaver, the web-weaving spider, and the like. Something is ascribed that the healthy normal specimen realizes in action under normal circumstances. Traditionally what is ascribed to the species with these sentences is a potentiality. Beavers have their unique dam-building potential, spiders their unique web-weaving potential, bees their honey-gathering potential, and so on. This, however, brings us to the question: What is a potentiality? Once more, we see that this notion, though needed in biology, cannot be defined in terms of the familiar notions of modal logic and tools of philosophy of science. A natural potentiality is not a mere possibility. Many things are possible for me now, including hanging from a chandelier (example borrowed from Iris Murdoch) that are not parts of my natural potentiality. Nor can one translate potentiality into probabilistic notions; natural potentialities may be manifested "usually" or may not. The internal structures of specimens can change so that the natural potential is only rarely realized.

Potentialities have a place within the larger genus of dispositions. An entity E has a disposition D if and only if under circumstances C the entity will manifest or realize that disposition. For example, our perceptual interpretation of the world is a series of dispositions to be realized. But of course not all dispositions are potentialities. To have a certain bone structure is for humans not a dispositional property. To see is. Seeing is a potentiality; it is a part of what we call the nature of the species. The disposition to scratch one's head once in a while is not a potentiality, though it is a dispositional property. Nor can we define potentialities as the necessary dispositions of a species. For there may be necessary dispositions, those needed for mere survival, which are nevertheless not potentialities of a species, since the latter, such as dispositions to feel pain, are shared across a wide range of species. Potentialities, as we see from the examples considered so far, have a teleological or functional aspect. Their realization admits of the "better or worse" assessment, and the realization also contributes to the specimens fulfilling as best as possible the functional needs that are parts of the nature of the species to which they belong.

One might try to analyze the realization of potentialities in terms of noncircular conditionals. If C'...Cn, then the beaver will build dams. But the difficulty is that the contents of the antecedent are either environmental conditions, in which case we are left with "the healthy beaver" in the consequent, or the contents of the antecedent are constituents in what it is to be a beaver. In that case the conditional is circular; it says, roughly, that if the creature is a well functioning beaver then it will function well–for example, build dams.

A survey of our general conceptual framework shows that defining kinds in partly functional terms is not unique to biology. We find at least three other areas in which such delineations play central roles. One of these is the genus of artifacts. It is difficult to conceive of the introduction of a new kind of artifact without some functional specifications. Humans produce things in systematic ways for some purpose, vague or specific. (This claim does not exclude occasional random production and aimless activity.) We cannot define 'chair', 'house', 'airplane' without functional specifications, purely in terms of observable properties such as size, shape, texture, and color. As Aristotle pointed out, we don't know whether a building is a house or not until we see how it is being used. Given that much, we can see that assessments of something meeting the standards of being a certain artifact will range over degrees of adequacy. We do not understand what a knife is without understanding what a good knife is. To be sure, we cannot talk in these cases about potentialities in exactly the same way in which we talk about this in biology. In biology the potentiality is grounded in the internal essential nature of certain kinds of objects. In artifact production that functional specification and hence the delineation of the analogue to potentiality comes from the designer and engineer or artisan. The locutions in both cases have the same semantic structure. "The size XYZ wrench can..." says that the well-constructed wrench of a certain size and shape and material can perform such-and-such tasks. Of course some types of wrenches can do this better than others; there are better and worse functioning wrenches, drills—we can say that much without postulating an ideal Wrench, Drill, or other tool.

Another domain for generics is constituted by human institutions in political, social, or educational domains. Universities, the presidency, Parliament, Christmas are all human institutions, and like artifacts have their built-in functions and rules for functioning. Without these, why would humans invent or design such institutions and roles? Spelling out, however, the rules for functioning needs be done with the help of the generic construction. The rules can only spell out how things should be going if all goes well. The actual functioning of a particular institution or role bearer may well be subject to Murphy's law (anything that can go wrong, will). For example, the American Independence Day is celebrated on July 4th, but one can imagine a case in which a gigantic earthquake or sudden war, plague, or other disaster necessitates postponement of the celebration. (The example is also interesting because the subject expression is neither of the "the F" type nor bare plural.)[12] The same can happen with Christmas, and though one can outline what the president of France would be doing, everything else being equal, things can always go wrong, someone invades France, or something else unexpected happens and if we phrase the role specification in terms of a universal quantification, it would turn out to be false.

Legal or ritual framework is not always needed for processes that are produced by human social forces and that need be specified in terms of generics. For example, harvests meet our description, or, as in our previous example, driving the cows to their customary summer alpine pasture.

In some cases we describe processes that are human-made in terms of bare

12. I am indebted again to Henriëtte de Swart.

plurals, but mean to say something only about frequency of occurrence or manner. Thus: "Demonstrations take place in good weather," is a generalization in terms of frequency, taking into consideration the level of enthusiasm people usually have for political or social causes, and their fear or aversion to getting wet, freezing, and so on. Let us look now at the ontology of the subjects of the various kinds of generics surveyed. Biological species are characterized by the following:

i. They have spatiotemporal location and their members are causally connected (relatives).

If we saw a species, such as the tiger die out, and then much later without any causal link at all saw another species develop that was in all essentials qualitatively like the tiger, we would not say that the species is continued now; we would classify it as a separate species.

ii. Species have members, the specimens, and this relation is neither the class membership relation nor the part–whole relation.

The relation cannot be class membership, since a class is defined by its members, but a species has a constantly changing collection of members and admits of counterfactuals of the sort "the species could have had this or that member (another offspring of this camel or this lion)." The members are not like functional parts of a whole; for instance, a tiger is not related to the species as an arm to the body. Nor are they related as parts to whole. The sum of two red objects is a (scattered) red object, but the sum of two tigers is not a tiger.

iii. Species admit of definitions and thus have essential characteristics.

The last property makes a species more like universals, but the first two make it more like particulars. We can take the path Richard Cartwright took, and say that there are entities "in between" universals and particulars, like types, which we contrast with tokens, and species should also be classified into this conceptual region.[13] Or we can take Peter Simon's suggestion and construe species as a special subclass of particulars.[14] In either case we have exis-

13. R. Cartwright, "Propositions," in R. Butler, ed. *Analytical Philosophy* (Oxford: Blackwell), pp. 81–103.

14. P. Simons, *Parts: A Study in Ontology* (Oxford: Clavendon Press, 1987).

tential import for the generics. There are no merely possible biological species, only properties. Species must have specimens.

Some of the conditions, such as causal interrelatedness, that we attributed to biological species are possessed by human institutions such as communities of various sorts like countries, professional associations, and so on, while others such as harvests, demonstrations, do not have these. But for our purposes the important point is that in all of these cases too we have existential import. For as in the case of artifacts, the origin here is human design and invention. We do not invent possible institutions with no functional specifications. Or if we do something that a person might want to describe that way, the correct account is that no institution or ritual has been invented; a person is merely dreaming, speculating, or doing something else. Until it is a part of spatiotemporal reality, it is not a human institution or practice.

So far we have dealt with what can be regarded, from any reasonable point of view, as legitimate kinds. Needless to say, a legitimate kind can also be put to bad purposes. (The generic construction allows us to formulate conditions under which processes, role bearing and so on can function well. This leaves open the question whether it is good to have that institution, and whether a particular individual is bearing a role for the benefit of others.) For example, rules in terms of generic constructions specify the functioning of royalty within a certain tradition. One can raise questions independently of this specification whether royalty is or is not a good institution, and one can raise questions about a specific person whether he was a good king, ruling effectively and wisely or not.

We turn now to cases in which groups of language users create alleged kinds, and specify these in terms of the generic constructions made available by natural language. Some of these activities can be called the creation of stereotypes. In many cases this kind of reasoning is harmful, and in some cases catastrophic. Pseudo-kinds are created like 'the Germans', 'the Jews', defined solely in terms of popular stereotypes, and the result is prejudice and hatred. In earlier days, similar misuses of the generic form appeared when people talked about witches. We should note that the rules of syntax and semantics apply also in these cases. What we said about irreducibility and untranslatability into logical form applies. So does existential import. This requires some explanation. Stereotypical thinking is not like thinking about dragons or mythical giants. It is thinking about actual people on groups. Furthermore, there is reference to kinds, even though these kinds are groups forced into a mental construction by the language user; a construction whose employment in this case does not meet the standards of rationality. The purported generics can be shown on further factual research and reflection to be either mere frequency reports or, just as often, plain falsehoods. But considering these uses of generics shows that the interpretation of subjects of generics can at times be merely in the mind. Genericity is "in the eye of the beholder," but this does not mean that all positing of kinds is equally legitimate. There are objective criteria that rank such positings along dimensions of justifiability. Furthermore, not all stereotypical thinking is harmful. In some cases we make up what some linguists call "ad hoc kinds." For example within a drive for funds for a local hospital we might use the generic constructions to talk about "the suffering poor" in the hospital. Once the fund drive is finished, the same collection of humans might be classified within a more complex classification. Generics on the surface seem to be value-laden. But the point of the examples and reflections just ended is that genericity is simply a construction made possible by structures of natural language. It can be used to express a rational articulation of kinds and species or irrational ones. It can be used to describe either temporary kinds for pragmatic purposes or kinds that are meant to be cornerstones of a science, for example, biology.

It needs stressing that this analysis of genericness does not lead to conceptual relativism. There are general rational criteria by which we can assess the legitimacy of a proposed use of the generic construction. Needless to say, the criteria–if well chosen–yield degrees of adequacy, not a simple all-or-nothing scheme.

As we saw, logical form does not guarantee truth. Logic allows us to express the true as well as the false. It is difficult to conceive of a state of affairs in which this could be otherwise. Likewise, the linguistic devices allow us to form adequate concepts of kinds, and also to form conceptions of pseudo-kinds. Again, it is difficult to see this could be otherwise. Above all, the existence and occasional misuse of these linguistic possibilities are not evidence for the legitimacy of any kind of relativism.

The use of generics and the generic construction should not be confused with two other phenomena discussed in linguistics and psychology at times.

One of these is the notion of "prototype," as used by Rosch, Lakoff, and others.[15] As an example, one might think of sparrows or pigeons as more typical birds than turkeys, and construct a psychological typicality scale along which birds of different kinds are placed. Such schemata are then meant to replace the notion of meaning as defining a sharply delineated class of entities in the denotation.

15. E. Rosch, "Principles of Categorization," in E. Rosch and B. B. Lloyd, eds. *Cognition and Categorization*, (Hillsdale, NJ: Erlbaum) pp. 27–48.

Some psychological work has been done to show that while the notion of prototypicality has psychological validity, it does not correlate with how people assign meanings to words, such as in the case of mathematical vocabulary.[16] Another argument against this conception doing a semantic job is that as in the case of birds prototypicality is likely to be sociologically influenced. For a child living in Brooklyn pigeons might be the prototypical–even the only or surviving?–bird, while for a child living in rural Iowa the turkey may be prototypical.

In any case, this psycholinguistic proposal is quite distinct from the conception of the generic construction as presented in this essay.

Another conception that might be thought to be relevant is that of the "representative individual." One might think of the cognitive construction of a representative individual embodying what we want to express with the use of generics, and think of this as the subject. But the difficulty with this is that the generics, when true, do not lead to the conception of an individual. They lead to the conception of a species, as explained previously. It is very important to note that within the characterization of a species partly in terms of generics there are a variety of individuals. Some differ in size, some in coloring, some in means used to achieve a state prescribed by "well functioning," and so on. There is no representative healthy beaver, any more than a representative healthy human. Healthy humans are different, depending on whether they are children or adults, teenagers or octogenarians.

There are also kinds with their own nature that are harmful for humans; such as cancer. This is a by-product of nature and has its natural potentials though very harmful for us. This, and other examples involving diseases, show also why the notion of prototype or representative individual cannot replace our analysis of generics. What would be prototypical cancer, or a representative individual for cancer?

First, there are many different kinds of cancer, so prototypicality would have to be explicated for each major type. Second, what is prototypical for an expert researcher may be very different from what is prototypical for a patient or layperson with a sick friend or relative. Then there may be also hierarchies of prototypicality among kinds of cancer, and these hierarchies will be different for physician and layperson.

Let us turn once more to the relation between our analysis of kinds and ge-

16. S. Armstrong, L. Gleitman, and H. Gleitman, "What Some Concepts Might Not Be," *Cognition* (1983): 263–308, and L. Gleitman, H. Gleitman, C. Miller, and R. Ostrin "Similar and Similar Concepts," *Cognition* 55 (1996): 321–76.

nerics that describe their potentials, and attempts at formal analyses of generics.[17] In formal semantics predicate operators indicate modes in which a predicate is possessed by the subject. An obvious example is the modal operator. Thus we can say: "John is necessarily a human", meaning that John cannot discard this attribute without going out of existence. Once a human, always a human, and a human in all possible worlds in which John exists. So why could we not have a 'healthy' or 'normal', or 'well functioning' operator so that we can say: if X is a healthy (beaver) than X can build dams"? Now the difference between a modal operator and an alleged "healthy" operator is that the former describes something, necessity, that is quite independent of the nature of a human or beaver. But the characteristics that go into being a healthy beaver are parts of what it is to be a beaver. In modern logic an entity either has or lacks a property. The idea of having a property well or not, completely or not, is not a part of the reasoning that modern logic is designed to capture. Some properties are quantitative, and in these cases we can attach a scale for size, weight, and the like. This helps with formal analyses of certain comparatives. But the notions of full nature, realizing full potential, are parts of a functional network of notions. We need these in some of the sciences, and to that extent such conceptions, whether in everyday or scientific thinking, do not fit modern logic. This is neither a drawback nor an advantage. We could introduce a H( ) operator, but it would be a purely ad hoc technical device, without any explanatory power such as possessed by legitimate predicate operators like "de re" modality.

These comments are meant to show the difficulties of accommodating standard predicate calculus and modal logic to an analysis of generics expressing potential. It is not an argument trying out a variety of different formalisms. There is nothing in principle that would make converting a primitive H( ) operator into something more informative and explanatory possible. This part of the chapter is designed to show the deep qualitative conceptions that underlie the notions of potentiality, and that of the normal or perfect or healthy specimen. The notions in question are not parts of traditional standard logical form. It remains to be seen whether a "logic of the potential" can be developed, or whether the notion of potentiality remains a primitive notion fundamental to human thought.

We can see, then, on the basis of what was demonstrated in this chapter, that with respect to certain features of natural languages syntax and semantics are

17. For discussion of these issues, see: H. de Swart, "(In)definites and genericity," in M. Kanazawa, C. Piñón, and H. de Swart, eds. *Quantifiers, Deduction, and Context* (Stanford: CSLI Publications), pp. 171–194.

not isomorphic. Different syntactic constructions can be correlated with the same semantic structure, and different semantic structures with the same syntactic structure. Furthermore, some constructions like the generic, cannot be given an adequate logical representation in set-theoretic terms. Finally, natural language sentences of certain kinds do not have logical form in the technical sense of this notion. This however does not prevent us from specifying logical expressive power in context, and thus reasoning deductively within natural language, with contextual semantic specifications given to some structures.

Montague first wanted to represent English as a formal language. Later he turned to "translating" English into an intensional formal language, defining different analogues to natural language constructions within these languages. I would question the notion of "translation" involved here, and the theoretical value of the exercise. Certainly as of now no interesting theorems about natural languages have been proven within this approach. Formalizations on a much more restricted basis can be useful, however. We can take certain configurations such as perceptual reports of certain sorts[18] or so-called branching quantifiers[19]–both of which can be found in natural languages–and prove interesting results concerning their semantic powers. But this is quite different from trying to construe, philosophically as well as technically, natural languages as formal languages. In the chapters to come, it becomes clear how rejecting this identification opens up a very different and constructive conception of the relations between mind, meaning, and natural language.

For the present, simply note that, as in the case of universal quantification and the lawlike versus the nonlawlike, so here too, in the case of essential generics versus frequency interpretations, the lack of isomorphism between semantic and syntax in natural language is an advantage. It gives syntactic stability to the language and at the same time semantic flexibility. As I said before, everyday use is more like the language of science in the state of research than in the state of presenting established results. We are not always sure of the semantic force of what we say, and it is good to be able to let context clear things up. The semantics too gives us some stability. In context we can reason deductively and inductively with it. But the phenomena we focused on in this chapter mirror the tentative and changing nature of some of our conceptual framework. And this too is an aspect of human thought.

---

18. J. Barwise and J. Perry, *Situations and Attitudes* (Cambridge, MA: MIT Press, 1983).

19. D. Gabbay and J. Moravcsik, "Branching Quantifiers," *Theoretical Linguistics* (1974): 139–157.

PART II

THE LEXICON, EXPLANATIONS, AND PRODUCTIVITY

CHAPTER 3

LEXICAL MEANINGS AS EXPLANATORY SCHEMES

This chapter presents a theory of lexical meaning. Within this theory lexical meaning is specified on three levels, rather than within the two-level meaning-denotation scheme. The reasons for this are, on the one hand, that on the first level meanings are explanatory schemes, rather than complete explanations or specifications. These schemes interact with a variety of contextual elements, thus yielding denotation-fixing contexts and finally contextual denotations. The hypothesis of lexical meanings being explanatory schemata is shown to be empirically justifiable and is then linked to the more general claim that humans are basically explanation-seeking and -forming creatures, and only derivatively information-processing entities. The hypothesis is defended in detail in Chapter 5.

This theory presupposes various theses that are justified in the previous chapters. First, at the foundation of this theory is the claim that an adequate lexical theory for natural languages must deal with the inner anatomy of lexical meaning with the help of both logical and nonlogical means. In formal semantics meanings are either not given an internal anatomy and are represented simply as functions, or if an internal anatomy is proposed, this has the shape of a collection of properties arranged strictly by the logical connectors of conjunction, disjunction, and entailment. Our lexical theory dissects lexical meanings with the aid of–among other things–of conceptual pairs like structure and constituency, happenings, and teleological (or functional) aspects.

The theory also presupposes that there need not be a isomorphism between syntactic and semantic rules, thus defending a version of the autonomy of syntax thesis. Such a conception is incompatible with Tarski's conception of a formal language.

In the previous chapters we had occasions to refer to the Oxford English Dictionary, and we saw that entries tend to include explanatory elements, some of the everyday variety, and some scientific. Our theory systematizes this insight, and gives the explanatory structures a clear description.

In formal semantics the analogy between proper names and individual constants is assumed, and singular terms are seen as fundamental to semantic analysis. Within our theory the proper names of a natural language are not seen as analogous to individual constants, and in general reference and denotation are not given top priority.

The proper names in a natural language that are of interest to a linguist, and should be of interest to any theoretician who is studying natural languages as objects worthy of explanation in their own rights, are those that come in systems and can be translated from language to language. Examples are, names for mathematical entities like numbers or names for the days of the week or months of the year. But though there are many interesting questions still unsolved concerning such linguistic expressions, it is clear that these terms can be defined, thus functioning like other terms with intension and extension; they are not rigidly fixed referential expressions without intensions. The best candidates for the latter category are demonstrative expressions. Clearly, there is no linguistic intension for each item in the Palo Alto telephone book, or for each use of 'this' or 'that'. But the uses of 'this', as well as 'here' and 'now', are highly context-dependent, and the context is to a large extent pragmatic–that is to say, dependent on the beliefs, intentions, and activities of speaker and hearer (intended audience), rather than on rules of language. For example, "give me this" is a request that cannot be understood in most cases except by reference to what went on in the previous conversation, the nature of activities in which speaker and hearer engage, and in some cases even the attributes of the hearer; for instances, one would use 'this' differently with blind people and with those with normal eyesight. Phrases like 'this scene', 'this accident', 'this disturbance', cannot be interpreted by referential intentions and semantic rules alone. Similar considerations apply to 'here'. In various contexts this word can refer to larger or very small regions; it can refer to regions on the surface of the body or inside ("Where is it bleeding? Here." versus "Where does it hurt? Here"–pointing to a part of the surface of the body, but being interpreted according to social convention, as being meant to indicate a region inside the leg or stomach). Communication is possible as long as the areas or objects indicated roughly correspond; unless the pragmatic context requires precision. When precision is required, the context determines the extent and nature of precision, and success for communication requires only sufficient overlap of conceptual framework so as to make possible coordinated activity such as an operation.

Similar considerations apply to names of persons. Very few names are translated across languages. And in many of these cases involving famous individuals, there is no clear agreement whether the name always covers the same person or whether there was only one person. According to the causal-intentional theory of names without meaning, we have to trace back the name to an original user/giver. But in the case of Homer or Shakespeare, it may well be that our use goes back to more than one name user or giver and in some cases the name users referred to one person, in some cases not. Homeric scholarship can proceed quite well without being quite clear whether the Homeric works were composed by one or two or many persons. No violation of the rules of language and no practical difficulty hinges on any of this. In the case of average individuals the highly pragmatic and nonlinguistic context-dependent nature of the significance of use is even more obvious. Only a relatively small number of people know the exact reference of a name in the local telephone book. Only a small number of people need to know. Which ones? That is not a matter of the rules of English but a purely sociological matter. In some cases we want a more systematic way of locating a human within a large collection. Hence the system of social security numbers in the United States. But even in the case of this practice, all we need to agree on is that for purposes of law, taxation and other official matters, a number singles out a legal entity. Metaphysical questions about personal identity and persistence are completely irrelevant. And if some unusual context arises for which the presuppositions on which the social security system works break down, then the naming use needs to be revised on the basis of practical considerations. An inkling of all of this is given by some of the family names used in English and other European languages. 'Smith' in one use at one point was simply the only blacksmith in a particular village. The same with 'Miller', 'Carpenter', 'Weaver' 'Baker'. After a while the community for whom knowing, roughly, the reference of a use of 'Miller' is relevant increases. So now "everyone knows" that by 'Miller' we mean the miller from this village, not the one from the village across the hills. That miller wears the name of, for example, 'Black' presumably because he has an unusual dark complexion. After a while these property-related connotations disappear, but that does not make the names rigid designators without intensions. Ordinary proper names become pragmatic pegs, usable only in a very restricted set of circumstances–restricted from a metaphysical or "possible worlds" point of view. What happens if Smith flies to Mars, becomes a different creature, appears in more place than one simultaneously? We don't know. Our ordinary naming practices are tied to much more practical and localized procedures that admit of no nonarbitrary extension to strange circumstances.[1] Our key concern is not whether proper names have sharply articulable or only loosely characterizable meanings, but rather whether they belong to a natural language at all, and how our competence in using them relates to our linguistic competence.[2]

I. OUTLINE OF THE LEXICAL THEORY

The details of this lexical theory have been presented elsewhere.[3] This outline will concentrate on the following two claims. First, on the first level of meaning there are complexes of properties that constitute explanatory schemes, and that these are necessary though not sufficient conditions for application. Second, these explanatory schemes lead to specifications of denotation-fixing contexts. A set of such contexts constitutes the second level. At the third level denotations are fixed partly on the basis of semantic and partly on pragmatic conditions.

The following show why the explanatory conditions mentioned should be necessary, rather than just "core facts" or other empirical information correlated with the use(s) of the term.

My theory admits that mere knowing of the general qualitative constituents of meaning is not yet to have a denotation also rigidly fixed. But it insists on the ability to use and understand the combination of descriptive words with quantifiers as one of the criteria for mastery of meaning. To understand the meaning of 'human' entails knowing how to use 'human' with universal, existential, and "generalized" quantifiers. It involves also knowing how to use 'the same…' over periods of time, related to the descriptive term in question (the same human, building, explosion, university).

But unlike the logical notion of identity, these principles of individuation–in Quine's terms, principles of how a descriptive term divides reference–are relative to the descriptive term they give structure to. To be the same human is not identical with being the same collection of body cells, even if the two spatiotemporal region. This is true as well for 'ring' and–in context–'pieces of gold'. It is not as if entities had their individuation and persistence conditions

1. J. L. Austin, *Philosophical Papers*, ed. J. O. Urmson and G. J. Warnock, (Oxford University Press, 1961).

2. J. Moravcsik, *Understanding Language* (The Hague: Mouton, 1975).

3. J. Moravcsik, *Thought and Language* (London: Routledge, 1990).

apart from the descriptive term under which they are considered. The link must be necessary; if we cannot agree even on how to count humans, virtues, or planets, there is nothing to describe and explain.

No lexicon without individuation and persistence principles. These principles vary from descriptive term to descriptive term. If we say, "This is how I individuate these entities now, but I may do so quite differently tomorrow, yielding quite different units," we fail to have a genuine subject matter. The different individuations will yield different entities.

Having seen, then, why some meaning constituents must be attached as necessary conditions to a term, let us turn to the second claim, and see what kind of explanatory schemes the first semantic level in our theory yields.

Our understanding of words is influenced by the variety of ways in which we relate to the world. We encounter something as observers, as users, as producers, as experts, or as laypersons. We call upon recognitional abilities in some cases and verificational procedures or discovery procedures in others. In still other cases, our interactions with specific items color our concept formation. For example, the concept of baseball will be colored differently for players, umpires, spectators, and owners. The concept of a lion has different features for zoo visitors, hunters, and zoologists.

This lexical theory is particularly suited to explain the intuition that in some sense the zookeeper and the hunter have, and in some sense they do not have the same concept of what a lion is. Similarly with kids playing baseball and umpires, concerning the concept of a baseball. What we called the salient explanatory necessary conditions will be shared regarding "lion" by hunter–and keeper, and regarding "baseball" between umpire and ball-playing kid. But there will be differences regarding what counts as lion or baseball in different contexts. The keeper knows how to diagnose illness in the lion, and knows how to keep the lion alive by cure. Hence he knows something about the persistence conditions that the hunter typically does not. Thus in terms of denotation there will be an overlap between the denotation assigned by the keeper and the one assigned by the hunter; but it will not be complete identity. The same holds for the umpire and the kid. Both will respect the regulations satisfying baseball, but only the kid, in his context of playing the game on some meadow, will call the ball made up of tightly strung rags "our baseball." Different contextual specifications lead to partly overlapping and partly distinct denotation ranges. Occasionally the ranges are completely distinct. Heat has different interpretations for physicists and average persons living in a cold climate.

Faced with this variety one might decide not to posit any necessary conditions as constituting meaning. Why not just attach to the word different procedures, and leave it at that? There are, however, reasons for seeking an underlying element that provides commonality and unites the variety of phenomenal experiences and procedures just listed. The main reason can be illustrated in the case of illness. Illness will mean–subjectively–different things to doctor, patient, nurse, and sympathetic relative. Yet it is crucial that they should be able to communicate with each other. Furthermore, what we know about an illness changes–we hope–with time. Yet there is a core meaning whose stability gives unity and direction to research. Neither of these considerations guarantee, a priori, that there *must* be a common denominator in the case of each word. But if we find the right common denominator then this gives us a more plausible theory then one that leaves us solely with procedural variety, bordering on chaos. A "dynamic" consideration calls also for a common denominator, for often in life we have more than one role or way of interacting with an item covered by the word whose meaning we consider. A doctor can also be a patient; a player can also be a spectator. Furthermore, we can change roles relevant to linguistic competence. A player can become an umpire; a layperson can become an expert; a spectator or observer can become an interacting agent. One could conceive of linguistic behavior that would involve the learning and relearning of new roles and ways of encounter, but this seems very cumbersome.

The theory proposed here posits a general explanatory scheme as the basic common denominator. Scheme does not mean complete explanation. The details can change; necessary conditions can be supplemented, in a variety of ways, with sufficient ones. But there remain basic explanatory features that provide a common core for meaning. If we look at the examples listed above, we see that activities take place in time and have temporal parts as their essential ingredients, while many of the items denoted by nouns have spatial extension among their essential properties. Items that are abstract cannot become concrete and vice versa, and such basic categorization remains constant across the variety of ways of relating to items denoted by language. Similar considerations apply to principles of individuation and persistence attached to words. In some contexts people know more and in some less. But the different phenomenological experiences do not, indeed could not, alter individuation and persistence. Of course, there may be cases in which a speaker is unclear about these principles attached to a word. But in such cases the speaker will be able to use and understand the word only in a very limited number of sentence frames. For example, the neighbor who has no interest in sports may not know the persistence criteria for a game of basketball. According to our lexical theory, understanding and using a word in a natural language is not an all-or-nothing affair. Some people can use and understand a word in a large variety of linguistic contexts, others less so. And in this situation it makes no sense to talk of an idealized speaker who understands the word in "all" sentence frames. What would that mean at any given time within the history of a language? Second, this would involve all kinds of extralinguistic knowledge, knowledge of games, physics, and other things that does not correspond to our intuitive understanding of what linguistic knowledge is.

So far, then, it has been argued that on one level semantic lexical representation should be construed as a set of necessary conditions that make up the general outlines of an explanation of what something denoted by the word is. In the next section we shall see what the categories for basic explanatory factors are. But we can see even at a cursory glance, that the basic explanatory frame giving us an outline of "what *w* is" even if it does not tell us the full nature, gives us information like: "it has to be viewed this way, because it is abstract," or "it must be taken in this way, because it has functional meaning."

The flexibility of having the explanatory factors filled out more or less, and in different ways is an advantage for the everyday uses of a natural language. We need not set sharp lines for just how much the competent speaker must know about the explanatory structures underlying accounts of the natures of this or that kind. These matters can change diachronically, and may vary across subgroups of linguistic communities, without causing chaos in the syntactic and semantic structures of a language.

The theory posits the fundamentality of explanatory schemes on two levels. First, it says that key elements of meaning are factors constituting explanatory schemes. Second, it says that among the variety of uses in everyday discourse, the explanatory role of descriptive words is fundamental. This thesis needs defense.

We often use words in contexts in which only a very shallow familiarity with the nature of what we talk about is needed. Thus we use words in contexts in which only recognitional skills are needed. But if challenged, such skills need be supplemented. "Why do you think that this is a tiger?" typically requires a response of the sort: "Appearances, activities, etc. of the sort experienced are accountable by judging the underlying agent to be a tiger." In general, word meanings for descriptive terms can be divided into the following categories from the point of view of offering explanations. Some words denote abstract entities. Thus various empirical manifestations are explained by being instances, exemplifications, or other manifestations of the underlying abstract element. Others involve phenomena that can be characterized as observational features with an underlying causal mechanism. Natural entities, artifacts, and activities all have this structure. Thus when we refer to whatever layer of the underlying nature meanings capture we give the full meaning of the word; and this comes up typically in sentence frames like "X if F, G, or can do Y, Z, because it is a member of kind K," where the notion of "kind" cuts across the spatial and temporal. In addition to the abstract or causal structures, functional specifications also constitute the essences of some items denoted by descriptive terms. These too are not purely observational features, but part of underlying posited natures. Hence again we can answer questions challenging why something should be usable for this or that purpose by referring to the essential functional features. We find chairs, tables in certain positions in rooms or houses because of their essential functional specifications. We see people going in and out of certain buildings and performing many of the standard functions of their lives because these buildings are houses.

Similar considerations apply to processes and activities. The merely observational does not tell one whether what we see is a case of walking, or machines moving, or some other activity. We need to know agent, intention, and other information. Thus again, it is the aspects of the underlying nature to which we refer in explanatory contexts. One might think however, that secondary qualities like shape or color or taste do not fit our sketch of how lexical items work. Is mere recognitional ability not sufficient to know how to use 'red', 'white', or some other descriptive terms? In answer we should be reminded of the fact that we use color terms typically in an objective sense. We talk about the color or taste of certain objects. This, in turn, brings in the issue of perceptual relativity. We see what is regarded by linguistic use as "the color" of an object only under certain circumstances. Thus in these cases too, mere recognitional capacity, though necessary, does not give the full meaning of color terms, and the full meaning is typically utilized in explanatory contexts. This same consideration applies to motion. Whether something moves is not merely the matter for subjective observation and we know this not only from science but from everyday experiences such as observing two trains next to each other with only one moving in the objective sense or similar experience with trucks. Similar considerations apply to allegedly simple notions like pain and pleasure. In typical everyday discourse–and not rarefied philosophical debates about "sense data"–these too are "theory laden" terms; we construe pain as having causes, typical effects, and other aspects. In dealing with symptoms of patients or friends we refer to the "full nature"–as far as the lexical meaning provides this–in order to explain experiential reports.

We talked about the explanatory and hence about explanation. As pointed out in Chapter 5, the notion of explanation invoked in this theory is holistic and not definable merely in terms of propositions arranged in a certain logical configuration (e.g., the nomological-deductive scheme). An adequate explanation and the resulting understanding is always more than a mere sum of propositions and logical relations.

At times philosophers think of our conceptual and linguistic framework as either atomistic or holistic, which means that either basic parts are intelligible by themselves or the whole system needs to be understood if any part is understood adequately.

According to the theory of this book the semantics of a natural language cannot be described either atomistically or holistically. It cannot be described atomistically, since the various items are interrelated via the semantic explanatory schemes, and these do not have an atomistic base. Nor can the semantics be described holistically, because as we shall see shortly, the lexicon is productive in the sense that new uses and senses are generated in predictable but not recursively enumerable ways. From a cognitive rather than a logical point of view the semantics comes in medium size chunks, depending on what, at any given time, we take for granted, what we see as problematic, and what we construe as having explanatory value.

Our analysis of lexical meaning also allows us to distinguish layers of meaning in a structured rather than a purely quantitative way. For example, we can admit of cases in which some of the explanatory factors stay fixed while others change. Obvious examples come from among terms for artifacts. The functional specification for 'vehicle' can stay fixed, while the factor yielding essential structure changes, as new types of vehicles are invented for the same general use. Within any one factor we can distinguish between more or less detailed accounts of essential conditions. Experts may know more details and some of these may become linguistically relevant.

We can also propose developmental hypotheses in terms of the layers of meaning the theory provides. For example, it is plausible to suppose that a small child associates in the beginning fairly specific functional essence with terms like 'mother', or 'food', and fills in principles of individuation and persistence only gradually at later stages. It would be interesting to see to what extent this is also true of the learning of names for domestic animals. There is also potential in this area for a beginning of articulating metaphorical structures. For example, when we compare the literal and metaphorical meanings of 'plough', we see the functional factor in the two to contain a large overlap, with the structural and individuating conditions differing.

Finally, we can articulate some historical semantic changes with the help of this way of viewing lexical meaning. For example 'communication' might have had a rather restricted range of necessary constituents, and necessary conditions about what kinds of spatial and temporal distances and obstacles between communicants were conceivable from lexical point of view. Gradually the restrictions were dropped or at least widened. What started out as people shouting at each other or leaving carvings for each other end up as global Internet communication. Function remains the same; necessary structure and constituents of the process are widened.

Our theory focuses on a phenomena that linguists and computational linguists like Jane Grimshaw and James Pustejovsky call underspecification, and shows how this phenomenon in various ways permeates all or most of our descriptive vocabulary. An accepted example of underspecification is 'use'. We do know what it means in general, but need linguistic and other contextual help to determine what in a given case use consists of. We use tools, help, institutions, our brains, and other means. When we fill in the linguistic contexts, the resulting complex phrases will have many different entailments.

This can be seen to hold to a lesser extent but still generally across the main syntactic categories. For instance, 'walk' is underspecified; it carries different implications when we talk about the first steps of a baby, a healthy adult's walking, the walk of an octogenarian, of an Olympic contestant, etc. With a little imagination we can see this also applying to writing, reading, and other such verbs. One can look at the examples handled in Chapters 1 and 2 also as illustrating a general kind of underspecification for expressions like 'snow', 'white', or 'refrigerator'.

We can link this phenomenon to what was said earlier about the incompleteness of the explanatory schemes, and the advantage of not dealing constantly with expressions whose meanings consist of complete explanations. There is no complete explanation to cover all cases of walking, writing, snow, water, emergency, or other expressions.

The specifications take place on the second level of our semantic analysis, with the third level yielding the denotations. We must not view the third level as yielding final semantic atoms. The specifications may go on indefinitely; depending on how our cognitive activities of taking things for granted, explaining things, and introducing explanatory schemes function. We shall see in Chapter 5 how these processes work.

Labeling cannot be basic, because it is highly context-dependent. The context is provided either by theories, and theory skeletons, or by contrasts without theoretical background. What we call running depends on whether the contrasting elements are walking and standing, or include cantering and galloping. What we call white, as we saw in a previous chapter, depends on what we describe: shirts, highway signs, races. What we label as a chemical depends on a certain theory that includes the table of chemical elements; but in other contexts we have commonsense contrasts as well, that does not presuppose that theory.

Thus we cannot start out with a notion of basic qualitative similarity, and then interpret labeling as picking out salient similarities. The reason is not only that philosophically the notion of similarity as a basic term is suspect, but also that what is salient will depend on changing interactions with the environment.

II. THE FOUR EXPLANATORY FACTORS

Having argued for the general thesis that lexical meanings have the conceptual structure of explanatory schemes, in this section we shall examine the specific proposal that these explanatory schemes consist of the realization of four explanatory factors, two of which are obligatory. These factors are:

i. The constitutive factor—that is, the necessary link between the given word and a domain within which the denotation ranges must be located.
ii. The structural factor. This consists of necessary principles of individuation and persistence, if any, and those necessary distinguishing properties that are required by at least individuation and necessary functional requirements.
iii. The agential factor. This obviously does not apply to all items; for instance, abstract entities do not have necessary causal powers attached to them. This factor includes those necessary causal properties of items within the denotation range that partially determine origin, causal powers involved in producing successors (e.g., modes of procreation), and those causal powers that are necessarily linked to how items in the denotations should function.
iv. The functional factor. This includes those functional properties that are necessarily parts of the meaning of the word; for example, that under normal conditions a knife functions to cut, and a cleaning establishment to clean.

These four factors are very general, and are meant to pick out key ingredients in explanatory schemes that specify the nature or "whatness" of an entity. At the same time, these factors also have linguistic impact; that is, one of the determinants of what is or is not in a natural language a semantically well-formed formula. However, the positing of these four factors needs to be defended against such objections as would claim that, for example, the universal particular distinction is also a very general distinction and has semantic impact, or that distinctions such as animate + versus –, or process versus thing, or artifact versus natural product are also distinctions with wide scope and semantic impact. In response one can point to the universal–particular distinction, and the property–instance distinction as not informative enough. Making that distinction can be read off from the four factors proposed, and by itself that dichotomy will not specify enough content for explanatory schemes. Knowing within what general domain an entity falls, what kinds of individuation and distinguishing properties it must have, as well as basic functioning and causal properties, if any, provides an outline of the nature of any entity. The universal–particular distinction does not do this. Not all spatiotemporal particulars have the same individuation conditions; those conditions depend on what kind the entity in question belongs.[4] The process–thing distinction is not exhaustive of all of reality, and again it can be read off our proposed scheme, since it is a part of the general distinction within the first factor of things within the spatial or temporal domain. The animate–inanimate distinction is marked in many languages, but its way of dividing entities up is highly variable. What about panpsychism? What about animisms of different sort? Time and space are basic dimensions of the nonabstract; there will be no debates on the everyday level whether something is an event or an object. Nor is there any debate over whether we should specify nature partly in terms of the domain to which a given item necessarily belongs. "Is it animate or not?" is not a question on the same basic level, and its answers do not bring out equally vital ingredients and differences between explanatory schemes.

The distinction between artifacts and natural products does have interesting implications, but these are restricted to a certain part of our interaction with the environment. "What is it made of?" is a question that applies necessarily to everything. "Is it natural or an artifact?" applies only to a certain range of phenomena and contexts.

The four factors are meant to pick out concepts the application of which we can assume to be innate. Humans need not be instructed to ask what something is made of, or how to apply to a kind term quantifiers like "many" or "all"; and "How does this work?" seems to come, in nonverbal form, to infants. On the other hand, several of the distinctions just listed may correlate to innate

4. Ibid, pp. 114–15.

ideas as well. The innateness of the four factors is a psychological hypothesis of this theory, and it does not exclude the possibility that many other linguistic distinctions also have an innate basis. Conceptual fundamentality need not correlate with psychological fundamentality.

One might think that the four factors provide explanations that are answers to "Why?" questions. But such a characterization is much too wide. We can ask "Why are you angry?" and the answer sought does not involve typically pointing to necessary fundamental ingredients of constituency, function, and so on. The explanatory schemes that we construe as parts of lexical meanings focus on explanations that present the nature or an aspect of the nature of a given entity. This specification does not exclude the possibility that the dichotomy of nature versus contingent properties is not sharp, and there are many borderline cases. As we saw above, within this theory linguistic, especially semantic, competence is a matter of degree; hence meanings too need not be sharply delineated in each case.

Let us turn to the first factor, namely that of constituency. Within this we differentiate not parts like leg or arm, but merely the domain within which an entity is necessarily located. Call this the m-factor.[5] Within it we distinguish only a small number of domains, namely the abstract, the spatial, the temporal, and the multicategorial. Thus numbers, properties, geometrical structures, types (vs. tokens) belong to the abstract domain. What we loosely call material objects belong to the spatial. Of course, these entities are also located in time, but it is in terms of spatiality that essential aspects such as being concrete, being things, or having concrete parts are described. Surfaces also belong to the spatial, and so do colors, smells, and other entities that are related to material objects but have an individuation of their own. The temporal domain is the "home" of happenings, events, processes, states, and activities. A walk may take place in some region, but its parts and hence the structure that defines parts and interrelations are temporal intervals and instances.[6] It would be a mistake to link this domain closely to any one syntactic category: within the domain we find births, battles, wars just as much as walking, eating, thinking.

So far, then, we have the domains for the abstract, the material object and its elements or dependent empirical entities (smell, etc.), and the basically temporal (including sound, and possibly mental events that have temporal but no spatial location). This leaves us the multicategorial. These are words that

5. This is a revised version of my *Thought and Language*, Ch. 6.

6. D. Gabbay and J. Moravcsik, "Verbs, Events, and the Flow of Time," in C. Rohrer, ed., *Time, Tense, and Quantifiers* (Tübingen: Niemeyer, 1980), pp. 59–83.

denote items whose basic domain cuts necessarily across the categories listed so far; they have mixed constituency. Three groups fall into this mixed domain: certain human institutions, certain events or activities, and the denotations of linguistic elements that function semantically as modifiers such as–in languages like English or German–some adjectives and adverbs. When we consider an institution like a university or hospital, we need to conceptualize it as the mixture of the abstract, the spatial, and the temporal, even if we restrict ourselves just to locating an item in its constituent domain. A university is made up of ideas, humans, regulations, buildings, and a history of mostly continuous activities. All institutions of similar, quasi-legal status have multicategorial domains. In some, instead of ideas, products form one of the contributing subdomains, in others, such as courts, ceremonial acts, "pronouncing sentences" will be among the constituents. The proof for the need for this multicategoriality is that it is needed to spell out principles of individuation and persistence. We can see that perhaps even more intuitively when we turn to the large class of adjectives that function as modifiers; that is, the semantics of which presupposes another semantic unit the content of which is modified by the semantic content of the modifier. The adjective 'wise' can be applied to agent, action, plans, and other notions. One can then reconstruct all the wisdom in this world as the sum of these instances in different domains of the abstract, the temporal, and the spatial. The same considerations apply to adverbs like 'slowly'. The m-factor will be whatever can have speed. This includes the temporal as well as the spatial. Finally, we find multicategoriality in the case of verbs of cognition. The verb 'expect' denotes a state that requires a set of temporal instances making up the temporal part of state, and an abstract object that specifies what it is that is being expected. Again, we can see that individuation will depend on these types of entities.

In summary, there are temporal configurations like events or actions, spatial configurations like lines, surfaces, or three-dimensional bodies, and abstract configurations like numbers. Then there are also the words whose meaning includes multicategorial bases. Understanding the m-factor without having a conscious theory about these things is an essential part of understanding the meaning of a descriptive word, since these domains help explain some of what we mean by explaining what the denoted item is, and also how that item can enter into explaining daily or scientific phenomena.

Let us suppose that we have located an entity in the abstract or temporal domain. The other key question that emerges is: What is the essential structure that holds the "stuff" constituting a region of the domain together and shapes it into a functioning entity? Quine, in both his ontological and semantic writings, stressed the importance of what we called individuation.[7] On the ontological plane this means that we have no adequate conception of an entity until we discover what distinguishes it from other entities, in particular other entities within its own genus. On the semantic plane this means knowing how to use quantifiers like 'many', 'few', or 'three' as attached to the word, and having some conception of the structures that in reality separate the entities in question and thus serve as the explanatory background for the use of the logical terms. Even if the word is a mass term like 'gold', or 'red', we need some way of characterizing the unity of a denotatum and separating it from other items under a higher count term; color, metal, and so on. These principles in turn entail having a variety of properties in addition to the ones explicitly mentioned in a statement of individuation. For example, two birds are individuated by the principle that each biologically functioning unit with birdlike characteristics is a separate bird–that is, it counts for one (whether it is separated in a purely physical sense or not.) This in turn, as we shall see, requires spelling out what the bird-making characteristics are. This introduces the s-factor, or–somewhat misleadingly–the structural factor. The key intuition does not depend that much on the ordinary meaning of 'structure', but on the idea that within a domain (in the sense of our m-factor) each entity has necessarily some individuation principles linked to it, and the embodying of these principles requires a variety of underlying properties. A key thesis underlying this approach, and defended elsewhere,[8] is that principles of individuation and persistence are based on kinds. That is to say, unlike identity which is a logical notion and is the same across all realms of reality, individuation is qua animal, vegetable, mountain, and so on.

Some of the properties listed under the s-factor can be best explained by contrast. We know on the commonsense level what a bee is by contrast with other insects like flies, hornets, wasps, mosquitoes, and so on. The range of contrasts is indeterminate. Some speakers of the language are well acquainted with the insect world, and some are less so. This is a matter of knowing about insects and not a matter of linguistic competence. It would make no sense to talk about idealizations in this context. It is not fruitful for linguistic theory and its relation to human cognition to posit an idealized speaker-hearer who is acquainted with the total vocabulary of all those areas in which some expertise is required such as wines, insects, wild animals, or minerals.

This is, then, another reason for rejecting the claim that lexical meaning

---

7. W. V. O. Quine, *Word and Object* (New York: John Wiley, 1960), pp. 91–95.

8. See note 4.

yields conditions that apply "across all possible worlds." As shown in the next chapter, this is not a reason for relegating lexical semantics to pragmatics.

Why should we not construe the combination of m- and s-factors as not only necessary but also sufficient conditions for denotation? As I pointed out previously, lexical meaning develops partly out of our interactions with the environment and among ourselves. These interactions cannot be summed up in a theoretically adequate way. The series of positive integers is infinite, but we have recursive ways of capturing the set. The same applies to the class of syntactically well-formed English sentences. However, the indefinite and infinite nature of all past present and future interactions among humans and between humans and nature prevents us from giving such characterizations. As the examples to follow show, we can give characterizations that provide the foundations for an explanatory scheme and place constraints on what can be parts of denotation ranges. It cannot specify completely the denotation ranges.

Having surveyed the two factors that must be present in the meaning structures of all kinds, let us turn to the two other factors. The f-factor contains what are the essential functional features that must be parts of lexical meanings. Recall the brief examples earlier in this section. Here we expand on this. For terms designating artifacts the f-factor is the use that we put these objects to, as designed and constructed. Chairs are to sit on, tables to put things on, beds to lie on, houses to live in. There are also many contingent functional specifications. In some contexts houses should be on stilts as protection against floods; in others utensils should be chained to the table so as to prevent theft (I know of one such restaurant which is–aptly–called: The Inn of Confidence). Vocabulary terms designating sports have as their f-factor specification of what is to be accomplished; what counts as activity in accordance with rules, what counts as winning. In the case of animals the f-factor is conceptually richer. It includes basic biological functional attributes such as survival, propagation, and biological persistence of individuals, as well as the more species-specific–such as web weaving for spiders, dam building for beavers, honey collecting for bees. These characteristics require some nonfunctional account of how these things are realized; such accounts or parts of these may not be parts of lexical meaning. Another class of term with rich functional meanings is terms denoting professions. Lawyers, doctors, government officials are described in their essentials as fulfilling this or that prescribed function. This is a good place to stress how different our lexical theory is from verificationalism. Lawyers, doctors, and others cannot be defined in terms of recognitional features. The words designating these professions emerge within the network of complex social and legal arrangements. Unlike words for secondary qualities like colors such as red or blue, there is no simple perceptual access to determine who does or does not qualify as a member of these professions. Philosophers at times emphasize the "theory-laden" nature of some of our vocabulary, but in that context we consider typically scientific theories. What is at issue here is not a theory in that sense, but a network of arrangements, some legal, that define roles, functions, ceremonial interactions, and so on.

In the previous chapter we dealt with generics. Here we can utilize this important semantic device. For spelling out the essential functional features of different kinds, natural or artificial, will have to be done in most cases in terms of generics. Just as not all beavers build dams, so not all chairs are used for sitting (a fact obvious to all those who visit occasionally the crowded offices of university professors, with at least half of the "chairs" serving primarily to have placed on them an indefinite amalgam of research material, unanswered correspondence, memos from the administration, material to be refereed, etc.). This goes for sports as well. What would be ordinarily an exercise achieving a certain level of physical or competitive excellence can turn into a spectacle for bloodthirsty thousands enjoying the efforts to please by humans vastly overpaid in terms of their utility to society.

The class of words with meanings requiring less generic constructions are activity words. Writing has a stable functional role even when used to evil ends; and the same goes for walking, eating, and other actions. The activities need not be those with human agents. The digestive system is to digest food, even when the food digested harms the human body.

This, then, is the f-factor. Some times the function is realized in terms of what something or someone does (carpenter) or again in terms of what a process accomplishes (building a house), or in terms of necessarily linked result (defeat). These functional aspects of meaning are independent of what the purpose or intention of the agent is at any given time. Healing has a functional aspect, and this is independent of whether the agent's main aim was healing or making money. Not all words, even apart from abstract ones, have an f-factor in their meaning structure. For example, 'motion' lacks such an aspect, as does any other word that can have meaning in a world of discourse within which there is no room for the teleological, functional, and purposive.

The fourth factor is the a-factor, containing elements that signify causal role of one sort or another that is necessarily linked to the meaning of some word. Obvious examples are: 'slice', 'move', 'produce'. To be sure, by and large every nonabstract entity is involved in some form of causal stream. This assumption, as stated, leaves open the possibility of a few purely random events, thus does not affirm determinism of any sort; nor does it rule that *out* on a priori grounds.

But apart from the causal streams some events have specific causal roles associated with them conceptually, and this is what the a-factor is designed to capture. The associated causal role may be necessary origin or possible reproductive mode, or a necessary effect without which the word in question does not apply. The factor is called a-factor to remind us of agency, a very broad term indeed, not linked to any specific theory of causation. Hence 'sculptor' has in its meaning an a-factor, since the sculptor produces sculptures, regardless of how closely or indirectly his activities relate to the product. Here again, as in the case of the f-factor, often the specification of the layer of meaning has to be couched in terms of generics. A sculptor, if all goes well, produces sculptures. Maybe war, persecution, or illness prevents him from doing this for years at a time, but this does not rob him of his professional designation.

There are different ways of affecting something causally. For example a musician plays some music, the composer composes it. The first is not creating the music she plays in the typical case but producing a performance of it. The second is a case of creating something but not necessarily performing it. Again, persuasion has a causal component. If one has not persuaded anyone of anything, then no persuasion has taken place. We can contrast this with pleading one's case. This takes place as long as one performed certain actions regardless of the causal consequences.

There are also the interesting cases in which a word like 'move' has both a transitive and a intransitive use. Within the lexical theory adopted here, this is represented by the differences in the s-factor, since in one case there will be one less argument place determining individuation, and also in the a-factor, since the necessary causal effects will differ among the two uses. It is important in such cases to keep semantics of a natural language and metaphysics separate. From a metaphysical point of view, perhaps every move involves a mover. This is irrelevant, however, to the representation of the semantics of everyday use. The semantics of English is indifferent to metaphysical puzzles whether something could have moved without its having been moved by an entity other than itself.

The semantic structure does not mirror exactly the syntactic one. For example 'write' takes objects like letters, warnings, or essays, and thus there is a causal element in the semantics of such verb phrases. But writing involves a different causal element as well. Writing is to produce symbols, even if the activity has no determined aim. One can just write words without any specific purpose, hoping that maybe something (a poem perhaps) will emerge from this activity. As linguists have noted, the causative element is represented in different ways.

III. EXAMPLES

We shall look first at one example in considerable detail and then sketch a number of others from different syntactic categories. Our example is 'baseball' and related expressions such as 'to play baseball'. This is an interesting case, since it involves activity, social convention, and multicategoriality. Furthermore, it is an interesting case for making the kind of distinction exemplified here by seeing the difference between understanding what baseball is, and understanding the word 'baseball'. What are the various uses of the term 'baseball', and how do these relate to the various points of view of those using the word, such as players, umpires who judge, spectators, and people with no interest in this particular sport? The use of the term is part of the competence of agents playing, different agents who enforce the rules, spectators who become emotionally involved, and competent users of English who fall into none of the aforementioned categories.

It would be a catastrophe if the differences in points of view would result in uses so different that we would have to assign to these a variety of meanings. There must be either a series of contingent overlaps or an underlying core meaning that facilitates if not ensures communication across roles and points of view. This point can be made even more emphatically in the case of patient, doctor, and researcher. They may have different points of view regarding an illness, but some common understanding is essential if the art of medicine is to function adequately.

It is also important to separate the puzzle we are setting up from the one involving differences between use by an expert and use by a layperson. There are experts in baseball, and there are mere laypersons, but that distinction does not coincide with the one between player, umpire, and fan.

Baseball is also a good example to show the inapplicability of a prototype-based approach to lexical semantics. What is a prototypical baseball game? A pitcher's duel, or one with many home runs? One with no ejections, or one with brawls? These are unanswerable questions; but so are their analogues if applied to other sports like football or basketball. As we shall see, there are interesting questions concerning how much departure from the rules of the game is allowed in different contexts, but the difference between a game played by official rules and deviations cannot be assimilated to prototypical specimens and less typical ones.

The following definition captures what I take to be the underlying core meaning of 'baseball' that can be used as the basis of understanding among people approaching the game from different points of view.

> a competitive rule-governed game for teams with a fixed number of players in which advantage is gained by hitting with a bat of predescribed dimensions a ball of predescribed dimensions and substance, thrown by the opposite team, so that it should not be caught the other team and should land within a predescribed area, thus advancing the hitter along a diamond-shaped path anchored on four stopping places, the fourth completing the course a batter should take in optimal contexts. Teams take the hitting and defending roles in order. Prescribed periods demarcate the change in roles, with the team with the more "runs" (batters circling all four bases) emerging as winners.

This definition, and its parts can function as an explanatory scheme. Various questions about why this team is "ahead," why the team is declared the winner, why fans are divided in their support, why the game has to be played within large areas, and so on can be answered by pointing out the baseball contains the features just listed. Of course baseball contains much more. If someone knows only what is contained in the proposed definition, she does not yet understand a great deal about the game. But understanding the definition enables one to be prepared to apply, with the help of contextual clues to which we shall turn, the term 'baseball' to the appropriate activities, and to use it in a large variety of sentence frames.

Let us see now how this definition can be analyzed along the fourfold semantic structure outlined in the previous section.

Since the entities denoted are games, one might think that the m-factor should be time. However, the "stuff" of which the game is made up cannot be described, as in the case of 'walk', as temporal stages containing motions with required agents. For the temporal stages are defined institutionally. An inning of a game, as in cricket, is not just a set of temporal stages with motions. Its start and finish are defined officially, by an umpire, and the motions performed are defined in terms of roles prescribed by the rules of the game. While there is no precise answer to a question like: "Where must the university be?" there is also no precise answer to the analogous question about a baseball game. If floods come, the game could have started in New York but ended in Chicago. Thus the multicategorality of this m-factor. It includes time, rule applications, agents, of various types, and spatial areas.

The s-factor has to specify principles of individuation, and persistence. As shown above, the latter is defined by rules applying to what the agents in different roles can or must do. There are limits of innings for a game abbreviated by rain, for a "normal" nine-inning game, and an indeterminate instruction of sequences of innings for a tie game. The beginning of a new game is, then, not necessarily a matter of different players, different umpires, or different places. In general, then, the persistence criteria are provided by rules governing activities of players, umpires, and arrangements for temporal continuity and legitimate gaps, and appropriate spatial container. The principle of individuation has to determine under what conditions there are two, rather than one or three, games being played. First, there is spatiotemporal distinctness; two games cannot be played at the same time in the same place by the same teams. Furthermore, one game cannot be played at the same time in two separate places. (This is not a general requirement on events, institutional or other. A peace conference, for example, can take place simultaneously in two places at the same time; the sections settling different kinds of matters, economic, issues of frontiers, etc.)

But *what* is individuated must also be part of the principle. This is provided by large parts of the definition offered. It must be a game with the characteristics and constituents listed, with the very important proviso that certain specifications of tools used, area of playing field, even numbers of participants, are specified indeterminately, in terms of appropriateness, fixed in context.

The elements giving us what is to be individuated and how, provide also ways of distinguishing a baseball game from other games. As mentioned above, these distinctions are dependent on a vaguely articulable conceptual context; to distinguish baseball from football, basketball, cricket, softball, or tennis, for example. It is senseless to ask for a definition distinguishing baseball from all other games "in all possible worlds." History is open-ended; as in the case of artifacts, so in the case of games, and sports, in particular, we have no way of delineating all of the logically possible games of the future of humanity.

The f-factor specifies what must be achieved in order for the motions, actions, including rule enforcement, to count as a baseball game. Since it is a rule-governed and competitive game, the f-factor must include what counts as a win, as a completion of a game, and the elements of achievement, hence function, that serve as constituents to the overall conceptual contour. Just how many of these should be included, and in what detail, need not be determined precisely. We can describe what it is to be a pitcher in terms of the required motions and underlying skills. There is also the functional requirement–that he is to get the batter "out" by getting him to miss the ball a required number of times or to hit it so that it is caught. The latter descriptions are parts of the structure of the game, the aim of the pitcher is a part of the functional structure, belonging to the f-factor.

The a-factor remains almost empty. Obviously baseball involves many causal processes, but the only essential causal link that is relevant to this activity is its being a human institution, hence not a natural process like osmosis.

This structure serves to sort out the different parts of the definition given above. At the same time, looking at the various definitional parts shows us why this is a complex of necessary but not sufficient requirements. The bat, the ball, must be of appropriate size, shape, and material. The playing area must be suitable. How rigidly is the number of players fixed? Granted that an umpiring role need be realized, how rigidly is the selection of such a judge fixed? In all of these aspects there is room for flexibility. This does *not* mean that in any one context there is that much laxness. Rather that along these dimensions we can specify what counts in different contexts as a baseball game. In the context of official professional or other organized system, the requirements are very rigid: nine players on each side, rigid rules about substitution, the need for an official umpire, constitution and size of ball and bat, and other details are all sharply delineated. But there are other contexts in which the standard of appropriateness can be relaxed without lapsing into semantic and practical anarchy. As we saw, the meaning of 'baseball' contains a heavy f-factor. The function of playing a competitive game involving teams, bats and balls, and so on can be fulfilled in a number of ways. There are "pick-up" baseball games at playgrounds, outings to state parks, informal league play in social organizations, and other matches. The bats need not be strictly up to standard, nor the balls used. Gloves become optional, and the area used for play admits of variation. Nevertheless, not "everything goes." Extreme departures from the official standards are not admissible. In short, not everything counts as baseball just because some people want to call their game by that name.

There is also the contextual difference between baseball for adults, and so-called Little League ball, designed for smaller children, with the area varying in size and shape and other differences.

We see, then, that the definition gives us salient explanatory necessary conditions, and that given the structure of the definition as articulated here, we can read off the general outlines of how denotation contexts and associated ranges emerge. The game involves winning by teams in a certain way, and in different social contexts, involving age, social or political setting (GIs playing on a field in war, between actions), the standards involved in the delineation of the s-factor are subject to change. What counts as baseball on a sandlot would not count as baseball in the so-called World Series. A clear case of such variance was illustrated to me by my observing in India children playing on a grassless area covered with mud, with balls made of rags, bats resembling broomsticks, and wooden structures hardly resembling wickets. In that context what they did clearly counted as playing cricket, even though the same activity with the same instruments and playing field would not count as cricket when planning a so-called test match in England.

Our definition will be associated by different agents with different experiences and different verification procedures. The spectator buys the ticket, goes to his seat, and expects to see certain objects, activities, and players. The player "knows" that he is involved in the same ball game through different means. What he sees and does is quite different from what the spectator sees from the stands, and does. One of the key points of lexical semantics is to explain how nevertheless spectator, player, and fan can talk about the same thing, and importantly, do more than that; they will give the same type of explanations to various questions about baseball, regardless of the subjective differences in their experiences relating them to the game. (There must be *some* commonality between the types of experiences that speakers understanding each other, have. Red Smith, one of the greatest of the American baseball writers started his career by writing a column describing the first night-time baseball game in Fenway Park from the point of view of a glowworm. While acknowledging the brilliance of this journalistic achievement, one must suspect a strong dose of anthropomorphism present in the account.)

So the denotation ranges are generated when we ask: "In this context, how much variation from quantitative standards of size, shape, constituency of objects, size of areas, number of players, and so forth can be semantically 'tolerated?" In some context this has practical implications; we do not keep records of number of "home runs" hit by people who use just any kind of ball and bat, for example. At other times, the definitional issue has hardly any impact on our lives, and can be left quite vague; for example, what game do sailors play on the deck of a battleship between naval engagements?

As we said earlier, understanding a word is a matter of degrees. This can be spelled out, for the degrees are a function of the number of kinds of sentence frames in which the speaker can use or interpret the word. Thus the speaker with no interest in sports will use the word in a more limited number of contexts than the player or umpire. It makes no sense to posit in these contexts an idealized speaker-hearer who can use the word in all legitimate contexts. For the ability to use and understand the term in a wider range of contexts is partly not a matter of linguistic but rather of nonlinguistic knowledge; it is a matter to an extent of knowing more about baseball, not of knowing English better.

Having seen how the denotational contexts can be generated by knowing something about certain elements of the definition and about the human interactions within which 'baseball' acquires its different uses, let us turn to how we fix denotation in specific denotational contexts, a matter discussed already in other publications.[9] We shall now focus on the question What kind of knowledge is required in order to participate in denotation fixing? What counts in different contexts as an emergency? Answering this question in specific contexts may require knowing about the speed and navigability of ships, or the speed of airplanes as seen by an air traffic controller. The same applies to baseball. To be able to fix what counts as baseball in a pick-up game on a playground requires knowing things about playgrounds as much as knowing semantics. Thus it might be suggested that this level of semantics really belongs to pragmatics rather than to that layer of meaning that should be labeled as belonging to linguistic competence.

As we see, there is a lot to be known and understood about baseball, and thus about 'baseball' and other similar words. Our fourfold structure is well suited to explicate the notion of having degrees of understanding of the meanings of words. In the standard Frege and Carnap inspired semantics one could articulate "intension" into layers of conditions and say that some people "grasp" more of these layers than others. But in our system we introduce more structure to understanding. For example, small children know some of the salient conditions falling under the f-factor for 'mother' ('mom'), but not some of the parts of the a- and s-factors. In the case of words for insects, like 'wasp', 'hornet', some people understand principles of individuation and persistence, but not the parts of the s-factor that distinguishes wasps from hornets.

These remarks raise the question: how do we distinguish within this lexical theory matters involved in knowing the meaning of a word from extralinguistic matters, that is, sheer information about the denotation? This question becomes even more acute within our system since it embraces Quine's view that there are no purely analytic statements. The distinction can be restated, however, even within this condition as two different kinds of revision; one of meaning and the other of mere information, even if the first does not cover truths that are supposed to hold "in all possible worlds." For example, general matters of propagation fall under the concept of meaning. The a-factor for 'koala-bear' includes that the animals denoted are marsupials. We could not have a situation in which we have one kind, named 'koala-bear', but some of the denotata are marsupials and others oviparous. Why is this? Within our account this can be explained by pointing to the fact that modes of propagation determine to a large extent the rest of the anatomy. We can contrast this with how much hair a person has. But this contrast assumes dealing with a world in important ways similar to ours, not with all possible worlds. In some possible

9. Moravcsik, *Thought and Language*, Ch. 6.

worlds, say in one in which the story of Samson and Delila is true, we would need different words or at least different meanings. But as long as hair determines so little of the rest of the anatomy, and modes of propagation so much, the latter is a part of knowing meaning, and the former not. Again, knowing the principles of individuation and persistence fall under the s-factor, and hence is parts of knowing the meaning of the word. Even in these cases, however, the line need not be sharp. Some people know more details about the principles of persistence of some items designated by parts of their language than others (e.g., physicians vs. laypersons.)

Understanding of the m-factor is part of linguistic competence. If one does not know whether the denotata are supposed to be concrete or abstract, then one does not have understanding of the word covering the denotata in question. We can see this in the case of intuitions involving so-called category mistakes. On my theory it is a part of linguistic competence to realize that "which takes longer, a soccer match or the number 2?" is an absurd question, while "Which takes longer, a cricket match or standard baseball game?" is not. There will be borderline cases; this is to be expected and is not a flaw in this lexical semantics. There will be also meaning changes that involve radical changes in a given factor. For, say, a tribe has a word for 'stick', which has as its f-factor use, if fighting, defense. As the tribe turns to an agricultural life-style, the f-factor comes to include use in various agricultural activities. We can not only locate the meaning change, but give it a clear specification; what changed and why?

We shall deal with the line between pragmatics and semantics in more general terms in the next chapter. But let us note here in connection with the example above that semantics does place constraints on what can be done with denotation fixing. All of the conditions of basic domain, and individuation as well as persistence, and the f- and a-factors remain intact. What becomes subject of variation are some of the less central elements of the s-factor–that is, those that function more as distinguishing factors rather than individuating factors. Should a game with only eight players count as baseball in a certain context in which informality and lack of continuity rein rather than an organized sequence of games? The extent to which we can be lax here is governed by the basic requirements on skill, effort, and what counts as winning. Maybe eight players will do (e.g., only two in the outfield) but not an arrangement in which there are no pitchers, and the ball is brought into play by some other means.

We shall look now at other examples, starting with 'bird'; this will be useful since its treatment was subjected to criticism by Mark Richard.[10]

10. M. Richard, "Reference and Competence: Moravcsik's *Thought and Language*" *Dialogue* 32 (1993), 555–63.

m-factor: spatiality
s-factor: biological organism with feathers, legs, body, beak, head, eyes; with the unitary functioning of a biological unit individuating, and the same structure, rather than e.g. sameness of parts, accounting for persistence
a-factor: natural entity, with its own mode of procreation
f-factor: maintenance of biological functioning, fly, move around on ground

We see from this that the meaning, as in the previous case, is a well-structured set of necessary conditions constituting an explanatory scheme. As such it is different from what are in Putnam's theory "core facts," associated by speakers with the word, not necessarily accurate or even true. The difference can be illustrated with reference to a list Richard gives as examples of what he takes would be "core facts" in Putnam's theory.[11]

sorrow is caused by misfortune
glass is fragile
chairs have legs
architects design buildings for a living
stones are found in the ground
playing is doing something for fun

It is difficult to see how any of these would fit into the fourfold framework of necessary conditions construed here as lexical meaning. Sorrow is a mental state, thus having time as its m-factor, and it does not have any necessary link to any causal origin. 'Chair' would be defined, as any word for an artifact, primarily in functional terms, and structural conditions vary from historical period to another as well as across cultures. Neither play nor being an architect would be defined in our system in the simplistic terms represented by the sentences above. What architects, mathematicians, lawyers, and others do would not be defined in terms of whether they make a living on what they do or not. In some cultures they do, in some they do not. Knowledge of such contingent associations is not a matter of linguistic competence.

Going back to our scheme for 'bird' we can see why the definition gives us only necessary conditions. Humans interact with birds in a variety of ways, and this will influence ordinary usage, even if it does not affect biology. Do we

11. Ibid, p. 559.

count as birds things that have no wings or do not fly for other reasons? Only if there is a plausible historical account of how they got that way (penguins, kiwi birds). How much damage or gene mutation would there have to be before we don't count in some context a birdlike creature as a bird? 'Bird', in science or common sense, is a theory-laden term, and hence subject to denotation domain generating factors, and different ranges. We cannot predict what new species will emerge in the future and what semantic legislation, at least in the form of denotation range fixing, will take place. Hence the same number of semantic levels is required for a word like 'bird' as for the other words we surveyed. We already saw this in the last chapter when we looked at 'water', 'snow', 'refrigerator', 'white', and other words. In each case, after a specification of meaning we were left with the task of specifying different denotational contexts, and asking, What should count as water, white, and so forth in this or that context?

Philosophy of language tends to get bogged down with few examples, most of which, like 'water', denotes concrete kinds. A much larger variety of examples has been given as illustrations of my lexical theory elsewhere.[12] Here we shall look only at a noun without concrete things as denotations, and a verb, thus applying our lexical theory to the kind of data familiar from the linguistic literature.

For the word 'joy', since it designates a state of mind, the m-factor is time. As for the s-factor, since this is a mass term, there is no principle of individuation; there are not "many joys," only many kinds of joy, or many occasions for joy. Hence the s-factor serves primarily as providing a way to distinguish joy from other psychological states. The distinguishing mark is a spontaneous emotional state of elation, not necessarily linked to utility or need.

This delineation helps to distinguish joy from such states as satisfaction, gladness, being pleased, and so forth. Again, we need to emphasize that the distinguishing mark cannot cover "all possible worlds." In this case this point is even clearer than in some other examples. For we do not possess any way of distinguishing or enumerating all human emotional states. Such classifications are related to human interests and to the variety of ways in which humans are perceived as interacting with the environment and with one other.

The a-factor specifies only that this is a natural psychological emerging quality. It does not necessarily have a causal effect, nor does its realization embody some causal effect.

The f-factor specifies that the functional end is inner harmony and a feeling

12. *Thought and Language* Ch. 6.

of wellbeing. These are, however, not construed as effects. As Aristotle saw[13] inner harmony or well-being are constituents of being elated in a certain way (as opposed to e.g. ecstasy). This is *how* we feel when experiencing joy, not that these are elements for which joy is a means.

Given what we have said about the s-factor, it is easy to see why we need a level of denotation range generation and denotation fixing. In different contexts 'joy' may be contrasted with different psychological states. Thus the denotation range will be that which is *not* covered by the contrasting elements. We saw that in the previous chapter when discussing 'white'. When it comes to shirts, the denotation range is so wide as to include much of what in other contexts we call yellow. Again, to talk about an idealized complete picture of all human emotions for all times makes no sense from a linguistic point of view.

The word 'expect' helps to bring out interesting contrasts. It is a word describing a cognitive as opposed to an emotional state. My joy may have causes; it does not have an object in the sense in which my expectations do. When I expect, I must expect something, and that object is typically described by a claim or proposition. Syntactically speaking, the objects vary. We can expect good news, a baby, a package, rain, and so on. But as Pustejovsky has shown, we can introduce devices linking syntactic variety to uniform semantic interpretation –in the case under consideration "type coercion"[14]–that accounts for such phenomena. Furthermore, the object plays a vital role in individuating expectations. Hence the m-factor is multicategorial: temporal and abstract. This captures the state and its object which is best characterizable as abstract–that is, the content of thought. Philosophical theories about the correct ontology of such abstract entities are irrelevant to the semantics of everyday language. Unlike in the previous example, here we do have principles of individuation and persistence. We individuate expectations by their objects; some expect sunshine, some rain; different expectations–and are thus even if the same person has both expectations. The cognitive state is one of judging that some event will take place. This distinguishes expectation from, for example, hope or mystic intuitions.

'Expect' is a very general word. We can add to it modifiers in at least two dimensions. It can be accompanied by positive feelings or by negative ones; thus we get 'anticipate', or 'dread' and 'fear'. Again, the evidence backing the expectation may be strong or weak. In English we do not have separate vocabulary

---

13. Aristotle, *Nichomachean Ethics*, Book X.

14. J. Pustejovsky, *The Generatice Lexicon* (Cambridge, MA: MIT Press, 1995), p. 111.

items to mark these states, but we could have. We can say "expect justifiably", or "expect without serious backing...".

What counts as expectation in different contexts? This depends on the different concepts of rationality that we invoke in different pragmatic contexts. The rationality of a judgment that an event is coming depends on one's conception of rationality. Again, not everything goes. In practical, theoretical, experimental, and other contexts we may invoke different criteria of rationality, but these criteria are public and interpersonal.

These examples show the full lexical theory that backs what we said about natural languages and formal languages in the previous chapter. It gives the positive alternative to the traditional philosophic distinction of intension and extension constituting alone semantic structure. It also shows that rejecting that philosophic view does not have to drive us either to construe the semantics of general terms as analogous to one of the logician's interpretation of the semantics of proper names, nor to retreating to the kind of mere data collecting that the so-called ordinary language philosophy featured (as discussed in Chapter 1.)

IV. TOWARDS THE PRODUCTIVE LEXICON

The introduction of our third level into lexical semantics made the lexicon productive in the sense that it does not merely delineate a fixed finite number of items as the vocabulary of a language, but in addition to listing a set of finite elements it also gives the basis of an indefinite number of denotation ranges, some already in existence, some emerging in the future. This does not leave semantic competence as a mystery, since the emerging denotation ranges are formed along predictable lines.

This multiple denotations structure should not be confused with meaning change. Meaning change is the diachronic analogue of ambiguity. But as examples of ambiguity such as 'bank' or 'hood' show, in these cases we have entirely different s- and f-factors, thus not assimilatable to the production of new denotation ranges that we saw.

To some extent the multiple denotation formation can be represented linguistically. For example, we can consider 'emergency' and its meaning, and then add 'naval' as an adjective, and get denotation specification. It may happen however, that within naval emergencies further distinctions have to be drawn (submarine, nuclear carrier, etc.). But the fact that adding a word to another can change meaning and create new denotations suggests the feasibility of introducing a technical term from earlier literature. In the semantics of Frege we find what can be called context-sensitive semantic rules, and in early Chomskian syntax we had context-sensitive syntactic rules. For example, for Frege "it is raining over Europe" had one meaning and denotation when standing by itself, and another when in the context of "John believes that…". Our examples suggest that we should add to standard representations of lexical meaning also context-sensitive semantic rules.

There is evidence of a different kind that drives us to the same conclusion. James Pustejovsky's recent interesting work[15] leads us to this conclusion by the analysis of the following kinds of examples:

> in "x baked a potato" 'bake' has a meaning that includes changing, or transforming in certain way a natural object–that is a potato.
>
> in "x baked a cake" 'bake' has a meaning that includes creating something, a new entity.

The difference has to do with the fact that in one case the object of 'bake' is a natural object, and is so marked in its lexical representation, while in the other case the object is a artificial entity which is marked that way in the lexicon, and comes about as a result of the baking.

The same phenomenon can be seen in "John began to read a novel" and "John began to write a novel". The phenomenon can be seen also in the case of other syntactic categories. For example, the differences between "we drove around the lake", "there is a path around the lake", and "there are grazing fields around the lake".

In each of these cases, the relevant semantic information can be given with context-sensitive rules. But, as Pustejovsky sees clearly, we cannot survey all of the possible word combinations, and especially not future contingencies that might introduce linguistic context affecting lexical meanings of descriptive items. Hence Pustejovsky's correct conclusion that within his theory the lexicon is productive rather than static. His proposal raises further interesting questions. What is the exact relation between the type of productivity posited by the lexical theory of this essay and his theory? What are the implications of productivity for the general knowledge-representation schemes the vocabulary of which Pustejovsky incorporates into his own, and which have currency in today's work in artificial intelligence?

---

15. Ibid.

These questions require a further book for their treatment. I have named this theory of lexical semantics the Aitiational Frame Theory (AFT), since it represents lexical meaning as explanatory factor (Greek AITIA) yielding structure. The theory can account not only for descriptive vocabulary, but also for words like 'in', 'around', 'all', 'and', and so on. We have seen already how 'in' needs to be analyzed as cross-categorial in its m-factor, and having its s-factor give instructions of how to generate determinate denotational contexts within which different configurations account for what counts as "in". The same phenomenon has been illustrated in connection with the word 'around'. We can now also apply the theory to the phenomena investigated in the early chapters. Thus, 'all' has the general s-factor as generality of the appropriate kind. We then saw different contexts for specification, such as the nonlawlike, the lawlike, and the generic. There are, of course, also other contexts for specifying generality.

Different conceptions of language and linguistic competence might draw the line between the languages of everyday use and science in different ways. Furthermore, one might ask why we need the third level in AFT and why we do not assimilate it to pragmatics. In the next chapter we shall consider different views on language that give different answers to these questions. Reflection on these will prepare us for the final main topic of this essay, which is the conception of humans as primarily explanation-forming and -seeking creatures rather than primarily information processing beings, and we shall see also what limitations on human self-understanding we must accept.

In summary, what do we gain with this new lexical theory? First, the richer internal structure of lexical meaning allows us to formulate more specific hypotheses about language learning, partial mastery, and certain types of language change. For example, we can investigate to what extent the f-factor plays a dominant role in early meaning learning, and when the s-factor emerges. We can formulate the hypothesis that in some cases commonsense understanding is based on the grasp of the f-factor and the m-factor but is hazy on the s-factor. We can see some language changes in physics as keeping the m-, a-, and f-factors constant but changing the s-factor (the principle of individuation). Or, conversely in changing the m-factor (from thing to event), the s-factor needs to change also.

Combining the Aristotelian structure with the three-level analysis we see how polysemy can be generated. We analyze the meaning of, say, 'emergency,' on the first level, and then see how some elements, say, "how immediate is the threat?" or "What counts as appropriate response?" form the basis of the second level; generating denotation fixing contexts. Thus we come to see that denotation will be different for naval emergency, earthquake emergency, or office emergency. This is no mere ambiguity, the meaning analysis on the first level ties the senses together and provides the guidelines for further denotation ranges.

The theory is presented in nonformal terms. One can probably formalize it, with suitable changes in different ways, depending on employment. Pustejovsky might do it one way suitable for computational linguistics, someone working on developmental cognitive psycholinguistics another way. For diachronic linguistics, in still a different matter?

Finally, this more articulate version of lexical meaning raises the exciting question of how lexical and compositional semantics might interact. Do we just collect features as we specify meanings for compounds (NP, VP, etc.) or in some cases do features drop out, become "overruled"? The current work done on this question is for another volume.

APPENDIX: TOWARD A THEORY OF FIGURATIVE LANGUAGE

The semantic analyses presented so far deal only with literal uses. In these pages the outlines of a theory of figurative language will be presented. One of the advantages of AFT (and of the similar theory in Pustejovsky's work) advantage is that it has the resources for analyzing nonliteral uses and shifts.

In recent work it has been shown that idioms are not always syntactic and semantic islands.[16] Hence we shall sketch treatments not only for metaphor and simile, but also for certain types of idioms. Since our main aim is to show how AFT structure helps in the details of analysis, we shall simply list the presuppositions of the theory, realizing that in a full treatment these will need defense. The relevant presuppositions are the following.

a. Idioms, metaphor, simile are three distinct modes of figurative speech, not reducible to each other.
b. Figurative language cannot be paraphrased without loss of meaning into literal use.
c. An adequate theory of figurative language has to show where creativity is involved and how this creativity differs from that needed for everyday use.

16. G. Nunberg, I. Sag, and T. Wasow, "Idioms," *Language* 70 (1994), 491–538.

Let us first sketch the treatment of idiom by considering the following example.

'he spilled the beans'

The AFT analysis of 'spill' includes as m-factors time and physical realization, while the s-factor–together with principles of individuation and persistence–has a content that can be paraphrased as: "careless letting out of appropriate container, appropriate small units of appropriate collections".

In the idiom consideration we switch the m-factor from: temporal-physical to temporal/psychological. This creative shift forces us then to restructure the s-factor as well. The appropriate letting out, container, units, and so forth will not be physical entities, but mental/psychological. Hence the spilling becomes the careless letting out of some mental content.

Now we turn to 'beans', which has a straightforward AFT analysis. The shifts already sketched forces us to reconstruct the relevant small units of things contained; the result: bits of information.

Putting the parts together yields: the careless letting out of information. This is, however still on level 1; we need to understand what it takes to be a case of "spilling the beans" in different contexts. The paraphrase just given is still underspecified. The imaginative/creative part comes in specifying what kind of carelessness of disclosing what kind of information will count in this or that context as "spilling the beans". The literal, physical case, language prescribes the constraints within which we determine denotation in any given context. In the case of the idiom, in the figurative case, we have much more freedom in determining whether an action fits the idiomatic description.

Finally, one might wonder why we should not take within the AFT account the whole phrase as a metaphor. The answer is that within the analysis, the choice of beans as the analogue of information is arbitrary and conventional. It could have been lentils, peas, or something else. Thus our analysis preserves both the arbitrary and purely conventional as well as the figurative aspects of meaning for idioms like the one discussed.

Let us now turn to metaphor. The typical examples are not of the simplistic: "A is B" kind discussed so often in the philosophic literature, but multiple, embedded ones. For example, out of "The Sounds of Silence" we take:

> "...flash of a neon light (split the night) and touched the sound of silence."

Let us start with 'touch'. Bodies can touch, so can surfaces, touching can be an action, and so on. The AFT structure gives as m-factors, time and physical realization, and as a part of the s-structure: "have/cause to have appropriate common boundaries between two entities A and B." Level 2, then, fills in the different appropriateness conditions, as we just saw. When we take the verb in a figurative sense, we go back to the underspecified layer of meaning in the s-factor; "A + B having common boundaries"; this allows us to change also the m-factor.

We need, however, to give the metaphorical interpretation of 'sound' and 'silence' in order to give 'touch' the right syntactic object. We consider 'silence' and take as salient for figurative purposes the functional specification within the AFT structure. At an underspecified level, the f-factor for 'silence' is: "the auditory experiencing of interval between sounds or noises". We do the same with 'sound'. In terms of human functional–in contrast with a physical, scientific–significance the sound of something is the auditory data experienced in contrast with what happened earlier and what will happen in the future.

Putting the two together we get as the level 1 analysis for "sound of silence" the "auditory experience of the interval between two noises or sounds". We then have to move on to the other levels and specify what counts as the sound of silence, for example, in the context of the song in question. Here the creative imagination takes over. For unlike the cases discussed earlier ('snow', 'refrigerator') practical and need-oriented considerations do not guide us in the figurative case to fixed denotation. At the same time the underspecified f-structures and consequently also the s- structures give us parameters so that "not anything goes."

How shall we now put together the visual–neon light–and the auditory–sound of silence–as appropriate candidates for the nonliteral "touching"? Since making the f-factor salient, our reinterpretation of what the words denote places this a is the level of phenomenological experience. Hence a new aspect of having common boundaries emerges; the before and after in our experience. With these shifts, we arrive at the interpretation of how the experiencing of the neon light and the auditory complex described can yield a case described in underspecified form as touching, and filled in on the specific level with what our creative imagination prescribes as light touching sound in this context. This filling in admits of variations depending on individuals, unlike the denotation fixing in the literal case on level 3.

In metaphors like this one, we first fall back on underspecified interpretations, and then add the component that makes the meaning of the relevant phrases figurative, namely the specifications of what counts in this context as sound, silence, and touching. The general properties under which we consider the elements of experience which the metaphor is meant to evoke leave principles of individuation and persistence indeterminate. Sound when considered within scientific or everyday use has its physical and phenomenal aspects, and its individuation and persistence specified in physical and perceptual terms. But in the metaphorical use we sketched the essential characteristic as the functional one we described. The manifestations can have a variety of physical and psychological properties, in some cases no physical property at all. Hence the manifestations, "what counts in this context as a sound," can admit of a variety of individuations. (Possibly, Pustejovsky's motion of "dot object" will become useful in this analysis.)

This point about the lack of fixity of individuation and persistence (How long is Juliet a sun?) separates metaphor from simile. In a simile like: "education is like being led out of a cave" both the denotation of 'education' and that of 'cave' remain fixed, as determined by everyday usage. The simile then says that these two items, coming from different m-factor ranges, have some salient characteristics in common. As we know, any two objects have an infinite number of similarities in common. For to be similar to something is to have a common property. Modern symbolic logic knows how to generate an infinite number of these between any two entities. Hence notions like salience and categoriality emerge when we attempt to characterize a sense of similarity that captures the intuitions of the competent speaker-hearer, and not only that of the logician. Aristotle thought that one could define quality as that in respect of which two things can be alike; for example, x and y are similar with respect of color, Joe and Susan are alike with respect to both being students. Some narrowing of similarity, both for the analysis of everyday use and for simile, is needed.

We shall bypass the enormous task of characterizing what counts as similarity for everyday and scientific contexts, and concentrate briefly on how similarity plays a special role in figurative language like simile.

In the simile under consideration two processes are compared. The simile is not just picking out "forgotten" common elements, nor is it creating new common elements.

It does either one of the following. It can point to likeness that needs to be spelled out in figurative terms. For example, "both lead to illumination"; in one case the illumination is physical, in the other intellectual. Thus we fall back on an underspecified meaning layer and then show how one can specify denotation conditions within the different contexts needed. In the case of the intellectual creativity is needed both for forming and for understanding the intended similarity conditions. There are different ways of thinking of education. Is it merely technological, or also humanistic? A successful simile has to make explicit which of the many potential similarity conditions we wish to make explicit.

The second structure for a simile is to consider an underspecified common characteristic between entities, and spell out new applications–on what we call level 3–that need not obey m-factor restrictions. This kind of simile is particularly important for diachronic phenomena in the language of the sciences. Hence the initially simile-type uses of 'force', 'mass', 'light'–terms that eventually become calcified, literal expressions, and eventually technical terms. It is a really bad mistake to think of figurative semantic structures as emerging only in connection with literature. Once we concentrate on the diachronic, rather than merely on the synchronic dimensions of scientific language, the importance of figurative uses becomes transparent.

This is a mere sketch of where a developed theory of figurative meaning within AFT is going. But it demonstrates the following significant points. First, figurative language is not all subjective, psychological, and so forth. Our theory leaves some room for creativity, but stresses fundamentally the generative potential of a natural language. Different denotation specifications, similarities no one thought of, and so forth are all potentially in the language, and could not be parts of our thinking without the rules of language, both syntactic and semantic. Figurative meaning is an aspect of the richness of linguistic meaning whose potential can never the exhausted.

Finally, AFT and Pustejovsky's qualia structures enable us to systematize the anatomy of metaphor and simile. Meanings are not just a bunch of properties logically related. Figurative language structures can be elucidated by showing what happens to the m-factor, how the f-factor can become dominant, how an a-factor can be taken out of the semantic layers, and so on. Not any meaning change can be turned into a metaphor.

CHAPTER 4

KEY ISSUES IN THEORIES OF LANGUAGE

The lexical theory presented in the previous chapter is centered around understanding and explanation. Thus it deals mostly with what philosophers and linguists call meaning. It deals with reference, and by implication what some philosophers call denotation, only at the last of the three levels of semantic analysis posited.

In this chapter we shall survey some of Chomsky's proposals made in his recent work. We shall see that Chomsky's new delineation of syntax, semantics, and pragmatics does not assign a central role to reference in the theory of meaning. In this respect it differs sharply from the philosophic theories that we surveyed earlier. The same holds also for the theory of meaning sketched in this book.

We will look at Chomsky's treatment of referring in natural languages within the perspective of his recent general theory of linguistic competence. Since his view also includes suggestions about how scientific reasoning and use of language differ from commonsense and ordinary language, we will also look at various relations between science and ordinary reasoning and language use.

In the last section of this chapter we will look at what referring is in everyday discourse, why one can describe matters of referring as performance systems, and how such an account is not incompatible with the lexical analysis of this book.

As an introduction let us contrast the standard philosophical view about meaning and denotation–as exemplified in Carnap's writings–with Chomsky's view. The former view is familiar already from the discussions in the introduction of the development of twentieth-century philosophy of language. This view has its origins in Frege's work and is then developed as well as modified in the semantics of Carnap.[1] Within this conception we distinguish semantics from syntax, with the latter yielding formation rules. The former includes theories of meaning as a set of necessary and jointly sufficient qualitative criteria for application, as well as specifications of denotation and reference, with these components derivable from a characterization of rules of meaning for descriptive elements of a language. In addition to syntax, semantics, and phonology, this conception also has the rubric of pragmatics. This includes aspects of meaning not related to truth and denotation, and conditions of reference related to individual-variant aspects of language use (e.g., intentions).

The second view has been presented in recent writings of Chomsky.[2] Within this conception Syntax has two parts; the compositional and the conceptual. The latter includes some of what would be called by Carnap the theory of meaning. The other part of language includes the rules of phonology. All of what the traditional philosophical theory describes as rules of reference and denotation is placed into the rubric of pragmatics, or as Chomsky calls it: performance systems. We can see now why what the philosophers regarded as semantics–that is, rules of meaning–can be seen by Chomsky as syntax, since he does not think that meaning relates language to the world, while this is a part of the definition of semantics in the Carnapian framework.

Underlying this whole conception is Chomsky's claim that the notion of a public language like English or German is just a piece of fiction, and not a very useful one at that. He thinks that for the purposes of linguistics it is sufficient to think of these public "languages" as the overlap between many idiolects, and these in turn are anchored in I-languages, the linguistic structures, syntactic and phonologic, that develop in individual humans on the basis of their genetic endowment, under normal circumstances. Chomsky admits, of course, that this development, while based on general linguistic principles, includes the kind of interaction with the environment that helps a human to add language-relative rules, both syntactic and phonological.

Chomsky thinks that there may be a fruitful applications of the notions of denotation and truth for the languages of the sciences. In this connection he considers also the existence of a separate human cognitive faculty, that of science development.[3]

Let us consider now the notion of I-language, and its possible uses in differ-

1. R. Carnap, *Meaning and Necessity* (Chicago: University of Chicago Press, 1956).
2. N. Chomsky, "Language and Nature," *Mind* 104 (1995): 1–59. From here on *LM*.
3. N. Chomsky, "Explaining Language Use," *Philosophical Topics* 20 (1992): 205–231. From here on *EL*.

ent debates about language and cognition. Some might think that accepting the positing of I-languages settles the philosophic debate about internalism–that is, whether a full description of the human mind and cognition necessitates talking about the human and the environment and the ensuing interactions, or whether the description can be complete if we restrict ourselves to talking only about what is internal to the mind and its physical manifestations. But one could accept the validity of the notion of I-languages and still be an externalist–for example, insisting that cognition must cover much more than logic and linguistic competence and has to account for certain interactions between mind and environment without which thinking could not take place.

Again, one might think that if the notion of an I-language is viable, then we have shown that reference and denotation do not fall under the concept of what a linguistically competent agent must master. But this does not follow. One could say that both the compositional part of what Chomsky now calls syntax and mastery of the denotational roles of parts of language are needed as ingredients in a full specification of human linguistic competence.

Finally, accepting the notion of an I-language neither commits us to nor leads us to reject the positing of a separate faculty of science making. The two issues are conceptually distinct.

These remarks should help to see why the theory of language that we will see in the last part of this chapter can remain neutral with regard to the matter of the existence of I-languages. Whether it is a useful notion or not will be seen in cases in which it affects linguistics or psycholinguistics, and in cases in which philosophers use it as one, but not the only, premiss in their battles over externalism, and adequate analyses of the semantics of indexical expressions.

I. SCIENCE, COMMON SENSE, AND MEANING

Chomsky writes:

> It would be misleading to say that we abandon the theories that the asteroid is aiming towards the earth, that the sun is setting and the heavens darkening, that the wave hit the beach and then receded, that the wind died and the waves disappeared, that people speak Chinese but not Romance, and so on, replacing them by better ones. Rather, the search for theoretical understanding pursues its own paths, leading to a completely different picture of the world, which neither vindicates, nor elimi-

> nates our ordinary ways of talking and thinking. These we can come to appreciate, modify and enrich in many ways, though science is rarely a guide in areas of human significance. Naturalistic inquiry is a particular human enterprise that seeks a special kind of understanding, attainable for humans in some few domains when problems can be simplified enough. Meanwhile we live our lives, facing as best we can problems of radically different kinds, far too rich in character for us to hope to be able to discern explanatory principles of any depth, if these even exist.[4]

Elsewhere Chomsky emphasizes the alleged difference between science and everyday thinking by construing the former as theoretic in the sense of its concepts and modes of reasoning being devoid of human interest and intention, while everyday thought is seen as tainted heavily by these factors.[5] Science, then, aims at truth, the uncovering of the real ontology of what there is, and hence needs forms of language in which predicates are correlated to and denote classes corresponding to real natural kinds, and their members. Everyday thinking ends up as encoded in what Chomsky calls performance systems that enable us to carry out plans, actions, and to relate to other human beings.

It is unclear why we should construe the sciences as presenting us with a real ontology of the world, or at least an approximation of this, and why the posits of common sense should be seen as not presenting us with an ontology. The answer is, presumably, because the former tries to get at aspects of reality beyond the mostly functionally defined notions of common sense, while the latter obviously does not do that. This contrast can be challenged on the following grounds. First, the ontological posits of the sciences are not independent of human nature and cognition. As we know, our observational evidence depends on our perceptual mechanism, and the terms we use. For example, in chemistry the labels for kinds are "theory-laden"; they do not make much sense outside of the theories in which these are embedded. Still, Chomsky might say that the basic human perceptual and cognitive structure is invariant across the species, while this is not so with human interest and motivation. In reply we can point to two considerations. First, some functional considerations resulting, say, in some artifact construction, even if in specifics these differ across cultures, seem universal. This is reflected in the lexicons of various languages.

Second, are the sciences really unaffected by human interest? Or do we have a variety of mixtures between the theoretic and the practical across different

4. Chomsky, *LM*, p. 10.
5. Chomsky, *EL*, pp. 211–12.

sciences? Furthermore, is common sense, or everyday thinking, always devoid of theoretic interest? Or shall we construe it as containing both detached attempts at understanding as well as practical interest, and then see different parts containing different mixtures of these ingredients? The following come to mind as examples of both an overlap between scientific and commonsense interest, and as having in them, elements of the theoretic and detached as well as the practical: mathematics, geometry, astronomy, and various parts of botany. For example, flowers are objects of both scientific and practical human interest. The same is to be said of the heavenly bodies. Furthermore, in many cases, even when the theories are different, they do not stand in conflict, but rather complement each other. For example, many of us enjoy classical music, and in accounts of this art form we distinguish different kinds, and concepts, such as opera, operetta and use notions harmony, scales etc. Correspondingly, one can spell out the physics and acoustics that underlie these notions and thus our enjoyment of such art.[6] Or again, we drive cars, and learn skills involved, while engineering and its application by mechanics gives the scientific theory that underlies or complements our daily activity and thinking. We enjoy planting gardens and caring for them, while botany gives an account of the hidden natures of what we deal with.

Chomsky emphasizes the differences between the scientific and everyday accounts, and the different viewpoints. But these examples show that in many cases there is a correspondence of concepts, and above all of subject matter. Are there *really* flowers? Numbers? Heavenly bodies? These questions do not make much sense to me, especially when the criterion for "really" is something like "completely independent of human existence and nature". It does seem absurd to suppose that the universe would not follow the same regularities that our physics and mathematics describe if humans were not around. The "realist" is right; we, humans, are not that important. But making this concession to the realist does not lead to claiming that the universe runs according to some specific scheme to be found in one or many of our sciences.

When we come to consider in detail Chomsky's examples of everyday use and what he says about these, we shall see how heavily the functional element in meaning affects terms introducing artifacts and our interactions with them. But the differences in points of view between science and common sense can be illustrated also with examples that do not invoke the practical. 'Sunset' introduces a concept under which we gather many occurrences of the part of the globe becoming dark at the end of the day. Chomsky could say that this will

6. M. Moravcsik, *Musical Sound*, (New York: Paragon House, 1987).

never be a term in one of the sciences. Now are there sunsets "in the world"? Can I not refer to sunsets? To be sure, the concept of sunset is formulated to include beliefs, feelings, and so on, about and toward a phenomenon *as* it relates to us. The phenomenon would exist even if we were not around, but it would not be described in this way. We respond to the phenomenon when viewed as a sunset, in a certain way. Can the phenomenon and our response be related to science? The answer is: not as an explanans, but certainly as an explanandum. What is to be analyzed, of course, is the phenomenon as it relates to human sensitivity. I agree with Chomsky that we may never have a scientific theory about that. But there is nothing about the phenomenon and our reactions that would push these *in principle* beyond the pale of science.

So far I have suggested that science and common sense do indeed differ, but I left open the possibility that the difference is more a matter of degree of presence of various factors, rather than a sharp dichotomy.

Chomsky's conception, quoted at the start of this section, conflicts with conceptions such as that of Stich, who describes common sense in terms of a number of "folk-" disciplines; "folk-psychology" and "folk-physics" among them and thinks of these as clashing with science frequently.[7] We can reconcile these conflicting views here by invoking the distinction between strong and weak common sense.[8] Roughly, weak common sense is a collection of empirical beliefs shared widely within a culture at a certain–time; for example, that there are witches, that the earth is flat, and so forth. We can cast these away without changing our fundamental and presumably universal conceptions of self, agency, space, time, causality, and abstract structures. It is clear from examples that this is not what Chomsky has in mind. His examples are better captured by the notion of strong common sense–a view of the world that has teleological or functional dimensions, the need for human interactions with the environment and each other, space, time, causality, and the need to exercise consciousness, the formation of beliefs or thoughts, and confronting daily life and needs in terms of agency. To what extent the vocabulary needed to encode these notions is invariant across cultures can be left open as an empirical question. The common elements are some ways of becoming aware of and talking about humans as agents–as deliberating, deciding, and acting beings. It does not make sense to claim that science can someday make us reject these basic concepts, though it can modify and refine these. (e.g., game theory, etc.).

---

7. S. Stich, *From Folk Psychology to Cognitive Science* (Cambridge, MA: MIT Press, 1983).

8. J. Moravcsik, "Conceptions of the Self and the Study of Cognition," in *Logic, Philosophy of Science, and Epistemology* (Vienna: Hoelder, Pichler, Tempsky, 1987), pp. 294–302.

This leads us also to the topic of intentionality. Since Brentano, many philosophers have claimed that the intentional vocabulary and our ascribing intentions to ourselves and others cannot be reduced to nonintentional discourse, and scientific treatment. In plain terms, this talk of intentionality boils down to seeing ourselves and humans as goal-oriented creatures; as William James would put it this is an unavoidable forced option for humans. But is it clear that viewing humans as intentional or goal-oriented creatures must remain a unique way of talking about humans only, and that science could never come to the conclusion that other elements of reality too should be thus interpreted? I have in mind not only the much debated issue of the extent to which it may be feasible to interpret certain kinds of animals this way, once we find out more about them, but more speculatively, whether there is any a priori reason why "science," whatever that is, should not some day construe some remote galaxies in this manner.

When Chomsky talks about the language of science and contrasts it with everyday language, the contrast is not analogous to, for example, distinguishing English from German or Chinese. At issue here are different types of languages that have radically different points of view and conceptions underlying them. The meanings of everyday use do not really function to help us confront reality "as it is." Rather, "a lexical item provides us with a certain range of perspectives for viewing what we take to be things in the world, or what we conceive in other ways; these items are like filters or lenses providing ways of looking at things and thinking about the products of our minds."[9] Does this correct remark apply only to the meanings of words in everyday discourse? Our human nature, the cognitive and perceptual structures act like filters. Do the filters or lenses function differently in science and common sense? Astronomy in some pure form presents a theory about the heavenly bodies and their movements that is not tied to our needs and interests. Then there is also the astronomy that is oriented toward what was earlier a burning need, namely guides for navigation. But it would be a mistake to think of these two kinds of astronomy as corresponding to the division between science and common sense. Science can be also influenced by the practical, and common sense has some of its roots in gazing and contemplation.

We have examined so far the language of science. But should we not rather talk about the languages of the sciences? This is not to say that we should assign to each science a separate language, but that we should discern different ingredients mixed in different ways in various types of scientific language.

9. Chomsky, *EL*, p. 221.

Mathematics is a field shared by science and common sense, and though the domain of the former is much wider than the domain of the latter, the overlap is important. For though we use calculation also for satisfying human needs, as in commerce, we also master from childhood simple elementary arithmetic, and learn its principles abstracted from issues of need and interest. The commutative law remains what it is regardless of how human interests change or endure. The same can be said for geometry. This science can be utilized in architecture or furniture production, but the child, the adult in everyday life, and the scientist can all partake of the pure contemplation of at least the simplest principles.

Physics brings us to the natural sciences–if indeed the apriori–natural distinction can be sharply drawn. Here the overlap between the scientific and the everyday conceptions holds mostly diachronically; some of the science of yesterday seeps into the common sense of today.[10] Does this mean that as such a shift takes place, the viewpoint associated with the concept in the sciences drastically changes as it is assimilated by common sense? Or are such phenomena further promptings to see here a continuum instead of a sharp division? Someone might think that the units of experience are different as carved out by the differing points of view of science and common sense. But this seems to be true only partly. To be sure, we think in terms of seeing cars or houses, while the scientist observes faraway galaxies, or atoms. But there is an overlap in the case of geometry. The scientist may be talking about points without extension and lines without width. But both scientist and layperson see points with extension and lines with width. The case of perception presents interesting problems for those wanting a sharp dichotomy. Ian Hacking's interesting discussion of the microscope forces us to ask: Is perception via microscope what the empiricists called information gained through the senses?[11] Furthermore, in the context of our discussion we should ask: is seeing an object through a microscope an experience within the everyday and commonsense way of looking at the world or the scientific one? Maybe yesterday only the scientist had this avenue to some observable, but today in many parts of the world every schoolchild beyond a certain age has had that experience. Does one's viewpoint of the world change when one stops seeing things unaided and turns to a microscope? What evidence is there for such dramatic sudden cognitive shift?

Similar things can be said about chemistry. Gold and water are objects of

---

10. I am indebted here to lectures by Ian Hacking. He should not be held responsible for my application of this idea here.

11. I. Hacking, "Do We See Through a Microscope?" *Philosophical Quarterly* 62 (1981): 305–22.

chemical analysis and are in everyday use heavily tied to utility and interest. But this is not true of all chemical elements and compounds. Furthermore, it is very difficult to draw a line separating those compounds that are also parts of the commonsense conception of things and those that are not.

As we move on to biology, we find both strong functional layers of meaning linked to many of the biological terms, and occasionally also metaphor, as in "DNA conveys information…". To be sure, we are told by some, though not all, philosophers of science that this is only a temporary state of affairs. But behind such promises nothing more seems to be lurking except a surreptitious dream of returning to the earlier reductionisms and unity-of-science movement of the positivists. Recent developments do not provide any evidence that such a return is likely to come off.

We considered so far theoretical disciplines and empirical sciences with causal explanations in focus. But what about theory of measurement? This is an empirical but noncausal branch of inquiry. Furthermore, there is a clear overlap between the use of language of the expert and that of the layperson. Our ordinary measurements may be less precise than those of the scientists (except perhaps at the Olympics), but this does not suggest a drastic difference in points of view.

The practical and theoretical is, then, mixed thoroughly in the applied sciences like engineering. Are we to interpret its language as providing us with points of view as do the more common words of everyday use, or are we to take this as also indicating the workings of the faculty of science forming?

We could go on, considering medicine, horticulture, and other disciplines. It seems that there are cognitive elements that one could describe as indicating the theoretical; pure curiosity, contemplation, nonfunctional explanation, and so forth, and though these are more prominent in the cognitive stances of what Chomsky describes as science, we find them mixed with other interest-related elements in several of the disciplines listed above, and we see that historically shifts occur that are difficult to describe as shifting suddenly from one to another mode of thought.

Chomsky's division of the sciences and everyday thought and language reminds one of Aristotle's distinction between the theoretical and the practical. By drawing this distinction, Aristotle started a philosophic debate that still rages, without any consensus that a clear and sharp dichotomy is viable.

To return to Chomsky's useful metaphor of meanings as filters, I see the filters consisting of amalgams made up of many elements, some at times more theoretical, some at times more practical. I fail to see, however, how one could draw and then apply to the disciplines mentioned a sharp line between the scientific-theoretical and the everyday interest-related filters, or even with regard to all of their elements.

We see, then that there are a variety of ways in which one might construe the relationship between science and common sense. These construals bear on how one interprets the relationship between the languages of science and natural languages like English. Both Chomsky's recent work and the lexical semantics of the previous chapter open up interesting ways to compare not only science and common sense, but also the respective languages. There is agreement between Chomsky's recent proposals and the lexical theory on the following two key points. First, any adequate analysis of the languages of science and natural languages has to be compatible with the possibility of a modular account of human understanding, including the possibility of a special science forming capacity. Second, it is wrong to view the language of science as an idealized version of everyday use, or to view the latter as a "polluted" version of the former.

In the next section we will look at some of Chomsky's examples of the variety of ways in which terms in natural language are interpreted, and we will see how my lexical theory would account for these.

II. CHOMSKY'S EXAMPLES

Chomsky gives in various places illustrations of how he interprets everyday use. The point of these illustrations is to show that understanding the meaning of everyday words is a matter of viewing things from diverse and seemingly incompatible points of view, coming to see how the meanings of these words are affected, and to some extent formed, by human interests and needs. The conclusion is that if we mean by the technical notion of reference a unique relation of designation between a descriptive word and elements of reality by themselves, then such a notion is not needed or is not to be found in the semantics of everyday words. Rather, we find the ordinary notion of reference in the sense of intersubjective identification, as embedded in a variety of performance systems. Hence these matters should not be described as parts of linguistic competence.

In our review of the examples it will be shown how AFT would analyze the words and their respective meanings.

One of Chomsky's examples is the word 'book' and what might be regarded as its meaning.[12] On the one hand, on the basis of examples like "this book weighs five pounds" Chomsky thinks that we construe books as concrete objects, while in questions like "who wrote the book?" we construe it as an abstract element. He thinks that this multiplicity of points of view is brought together in sentences the interpretation of which is a task for performance systems especially geared for such tasks, namely sentences like "the book he wrote weighed five pounds".

Within AFT, it makes no sense to regard the book as either abstract or concrete. Books are primarily functional entities. They serve normally for the recording, preserving, and disseminating thoughts and complexes of thought. In this respect, books are analogous to what I earlier called cross categorial terms, such as 'university'. In that case too, we distinguished a variety of ingredients, including buildings, lands, legal charter, faculty, and ideas. It makes little sense to say that we construe the university differently from different points of view. Rather, in some of our statements we concentrate on spatial parts, in others on the abstract contents produced by members, and in still others on the biological entities that are also parts.[13]

Since books are used normally as described above, they will have abstract as well as spatiotemporal parts. These parts, in turn, will be defined partly in functional terms. To be sure, there may be books with only empty pages, but these cases can always be given special interpretation; the text never got put on the pages, the book was given to someone to write in it, but that person died prematurely, and so on.

Books are a vehicle for expressing thoughts. Both symbolic representations and material realizations are parts of it. Hence the cross categoriality. The m-factor in the meaning structure is both the spatiotemporal and the abstract domains. The s- and f-factors fall out of the characterization given above. That characterization entails the need to apply the type-token distinction to the items in the denotation. According to AFT, we need to move to levels 2 and 3 because of the qualifications that there must be appropriate size, kind of message, quantity of message, or thought expressed among other things. In different but predictable contexts different items count as books.

Chomsky might say that his example illustrates beautifully the distinction he wants to draw. Science does not study books; it studies various aspects of books. Physics studies some of these, chemistry still others, and geometry still others. An adequate theory of linguistic competence should also enable us to give a partial interpretation of the representations of thoughts contained. The

12. Chomsky, *EL*, p. 207. Examples like this were also discussed by Geoffrey Nunberg and others.

13. On analysis of 'university' see Moravcsik, *Thought and Language*, p. 249.

layperson, then, in ordinary language use, combines these diverse aspects and elements into a functional unit, from the point of view of human needs and interest. Furthermore, though the technology of book production pays attention to functional aspects, the sciences, insofar as they study the various aspects mentioned, abstract from considerations of human interest and need.

In reply one could point out that the diversity of "aspects" certainly cannot be divided into just two classes "concrete" and "abstract". Geometry studies some abstract aspects of books, physics some spatiotemporal properties, chemistry still others, and the study of content brings with it language interpretation, in some ways abstract but not in the same sense in which geometry is. So far there is no mystery. The principles of individuation and persistence for types and tokens yield the same respective units across these distinctions, with a complex set of parts of different kinds. It is a fact about natural languages that in some uses of some terms we have primarily this or that part as the subject, and the finding of the subject is a matter of considering the meaning of the predicate ("weighs five pounds", "is profound").

Chomsky's key point, thus, for relegating the semantics of 'book' and similar expressions to the performance systems, must be the claim that such units could never become objects of science. First, as we saw, physics and chemistry too are not altogether independent from interests and needs. Second, why couldn't a science someday develop that studies ways in which various media can represent thoughts and ideas? Must the units be spatiotemporal, or at least temporal (like speech)? There is no reason to assume that in principle units of containing thought expressions like books, manuscripts of other sorts, communication by making speeches, and so on cannot become objects of scientific study. Perhaps a part of archaeology will someday develop into this kind of study.

The same considerations apply to the example of 'house'. Chomsky says again that this is in some ways a concrete object and in some ways not. But in fact the case here is even simpler than 'book'. There we have the aspects of concreteness, functionality, and thought representation. In the case of 'house' we have only two: some spatiotemporal and functional specifications. An entity qualifies as a house only if it possesses both aspects. Without the functional the "house" is just a building. A house is something that provides, or at least is designed to provide, or used to provide, shelter. As Aristotle remarked, we don't know whether something is a house or not until we see how people use it. We at times pay more attention to its spatiotemporal dimension and at other times to its function in terms of giving shelter. But it would be a mistake to think that common sense or everyday use does not involve studying both. We can look at a house as what obstructs the view from the next one, and also as where our friends live. A study of what can function as a house can certainly be also a matter for scientific or "naturalistic" study.

These points come out sharply when we turn to the contrast Chomsky mentions between 'house' and 'home'. Both of these words are–in AFT–partly functionally defined, but 'home' has a more dominant f-factor in its meaning structure. A house is a shelter of a certain sort. A home is simply whatever a creature–human or animal–regards as its stable seat of residence or most important seat of residence, with some features defined in context as providing some shelter. Houses can be homes, but so can–as in Sophocles' Philoctetes–a cave, or a tree, or any of a other large number of types of things. Not all houses are homes, and not all homes are houses. There is in some cases coincidence. That does not mean that the two are the same entity. They may coincide for some time, and then their life branches may part. For example, something may remain the same home, even though after so many rebuildings it would be regarded a different building.

Lack of accuracy is not a general characteristic of ordinary uses. Concepts are as sharply or as vaguely delineated as need be. For instance, in monetary transactions, or tailoring clothes, we are and can be very accurate, while in other contexts what counts as this or that can be left partly indeterminate.

Chomsky uses the example of 'house' to examine also the pair 'interior' and 'exterior'.[14] He points out rightly that this contrast is drawn in different contexts in different ways. But this should not lead us to posit relegation to performance systems. The two elements of this contrasting pair have–like the other examples–a functional ingredient in their meaning structures. What counts as exterior depends on human perceptual capacities, activities like building or painting, and normal conditions of daily life in a given culture. How much of the exterior walls of a building count as the exterior of the house? In the case of painting, the visible outside surface. This is not arbitrary. It follows from the fact that painting an object means in most contexts painting its outside surface. What counts as surface? Again, a large variety of contexts yield different answers, but the variety is not arbitrary and unpredictable.[15]

Similar observations apply to 'interior'. How much of the containing elements and what is contained count as the interior? The interior decorator decorates only the outside surface. You could not ask how much of the walls (what thickness) count as parts of the interior in that context. In some contexts we

14. Chomsky, *EL*, p. 220.

15. A. Stroll, *Surfaces* (Minneapolis: University of Minnesota Press, 1988).

think of the interior as an area contained, in other contexts we think of it as including the items within the contained space (chairs, desk, etc.) These linguistic practices are linked to nonlinguistic practices and are not arbitrary. The fact that a use is linked to a nonlinguistic practice is not a reason for thinking of the analysis of the use as falling completely outside of linguistic competence. Much of our vocabulary of mathematics is dependent on the practice of calculation, but this is not a reason for regarding mastery of the meanings of mathematical vocabulary as outside of linguistic competence.

III. REFERRING, TRUTH, AND DENOTATION.

In this section we will explore the notion of reference as employed in ordinary discourse, and see its implications for the analysis of proper names and definite descriptions in natural languages. We shall also look briefly at the notion of truth in its ordinary and technical senses, and then consider the notion of denotation, showing how it has primary intelligibility and application in the context of the structures of formal languages in the sense defined earlier. Since in the earlier chapters it was argued that natural languages are not, and should not be represented as, formal languages, the utility of employing denotation in the analysis of the semantics of natural languages becomes problematic. These reflections show why Chomsky regards the referring functions of natural language parts as matters of various performance systems, and how the AFT lexical analysis is compatible with this, since on the third level reference specification becomes a matter of arguments based partly on nonlinguistic abilities.

Chomsky writes:

> It is reasonable to suppose that naturalistic inquiry aims to construct symbolic systems in which certain expressions are intended to pick out things in the world. But there is no reason to believe that such endeavors inform us about ordinary language and commonsense understanding.[16]

In this quote Chomsky separates the task of specifying the expressive power of a language designed to embody a theory such as mathematics, or physics, from the task of characterizing the linguistic competence possessed by compe-

16. Chomsky, *LM*, p. 46.

tent speakers of natural languages. A natural language is not designed to embody one theory. Rather, it is designed for many different tasks, including the challenge of being able to communicate across different theories. Though they disagree on many other topics, both Chomsky and Wittgenstein in his later phase are maintaining that there is no one fundamental task for natural languages such that all other uses could be analyzed as derivative from this one. A number of uses of everyday discourse are on equal footing as far as fundamentality is concerned. Wittgenstein uses this observation for his own peculiar philosophical therapy. Chomsky uses it as a key principle for the characterization of linguistic competence as applied to natural languages. Furthermore, he thinks that this is important for the explication of what he regards as related performance systems. It is agreed by everyone studying these matters that we occasionally use parts of natural language to refer or to identity what are purported to be elements of reality for each other. We shall now turn to the analysis of some salient properties of such practices.

"The terms themselves do not refer, at least if the term 'refer' is used in its natural language sense; but people can use them to refer to things, viewing them from particular points of view..."[17] In this passage Chomsky takes over the analysis of referring in its natural sense that was made prominent in the philosophical literature by P. F. Strawson.[18]

The characterizations given here are in agreement with the Oxford English Dictionary which defines one sense of 'referring' as directing a person to something by directing attention to it, or pointing it out. This description justifies Strawson's approach to reference via the notion of identification. We can build up the full force of identification by approaching it in layers. The simplest case of identification is the one in which a speaker identifies an entity that is sensibly present to him and to an intended hearer. Still, we should note that even such simple cases assume quite a bit of shared background information and cultural practices. There must be at least a large area of overlap in the conceptual material that speaker and hearer associate with a number of relevant expressions, there must be some agreement on how to convey intentions involved in drawing attention to something, and so forth. In short, even this case requires quite a bit of context-dependent interaction between speaker and hearer. Even in the case of speaker and hearer sitting in front of a fireplace, staring at a cat lying there, and one person referring to this cat, there must be successful "meeting of minds" on the significance of certain words, gestures, tone of voice, and so on.

17. Chomsky, *EL*, p. 221.

18. P. Strawson, "On Referring" *Mind* 59, (1950): 320–44.

The speaker must have correct views on what counts in that context as a cat for the hearer, what kinds of descriptions will be intelligible to the hearer, and so on.

Even though we ordinarily assume that in a case like the one under discussion the reference has existential import, in general this is not so for identification. As long as there is intersubjective agreement on which purported references should be taken by members of the linguistic community as veridical, successful reference can take place. I can identify something to another person who has beliefs similar to mine, even if from some objective point of view the entity we assume to have been identified does not exist. Communication can be successful and coordinated activity can ensue from one drunk identifying to another an alleged pink elephant that is thought to be pursuing both. People, we think, have been wrong about Greek gods, witches, phlogiston, the Yeti, and so forth, but one could hardly say that identification and communication among believers in these entities has not been successful. Identification in communicative contexts requires only that the purported entity should be believed to exist.[19]

The next step in the analysis of identification is reference to an object not sensibly present to either speaker or hearer. These are, in fact, the most common types of identifications. In describing, instructing, warning, and so forth we typically talk about things we believe to exist that are not present to the senses. The entity identified may be abstract or concrete. Successful communication depends heavily on a common understanding of vocabulary, but also on all of the contextual elements mentioned above. It might even require discussion on what should count as an element purportedly identified. For example, in a given context what should count as rain, storm, or only drizzle? Success demands also that the speaker should be aware of which range of characterizations of the purported entity will be familiar to the intended audience.

Further complications apply to other types of identification. It may be that the speaker is not sensibly present to the hearer, or that the intended audience is not clearly definable. In all of these cases what was said about contextual requirements and the failure of existential import not obliterating the communication still holds.

The most general type is identification with an unspecified audience. I report in a newspaper or in a professional journal or an autobiography some

19. J. Moravcsik, "Strawson and Ontological Priority," in R. Butler, ed., *Analytical Philosophy*, Second Series (Oxford: Blackwell, 1965), pp. 106–19.

event or sequence of events, thereby attempting to draw attention to some entity or entities. We interpret communication like this every day. Still, even in these cases various conventions and intersubjective expectations must hold in order for the referring to be successful. Referring takes place in an intersubjective environment of a linguistic and pragmatic community. This is true regardless of whether any explicit specification of the relevant communities is given. I can say "it is hot in here", and not specify to whom I am talking. Still, if I am to achieve anything with the announcement, I must have some more or less specific hypotheses about what the people in my environment would understand, what counts as "hot" in that pragmatic context, what if any negotiations about reference fixing in that context would be fruitful, and so on. What is unbearably hot in a room is a subjective matter, and yet not anything goes. Reference fixing results in an agreement that often represents compromise between those enjoying the occasionally healing powers of heat, and the "polar bear club," people who want the temperature as low as normal public context will allow it.

Temperature may be an extreme case in that the need for intersubjective agreement is clear, and the necessity of invoking nonlinguistic dispositions is also beyond question. But differences between this type and others are just matters of degrees. Even what may seem to be solely a matter of linguistic data and independent of pragmatic considerations like: "I want to talk to the smartest lawyer in town" turn out not to be that. Does the speaker realize that some lawyers now specialize in "theft of ideas" types of lawsuits, and that in fact the smartest can be found in that group? It is most unlikely that the person who needs a lawyer in everyday cases is looking for *that* type. Different kinds of shrewdness are required in different of legal contexts, and the number of legal specialties in a modern society is in constant flux. Fixing what we really want is not primarily a matter of linguistic competence.

There may be some types of cases in which purely linguistic matters achieve unique specification. For example, some mathematical referring activities may be of this sort. But it is a mistake to take these cases as paradigmatic of everyday reference, and then construe the less abstract cases like referring to the hot room, or the angry people in that room (what counts as anger in that context?) as somehow derivative cases.

As we indicated before, referring is not an arbitrary matter. There are systems of referring practices, such as baseball umpires calling pitches, signal systems in the military, and even less rigidly structured ones, like systems of evaluations in different walks of life, and weather forecasts. In general, we must keep in mind at least three types of conditions for successful reference:

a. The linguistic constraints, both syntactic and semantic. As we saw, words can be polysemous, but not arbitrarily, and referring expressions have their syntactic categories.
b. The pragmatic factors, such as what is intelligible to whom, what counts as what in various contexts, and what are acceptable modes of reference fixing, from degree of heat in a room to the scope of what is an emergency when the departmental chairperson goes on vacation.
c. The responsibilities that need be shared among those involved in the communication. The speaker should have an overview of what identificational resources the situation requires and how much of that is in fact available.

The last point can be used to stress the fact that referring can end in failure, not because of lack of existential import, but because the linguistic and pragmatic resources needed were not present, or were not used correctly by the persons involved. In this respect referring is different from such cognitive activities as calculation. As long as one knows the language of mathematics, and one knows some mathematics, one can calculate, even if nobody else understands the calculation. But it makes no sense to say that Jones was referring to the stuffiness in the room, even though he ignored the pragmatic factors required in that context to make the reference successful. The following are the syntactic categories within which the term typically used for referring fall: definite descriptions, proper names, pronouns, and demonstratives. The last of these has received a lot of attention in recent philosophy, and therefore it should be stressed that for ordinary purposes of referring, the use of demonstratives is subject to the same conditions as the other items we mentioned. In the case of these expressions, it is also true that using them in referring will not carry existential import, only intersubjective agreement about purported import. In terms of a vocabulary made familiar to philosophers by Quine, referring does not depend on ontological import, but only on shared ontological commitment, and shared conception of the practical implications of what is taken as success. For example, one can say "that is a scandal", and if the kind of conditions mentioned already obtain, the reference will be successful. In this kind of an example, it seems strange to ask if the entity referred to "really" exists. There are regular and predictable procedures we go through in order to convince ourselves that indeed a scandal is about to break. Furthermore, mere agreement is not sufficient for saying that there is a scandal. There could be situations in which an outsider can criticize a community, and insist that though they all agreed that there was a scandal in government circles, in fact, what went on should not be regarded as such. But if the people involved in the agreement went through all that can be expected of them in such contexts, and agreed that there was a scandal, then we ought to take that as the final word.

There are also other cases in which it seems strange to ask about existential import. In the Homeric texts, as well as contemporary weather forecasts, there are many references to the sky, or in the Homeric case especially to "rosy-fingered dawn". What shall we say about existence? Are sky and dawn entities that exist? It certainly seems strange to *deny* their existence. To make sense out of assertions like "there is no sky" or "there is no dawn", we require very unusual contexts. (For example, when someone wants to say that what "really exists" must be a part of what a science is about–a dubious claim at best). Homer refers to the sky and the wrath of Achilles to his audience and to posterity, and we do know what he is talking about, and enjoy the epic. One can take the epic as fiction, but others might not. In either case, it would be pointless to ask whether the sky or the wrath of Achilles really existed. It is sufficient to agree that these items are among the sorts of things we can ordinarily talk about.

Philosophers focus often on the singular expressions 'this' and 'that'. But from the point of view of sound linguistics, these are just members of a larger family that will include also 'these' and 'those', as well as compounds like 'these three', or 'those four'. Furthermore, such expressions can combine with nouns or noun phrases to form: 'these five soldiers', or 'that dozen vicious thugs'. Reference can be singular or plural, and within the plural, we can have reference tied to any of the positive integers.

In this way we can see the semantic transition between these referring expressions and what logicians call quantifiers. Among these we count not only 'all', 'every', and relatives, but also 'few', 'two', and so on. All of these can be used for referring or as essential components in complex expressions used for referring.

One typical expression used for reference is a quantified noun or noun phrase. But in order to know how to use 'all humans' and 'all body cells of this human now', we must attach principles of individuation and persistence to such expressions. This is to say that the use of these expressions assumes criteria for what counts as 1, 2, 3, men, and for what counts over time as "the same man", "the same tree", and so on. Different nouns come with different principles of individuation and persistence. The same spatiotemporal continuum can contain one human body and a hundred thousand body cells. Spatiotemporal contiguity or separateness by themselves do not guarantee across-the-board individuation or persistence.

These reflections show that there is an important linguistic and semantic underpinning for referrings of various sorts, namely that there must be agreement on the relevant principles of individuation and persistence. There may be an indefinite variety of emergencies, but there will be an underlying principle of individuation for these. At the same time, it is important to note that the use of quantifiers and quantified phrases in everyday discourse does not guarantee existential import, only purported import. We can talk successfully about all the scandals or the dawns of the past twenty-five days, and all that is needed for successful communication is intersubjective agreement on what we talk about. So the specifications on the third level of the lexical theory presented and in Chomsky's performance systems account for what is described in everyday discourse as referring, the same subject that Strawson analyzed, without seeing the point about lack of existential import. We see here also that referring expressions and their link to quantifiers in the broad sense shows the strong linguistic, or as Chomsky might say, conceptual, (syntactic, in a broader sense) background that referring requires.

It is interesting to see how names play roles in everyday acts of referring. There are two main types of names, those that come in systems, like names for numbers, shapes, months, weeks, and those–such as for humans, pets, ships–that do not. In the case of systems like numbers or shapes, securing ontological import comes by necessity. Finding numbers and shapes is not like finding mountains, exotic species, and so forth. It is a conceptual matter. Even in these cases, there may be questions about what counts in this or that context as a number. We talk to children about all numbers and do not mean to include negative numbers. Furthermore, there may be questions to be negotiated in cases of empirical application. In what contexts does a shape count as an instance of hexagonality, and in what cases does it not? But apart from these matters, we define numbers and shapes in systems, by finding relations that tie members of the system together (e.g., the successor function for positive integers). The systematic nature of interdefinition applies also to units of calendar, such as months or weeks. And, of course, since we are dealing with temporal slices, in referring with the use of such terms, questions of appropriateness, delimitation of the relevant time slice for this or that practical context also apply. For example: "When is the examination paper due?" "On Wednesday?" Such an exchange, unless rigidly specified for that particular context, can open a host of questions about the conditions under which one can say that the paper was handed in on time.

What was said about the oddness of asking about existential import in some contexts applies once more here. What sense can one attach to a question like: "Does January really exist?" It is odd to say that January does not exist, but it is also strange to insist that it exists. In what everyday contexts could such questions be raised? If the question makes any sense at all, it should be construed as a question about the local calendar system. The Chinese have one, some Western countries have another. Furthermore, we do refer to months and weekdays frequently in everyday commerce. Intersubjective agreement is all that is needed for successful reference and identification in these contexts.

With regard to referring by the use of ordinary names for persons, places, and so on. we find a wide variety of practices, or as Chomsky might put it, performance systems. Some names name famous persons, others do not. It would be absurd to say that knowing the putative referent of each proper name is a part of linguistic competence. In that case it would have to be a part of knowing English who the referents are for all of the names listed in the San Francisco phone directory. Linguistic competence is relevant, as we saw in the other cases, for use of quantifiers and thus knowledge of relevant principles of individuation and persistence apply in these cases also (for humans, mountains, respectively). But settling on who or what the referent is to be taken is a matter of nonlinguistic considerations. When we work on the history of philosophy, 'Aristotle' is used as the author of all or at least a large number of the works regarded in the tradition as Aristotelian. If it turns out that the author was not called Aristotle, that would be irrelevant, requiring only a small corrective footnote in history books. Still others are known as agents in key historical military matters. Here too, the same considerations apply. If it turns out to be the case that the agent we associate with Napoleon's early deeds is not the same as the agent to be linked to later military efforts, we would again just add a small footnote to the books. "Who really was Aristotle?" under those conditions would be a senseless question.

There are also quite different contexts in which biological continuity is crucial. This is not because some alleged metaphysical priority of such causal strings, but because of practical issues like inheritance, or other legal matters. So in the case of fame for a great composer or philosopher, authorship matters; in the case of a paternity suit, genetic criteria matter. In still other contexts such as financial responsibility, in which a name might be linked to role bearers, biological continuity and other matters. may be irrelevant. The chief executive is to be called on the carpet, and the question of whether this was one person biologically speaking, or a succession of three, is neither here or there. These examples should show that in terms of analysis of ordinary language, there is no such thing as a "basic reference" for names of humans. Positing such "basicness" is at most the result of materialistic metaphysical prejudices. Common sense is neutral with regard to those.

Examples could be multiplied indefinitely. Do we name strikes and balls in baseball? We certainly refer to them. Does it make sense to discuss their existence in general? What about emotional states like fear? What is seen as fear from one point of view may be construed as appropriate caution from another.

Referring, then, in everyday language is a matter of linguistic competence and a variety of systematically organized performance systems. Both convention and agreement, at times quite specific to a situation, play a role in success. To raise the question about the reality of what is referred to either is unnecessary or in some types of cases quite strange. As we shall see, in all these respects the notion of denotation as introduced by philosophers is quite different.

Before turning to denotation, we shall take a quick look at truth, because this notion plays a role in common sense as well as in formal semantics. The respective roles are different, however. Needless to say, we will not even touch most of the difficult problems involving philosophical theories about truth. What follows is restricted to showing that the ordinary uses of 'true' are compatible with what has been said about referring, and that the utility of bringing the technical notion of truth from formal semantics to bear on ordinary reference is yet to be shown.

In ordinary use 'true' does carry the implication that what has been expressed corresponds in some way to some extralinguistic bit of reality. But beyond that, what counts as true depends to a large extent on context and points of view. The same thing can count as true in a history book and false in a paper on chemistry. Furthermore, the ordinary use allows qualifications like 'this is true in a way', or 'this is more or less true', or even 'this is almost true'. Furthermore, one could not single out a usage and then construe all the rest as somehow derivative. Mathematical truth does not have such a privileged status in common sense. It is also important to separate the point about contextuality and different points of view from vagueness. As we saw in the earlier chapters even if we could fix the range of application of a term like 'white' so that no borderline cases can arise, this would still leave us with the variety of contexts in which different ranges count as white, whether these are vague or not.

In contrast, the technical notion of truth does not allow the qualifications we listed above, and there is no room in it for truths judged from different points of view. Tarski's scheme demands a clear, sharply defined, unambiguous and polysemy-free notion of truth, or truth relative to a formal language.

For special purposes, such as to characterize the expressive power of a part of language under idealized conditions, one might want to retain the technical notion of truth. For example, this comes up in investigations of whether so-called branching quantifiers can be represented in natural languages like English, in ordinary use. But these explorations are not designed to give a general characterization of natural language competence. At best they present some structure the mastery of which needs to be accounted for by any adequate theory of linguistic competence.

This discussion of names and other singular terms provide a good bridge to the analysis of denotation, or "satisfaction", technical terms from Tarski's conception of formal semantics. Within formal semantics denotation is the relation that links descriptive terms to their domain of application, as specified by further conditions on what a formal language has to be. The denotations play a key role in presenting the semantics of a formal language. The assignment of a denotation to a term carries existential import, and once we reflect on the nature of a formal language it is easy to see why this is so.

For a formal language those constructing it specify the domain of application. Examples include sets under some restriction, or numbers, or space-time points. The domain can be also a specific kind of entity, such as cells of organic entities, the nature of which the theory embodied in the formal language is to explain. In these cases existential import is not an open question. The descriptive parts of language are simply assigned entities the existence of which is within the theory a necessity. Thus predicates are assigned sets as denotations, and individual constants are assigned particular entities. Thus the matter of whether a name has a reference, or denotation, and what it may be, does not arise. Given these assignments, or given interpretation, truth can be mechanically defined for the sentences of the formal language.

As we saw, none of this is true of natural languages. What is a natural language about? Everything, as Tarski remarked a long time ago. But we humans, living in "midstream" and thus being confronted with a reality much of which we will most likely never know, use our descriptive terms without having guaranteed extralinguistic correlates. Furthermore, unlike a formal language that is designed to embody a theory like mathematics or physics, a natural language enables us to do a variety of things besides theorizing, and even in the case of theories it must serve as that which enables us to communicate across different theories, with their different points of view. We have no control over what kinds of entities we might be led to talk about in English, German, or any other language.

We can see now how these reflections are linked to the arguments in the earlier chapters showing that natural languages are not and cannot be treated as formal languages in Tarski's sense. In formal languages the domain about which we talk is fixed. In a natural language the semantics features a number of productive devices that enable us to construct meanings and ranges of applications as we go along. This characterization of natural languages fits well both with what Chomsky says about referring and performance systems, and with the presentation of the lowest level in the lexical analysis presented in this book.

PART III

EXPLANATION, THE PRODUCTIVE LEXICON, AND LIMITATIONS ON UNDERSTANDING UNDERSTANDING

CHAPTER 5

HOMO SAPIENS = HOMO EXPLANANS

Earlier chapters showed that natural languages are not and should not be represented as formal languages in Tarski's sense. I had three main reasons for this. First, formal languages require rigidly fixed vocabulary items. Ambiguity and only vague correlation of meaning and denotation are not tolerated. Second, building up semantic complexes out of simpler elements must be done via the logical connectives. Third, the whole semantics must be explicit. Whatever involves contextual specifications, such as speaker-hearer relativity or cultural assumptions must be relegated to pragmatics.

In contrast, I articulated a conception of semantics for natural languages within which the semantics of lexical items was generative; that is, its structure is built so as to enable us to construct polysemous complexes without introducing endless lists of separate meanings. I showed also that in addition to logical complexity, there are other key semantic relations, such as part–whole constructions in which the whole is not a mere sum of parts. Finally, my semantic proposals are designed to build structures that describe semantic content but without omitting contextual matters. Semantic content and contextual contributions jointly articulate full meaning.

In this chapter we clarify the key cognitive conception that underlies the work on the lexicon. This is the conception of humans as primarily explanation seeking and forming creatures. This project involves showing that explanations are not just generalizations with logical connections. On the psychological side, this entails that understanding is not just a collection of beliefs arranged into logical organizations.

On the positive side, we show that explanations are more than mere logical structures. They constitute holistic units in which the whole is more than its logical parts.

After we articulate what explanation, and its counterpart, understanding, are, this conception is injected into a conception of basic dynamic human cognitive states and processes, the foundation of which is human thinking as basically taking some things for granted, seeing some as problematic, seeing others as having explanatory force, and then applying the latter to the former so as to gain cognitive patterns and belief-forming potential that we can use in a variety of ways.

The chapter shows also how this conception of human cognition interacts with our conception of generative aitiational (explanatory) schemes. At the end I argue that beliefs can be explicated fully only against the background of the kinds of explanatory structures that are sketched in the main body of the chapter, and hence that beliefs are not the only or most fundamental elements out of which all cognition must be constructed.

I. WHY INFORMATION PROCESSING CANNOT UNDERLIE OUR EXPLANATORY SCHEMES

Let me first sketch briefly in rough outline the picture that is opposed by the views of this book. A typical conception of the information-processing structure and related activities can be summed up in the following.

The basic cognitive elements are concepts and beliefs. Concepts are formed by humans noticing similarities among the entities they encounter. These similarities are supposed to be captured by concepts. We know, however, that between any two objects there are an infinite number of similarities, since the only logically clear notion of similarity is that of entities sharing a property. If there is a property correlated to every predicate expression in a language–including, for example, the property of not being identical with Napoleon–then unmanageable similarities between any two entities will follow. This has been noted by philosophers like Quine, who then sees the need for adding to the cognitive mechanisms proposed an "innate quality space"; for example, a way of arranging colors according to similarity.[1] As we move away from the perceptual, properties like "looking tired" make this account difficult to maintain.

Beliefs are then representations of objects subsumed under concepts, or concepts related to another. Beliefs are then related according to the rules of inductive and deductive logic.

1. W. V. O. Quine, *Word and Object* (New York: John Wiley, 1960) p. 83.

Information processing of this sort is not construed as taking place in a vacuum. The incoming information is to be assimilated to what we know or believe already. But this assimilation is simply a matter of subsuming newly discovered material under concepts already possessed, or creating new concepts, and ordering the new beliefs into the logical web already at hand.

Explanations within this picture are lawlike generalizations arranged in hierarchical order.

This conception has been seen as inadequate by various philosophers of science. Recently two additions to this construal have been proposed. One is that the explanatory unifies what have been seen prior to the introduction of the new scheme as separate domains of facts.[2] The other is that within an explanatory nomological scheme there must also be underlying causal mechanisms posited for key phenomena.[3] The following questions arise, however, in connection with these proposals.

Apart from whether one could make the notion of unifying phenomena sufficiently rigorous, it seems that at times unification helps, and at other times adding much detail is more explanatory. For example, in classifications both finding appropriate genera and obtaining an illuminating articulation of a network of species are of equal importance. At times one, at times the other brings more illumination. It would be also difficult to separate the need for unification and the alleged need for reductions. If a reduction of biology to chemistry and physics could be attained, this by itself might not bring any illumination; at times reductions of this sort, and analogous "moves" in the foundation of mathematics, result only in explaining the obscure by something even more obscure. In phonology, for example, scholars have been looking for general characterizations of the sound patterns of all human languages for some time. But only in recent decades have we obtained a sufficiently illuminating articulation of both unity and variety. The same holds for chemistry. The unification is no more important than the details obtained by the table of chemical elements.

If the table of chemical elements gave us only a common denominator for all of what we call chemicals, this might not be explanatory. One of the strengths of the table is the analysis of seemingly simple stuffs into a complicated underlying complex structure, constituted simples that can be theoretically illuminated. Classifications according to genus–species structures may or may

---

2. Ph. Kitcher, "Explanatory Unification and the Causal Structure of the World," *Minnesota Studies in the Philosophy of Science* 13 (1989): 459–507.

3. W. Salmon, "Four Decades of Scientific Explanation," *Minnesota Studies in the Philosophy of Science* 13 (1989): 3–196.

not be illuminating, depending whether these are based solely on observable features, or also underlying elements not detectable by everyday observation. Adequate explanations seem to involve the appearance–reality distinction, but this is already an extralogical element. We shall return to this later.

The proposal to add to the laws the requirement of causal mechanisms affects only a part of what the theory of this essay is to cover, namely the natural sciences. But even here the requirement of causal mechanism is both unclear and unduly restrictive. It is unclear because we might mean by this mechanistic systems, or more plausibly, probabilistic correlations. The hypothesis that every natural phenomenon has mechanistic systems underlying it seems absurd in the light of the development of sciences over the past two hundred years. The requirement of probabilistic correlations is illuminating or not, depending what the correlata are surface phenomena, as in behavioristic psychology, or interactions among entities way beneath the level of the everyday observable. Furthermore, in many cases the development of measurement and refined measurement techniques bring far more illumination and insight than mere correlations. The ancient Greeks had many correlations of elements used in architecture. Still, great explanatory power was added with the discovery and invention of precise units of measurement and techniques of implementation.

Relevant to this discussion is the point made by Charles Taylor, that in some societies explanatory efforts center on seeking causal order while on others insight is construed as centering on finding mathematical order, symmetry, or in some cases teleological structures.[4] There is no noncircular way of establishing priorities among these general conceptions of explanatory pattern.

Let us now consider a few key objections to this picture. The most general point has its roots already in vocabulary. The French "savoire" versus "comprendre" distinction as well as the English "know" versus "understand" suggests an underlying intuition that two distinct mental states are covered by the contrasts. Though the story of the French diplomat who contrasted himself with his nearest rival by saying: "He knows everything but understands nothing, while I know nothing but understand everything," is a mere anecdote, it is worth exploring whether under its smoke there is also some fire.

Let us consider–as an idealized abstraction–a collection of singular propositions that would cover all entities of reality and all of their properties. Such a collection could be called a "book of simple truths." Knowing the content of this book clearly would not yield understanding. It would not tell us "why." Adding inductive generalizations, lawlike projections, and deductive relations

4. Charles Taylor, "Rationality" in Charles Taylor, *Philosophical Papers*, vol. 2, ch. 5.

among the generalizations, with the help of some theoretical vocabulary, still would not give us sufficient structure to enable us to claim that we have understanding. One could always ask of such structures: "Yes, but does this really explain what we find problematic?" Such structures would–ex hypothesis–give us truth. But mere truth does not by itself yield insight and understanding.

The second objection is related to the first. If mere truth does not yield understanding, what does? Our ways of assessing adequate explanations point to the answer. An explanation, unlike a set of simple propositions with logical interrelatedness, is not simply true or false. To be sure, an adequate explanation should consist of elements that are true. But adequacy is then claimed when we can say also of the purported explanation that it is deep, insightful, has larger significance, helps us to "make sense" of the domain under consideration. These notions, in turn, are not analyzable solely in terms of truth and logical impeccability.

One might join these two objections and reply by saying that the "extra" elements that our ways of assessing point to are not parts of the general objective part of rational assessment of the claims of science or common sense. The additional elements are subjective.

Let us get clear about what is supposed to be subjective and what a claim of objective content amounts to. According to the analysis to be presented in more detail, both explanations and their cognitive counterparts, states of understanding, are holistic in nature; that is, they cannot be analyzed exhaustively as the mere sum of their parts. For example, understanding a proof is more than merely knowing the premises and the rules of inference. If one really understands the proof, one can assess its significance, alternate ways of constructing it, and so on.[5] Likewise, a theory in a science is more than the laws, definitions, and predictions. One has to see why the theory has explanatory force while other theories accounting for the same phenomena do not.

Adjudicating rival proposals is made difficult by the fact that those denying the objective validity of the experience of having gained insight and understanding typically also deny the "additional" transpropositional (a better term than nonpropositional, which I used in previous publications, since I do not think that one can simply have these nonpropositional insights apart from knowing a great deal about the subject matter) ingredients in proofs, explanations. Thus the issue comes down to whether one can identify the objective explanatory content with the mere formalism that present the proofs, theories, models, and so on. Are the judgments of insightfulness, adequacy, depth, sim-

5. J. Moravcsik, "Understanding," *Dialectica* 33 (1979): 201–16.

ply a matter of changing tastes and individual variation? Objectivity hardly requires universal consent. We lack this in any other domain, and are not surprised by it. Not every human in the world assents to the truths of simple arithmetic or physics.

The only way one can examine the rival claims is by looking at efforts of historians of science. I cite here only two theoreticians who seem to be on my side. In an influential article Georg Kreisel has stressed the importance of basic intuitive concepts like those of number and set, in addition to and apart from varieties of formalization. He stresses the importance of these in contrast with conceptions within which formalisms are the highest goal.[6] Again, writing about mathematical knowledge and practice Kenneth Manders writes with respect to mathematical conceptualizations "The essence of these accomplishments is the overall intellectual grasp which they enable. Overall intellectual grasp, in turn, is the essence of the theoretical component of human knowledge generally."[7] He complains that excessive concern with the nature of evidence and reliability led to a distorted theory of knowledge. As far as I can see, Manders uses different terminology, but on the basis of careful expert examinations of specific cases in the history of mathematics and geometry he comes to the conclusions I advocate here, namely that classifications of the reliability and evidential basis of propositional knowledge is not sufficient to understand human understanding. In several places Manders considers instances in which two theories in geometry account for the same set of facts, but the experts agree that one of them gives us much more insight and explanation.

The point can be illustrated also in other domains. In the case of illnesses, our accepted explanatory pattern is the positing of underlying elements that account for symptoms. The implicit appearance–reality distinction is not a matter of propositional knowledge, nor a matter of success in predictions. In fact this pattern was accepted at historical stages in which regular predictability was still out of the question.

On the basis of these considerations, I reject the notion of explanation and understanding that reduces these concepts to what is covered by information processing as sketched above. On the contrary, it will be shown that information processing functions well only when couched within general explanatory patterns and a cognitive context within which we can make–generally–sense of what we encounter.

---

6. G. Kreisel, "Informal Rigour and Completeness Proofs," in I. Lakatos, ed., *Philosophy of Mathematics* (Amsterdam: North Holland, 1967), pp. 138–157).

7. K. Mander, "Logical and Conceptual Relationships in Mathematics," *Logic Colloquium '85* (Amsterdam: Elsevier, 1987) pp. 193–211.

II. EXPLANATION AND UNDERSTANDING

We can explain and understand many different types of entities and formulate explanations as answers to different types of questions.[8] We shall concentrate on explanations why something seems to be the case, how certain phenomena can come about and what various conceptual complexes are. For example, why did the flood come about? Explain what electricity, or magnetism, is. Explain how osmosis takes place.

One might think that the answer to an "explain what?" question will be simply a definition. But this is illusory. Definitions can be more or less illuminating; providing more or less explanatory power. For example at an early stage some Greeks defined a straight line as one that, when viewed from the end, has all of its constituent points behind one another so that one can see only the first. Subsequently the definition of a straight line as the shortest distance between two points was accepted. Understanding that the second definition is deeper and more insightful than the first requires knowing a bit about geometry but is ultimately a matter of insight and understanding.

Likewise, understanding why a certain property is the "right" choice as a primitive in a system (e.g., numerosity) is a matter of "seeing" how it relates to all of the other relevant properties and notions. Thus such choices are not merely a matter of convenient formalisms. Deep intuitions, surviving the passing of time, are the ultimate criteria.

This is shown by Plato in his treatment of so-called divisions.[9] For example he considers a general notion, and for his analysis of knowledge a fundamental one; that of "techne" or rational discipline. In his presentations he points to two key observations about the analysis of such concepts. First, there is an indefinite number of ways of analyzing such a concept into ingredients, and some of such analyses are more insightful than others. (As he says, in some analyses the ingredients are real wholes, in others mere parts.) Second, there are no absolute minimal parts of concepts, or properties. We make as many sound distinctions as seem theoretically advisable because they increase intelligibility but further distinction, even if in some cases trivial ones, are always possible.

Much of this conception relies on our reaching–after much reasoning and gathering of knowledge–sound intuitions concerning what is deep and explanatory and what is less so. Rational discussion of such questions is possible,

8. S. Bromberger, *On What We Know We Don't Know* (Chicago: University of Chicago Press, 1992).

9. J. Moravcsik, *Plato and Platonism* (Oxford: Blackwell, 1992), ch. 6.

but it is neither pure formalistic deductive reasoning, nor merely gathering evidence. Plato's term "dialectic" for this is no longer in fashion, but we have not really come up with an adequate substitute.

There are a variety of structures that embody and lead us to understanding. Proofs, theories, diagrams, models, all contribute in different ways. The latter two are of special epistemological interest, for if we understand these well, we must also see that they point themselves. The insights we aim at are not about diagrams and models; but these structures can lead us to grasp the abstract structures that form holistic units, and thus the appropriate objects of explanation and understanding.

Herewith some concepts and distinctions the appreciation and utilization of which requires "transpropositional" understanding and grasping of what adequate explanatory power is. One of these is the distinction between appearances and underlying reality that is already implicit in pre-Socratic thought, is made explicit in Plato, and dominates all subsequent Western science. The "appearances" are the observables; the explaining is done by underlying elements and their interrelations. These may be genuinely abstract mathematical structures or unobservable spatiotemporal elements. There is no inductive or deductive proof of why we should interpret reality in this way. To say that this approach has been successful begs the question, for it leads immediately to the further question: Why do we regard what this organization led to as success?

Another such distinction is between an idealized account of a collection of phenomena and the accounts we give of the actual phenomena as we encounter them in scientific or everyday experience. There are at least two reasons for not ascribing the preference for such explanatory schemes to practical considerations. First, there is no clear evidence that practical needs and manipulations could not be served equally well by accounts based on different patterns. Second, the history of the sciences does not show that the main motive for such two-stage explanations is based on practical considerations. Idealizations serve primarily pure understanding. We get a better comprehensive picture of a certain domain when we view it under idealizations, be this the phenomena of gasses or of linguistic competence. Furthermore, some idealizations are more insightful than others. Here again, we decide on the basis of what is intuitively more satisfying. (Efforts to select the "better" theories on the basis of economy, elegance, or more predictive power have failed in the past decades.)

Still another practice whose introduction is primarily a matter of gaining better understanding and deeper explanations is measurement. Measurements of various degrees of exactitude, and applicability to different domains, have been introduced gradually, over long periods of time. In some cases systems of measurements with considerable exactness have been also of practical use. But this is not always so, and again, the main motivation in many cases is not technological.

Why should magnitudes subjected to precise measurements be more intelligible to us than these same magnitudes viewed simply under "mass terms"? There is no non-circular answer we can only say that it is "clearer" to us that way.

Finally, another example illustrating the irreducibility of understanding and explanation is the debate over the relationship between quantitative and qualitative notions. For example, as in many other sciences, in economics many of our notions about economic practices have been given quantitative interpretations. Still, one could demand that at a foundational level qualitative concepts like property, planning, or communal values, should be included in an adequate account of economic practices. Even apart from foundational issues, this can be illustrated in connection with debates about what constitutes a raise or decline in the quality of life of a community. Some researchers tried to define this solely in terms of money and other material gain, while others have pointed out that we need to include also such notions as security, a sense of community, or self-respect.[10] These issues too raise fundamental questions about what we find clearly intelligible and "making overall sense."

The phenomena related to explanatory power and understanding emerge on relatively simple levels in an introductory mathematics class, or in debates by experts about logic, or any of the natural sciences. An industrious student may know a lot about a certain proof, but it takes a certain illumination (an "aha" experience) when "it all comes together." This happens also frequently with philosophy courses, where only within the final overall review do some items finally seem "clear" to some students.

We must not take the phenomenology too rigidly. The experiences mentioned can in some cases be illusory. There is no litmus paper test for the veridicality of such experiences; in this respect these are no different from most other types of cognitive experiences.

In these reflections it becomes clear that understanding and explanatory power are matters of degrees. This by itself shows that these notions cannot be reduced to truth and logical structure, since those complexes are not matters of degree. Something is either true or false, either valid or not. Things can have degrees of probability, but that is quite different from the kinds of degrees that we involve when talking about insight.

The difficulty of saying anything precise about explanatory force and un-

10. A. Sen, "The Standard of Living," *Tanner Lectures on Human Values*, vol. 7 (Utah: University of Utah Press, 1986), pp. 1–54.

derstanding is mirrored by the difficulty of specifying what needs to be explained and understood. It is a mistake to think everything we encounter calls for explanation and illumination. As a rough initial description we can say that what is *problematic* calls for explanation. This, of course raises immediately the next question: What is problematic? There is no general characterization of what will seem in this or that context problematic to the human mind. But in any case the problematic involves seeing something strange in light of some explanatory structures and beliefs that we have already. Lest we get involved in an infinite regress, we can posit as innate certain explanatory tendencies–such as those embodied in our lexical AFT or qualia structures. But to describe the normal flow of cognitive life, we should use a modified version of Neurath's analogy, used so successfully by Quine. Maybe every plank is open to question and revision in principle within our conceptual frameworks, but at any given time, we must keep some planks fixed–convictions taken for granted–while viewing others as problematic. A ship in which all planks are torn up simultaneously–even for such a laudable purpose as repair or replacement–sinks.

We illuminated so far in some ways notions of explanation and understanding as both semantically and cognitively holistic structures. At the same time we have not denied the importance of forming beliefs and organizing these partly into logical structures. We shall now turn to arguments showing why the explanatory frameworks must underlie belief formation and maintenance.

We have seen already that explanation and understanding cannot be built up solely from collections of beliefs and logical structure. In short, understanding and explanation are irreducible notions, given current alternatives. From this the fundamentality of the explanatory does not follow. We could have two systems, mutually dependent on each other, and neither more fundamental than the other. Or even the explanatory as not reducible to belief and logic, but in some way less fundamental than these.It has been said often that beliefs are "theory-laden." This can mean many things. By itself it does not show the priority of theories and models as interpreted in this essay. The theory-ladenness invoked here could be given and interpretation within the information processing model. Beliefs can be theory-laden in the sense that some of their constituents must be concepts already within our conceptual framework, and that the beliefs will be fitted into the logical web we have already, thus achieving coherence–as far as possible.

In order to show the required priority we must show that beliefs, in the ordinary or technical senses of that term, are embedded into the kind of patterns of explanation and understanding that we have been sketching.

In any reasonable sense of 'belief', beliefs and their contents either relate concepts to concepts or concepts to particular spatiotemporal entities. But concepts representing meanings in everyday or scientific uses have the structure delineated by AFT or Pustejovsky's qualia structure. Hence the content of a belief relies on the kind of explanatory schemata that is contained in the meanings of the descriptive vocabulary. Hence beliefs are embedded in a non-trivial sense in explanatory structures. Concepts "cleansed" of all explanatory force are not idealizations but distortions of human cognition.

Let us consider examples showing that if a putative belief is embedded in different explanatory structures, it will have different content.[11] We see this in the case of descriptions of illness. Suppose one says, "Jones is sick". This will mean one thing if the notion of illness is analyzed as an explanatory complex including the symptom–underlying cause relation, and something quite different if "sickness" is interpreted strictly on the observational level, with searches for cause remaining on this plane ("behavioristic medicine?"). This applies also to the so-called observational level. What I see, I *see as* for example a symptom, a malformation, or the manifestation of a healthy constitution. I "observe" the "same thing" in an ordinary sense even if I don't have the symptom–underlying cause (bacteria, virus, etc.) scheme as my interpretation, but this is not strictly speaking true. I may be exposed to the same sensory stimuli, but the mental representation of the content of the belief will different in the two cases.

Thus a belief that Joe is sick acquires different contents in different explanatory contexts. In a context in which medicine and illness is understood as relating behavioral events to behavioral events only, it is understood one way, but within a conception of medicine in which symptoms are construed as just symptoms, to be related to underlying, and possibly only partly observable, causes, the belief content is different. To be sure, after a while the medicine that attempts to treat symptoms only on the observable level with observable means, and the related commonsense conception of illness and healing, will disappear, since most human illnesses cannot be treated at that level. But we cannot count on the "bad" explanatory scheme always disappearing. Competing explanatory schemes can survive and coexist for long periods of time.

Another example illustrating the same point is a belief that tonight we have a nice sunset over the ocean. The content of this belief must relate what I see to the concept of a sunset. This, in turn–assuming that I can express my belief in verbal form–must contain explanatory structure. It is then not just the truism

11. A similar point is made in K. Manders, "Diagrams, Contents, and Representational Granularity," to be published.

that two people can interpret and classify the same sensory stimuli in different ways, but that the difference must reflect explanatory patterns, ways in which the world makes sense to us. Furthermore, there is nothing in this claim that would entail some kind of cultural or conceptual relativity. People who see the world in different ways can compare notes and come to understand each other. It happens between historical periods why should it not happen among humans living at the same time?

This priority claim for the explanatory (or as I called it in earlier publications, the "aitiational") does not entail that we cannot offer different explanations for the same belief. What it says is that this "belief" or its content is itself embedded partly in explanatory assumptions, and that the people seeking complete explanations share some of these assumptions. For example "it is raining" will be explained differently by those who believe in modern physical explanations and those who think that this is a matter of the gods being angry. But both will share explanatory patterns within which we regard as nonproblematic that things can fall towards the earth, that some liquids are natural and not artificial, and so on.

Hume's insistence on the fundamentality of secondary qualities was not merely a demand to reduce things to the observable, but also that the elements of cognition should be reducible to concepts lacking in our sense explanatory or functional content, at some fundamental level. Both Chapter 4, and the material presented in the present chapter deny that this is the case.

III. THE COGNITIVE LIFE OF HOMO EXPLANANS

Our cognitive life results in our articulating reports, observations, descriptions, plans, predictions, and so forth. All of these have beliefs as a common denominator. But, as we saw, in the previous section, beliefs are embedded in explanatory schemes. However, we cannot have explanatory schemes without beliefs as ingredients. Do we have a vicious circle here? This can be avoided if we assume that a few basic explanatory structures, like the four involved in the AFT lexical representations, are given innately. That would mean our starting to process information, input, sensations, from the start into certain explanatory schemata. This assumption has a long tradition, starting with Plato, and persisting today in the works of Piaget, Chomsky, and others.

The embeddedness of beliefs in explanatory schemes does not mean that humans are interpreted as spending all of their time and energy on seeking and forming explanations. We posit, however, a scheme like AFT, and assume that humans can fall back on this when needed, and maintain it by continuous work that goes parallel with other cognitive processes such as describing or reporting.

Presumably our cognitive life (mind/brain activity) is a constantly ongoing process. This was recognized already by earlier philosophers like Plato and Descartes. In terms of beliefs, this means a steady stream of new beliefs, leading from time to time reconstructing beliefs already held, and reorganizing the whole set of beliefs we hold. The main reason for this is the constant influx of sensory input. Every movement of my body forces me to have new beliefs. In this respect the formation of explanatory schemes differs from belief formations. The constant influx of sensory information does not force us to come up with new explanatory schemes. To be sure, some of our cognitive energy will be spent on maintaining the schemes we have, and providing contexts for the new beliefs. Occasionally we do change explanatory schemes, and at times come up with new ones. The new schemes either have the role of accommodating new information, or interpreting what we believe or know already in different light. It is a fundamental fact of our mental life that if necessary, for example from the point of view of justification, we can fall back on the explanatory schemes that we embrace and which we need not have consciously in mind for most of our waking hours.

AFT is a combination of Kantian and Aristotelian intuitions. It is Kantian to the extent that one can view Kant's categories as apart from claims about the transcendental and the apriori synthetic, and construe it as the positing of a set of innate ideas. It is Aristotelian to the extent that the four key factors are considerably modified version of Aristotle's conception of "key causes" or better put, explanatory factors. Explanatory may be a misleading phrase since today we think of explanations as invented by humans, not as impressed on the human mind by nature. Cause is, however, just as bad if not worse. Innate explanatory scheme is perhaps the least misleading description of what is posited here.

We utilize AFT or qualia structure in the following way. Our cognitive life has the following four stages:

1. We take certain things for granted.
2. We construe some things as problematic.
3. We regard some structures as having explanatory power.
4. We apply elements of stage 3 to elements of stage 2, and proceed with our usual cognitive activities.

Under stage 1 there will be mere beliefs as well as explanations, for example, beliefs about the uniformity of nature, a general reliability of causal explanations, the validity of some rules of inference, etc. What we take for granted can be very general or quite specific (taxes, greed for money). Furthermore, nothing must remain in stage 1. In some context any item might become problematic, but not everything at the same time.

In stage 2 as well we can have observations, connections between events, new types of phenomena, or just old ones that suddenly are seen as having puzzling features (surface of the earth, Euclidean space, etc.) What becomes problematic and why is one of the mysteries of the human mind.

In stage 3 I assume some items remain fixed, but others change, and even among the permanent some factors are seen as having priority at one time and not at another. For example, in earlier stages of history explanation by origin was dominant, while today explanations in terms of constituency (abstract or concrete) or properties are seen as having deeper and more general explanatory power. Some explanatory structures are specific, like DNA or molecular structure, others are not.

This fourfold classification represents an interpretation of what we called the modified Neurath-picture. In stage 1 we find the planks that are for the time being fixed and not moved while in b) we have the planks to be seen as needing repair or replacement. In stage 3 we find whatever at a given stage in history is accepted as having explanatory force; one hopes that *some* elements always do, such as a class of deductive proofs.

Stage 4 represents the ship running, as best it can. I wish to add, however, another hypothesis about the shiplike human mind, namely that it does not use all of its equipment at all times. Meanings are represented–in ways not well understood–in the mind. Thus meanings–in the sense of AFT, as shown in Chapter 3–in our minds are psychological structures. We can utilize all or some parts of these for interpretation. In some contexts in which much is taken for granted on the basis of habit and external cues, we can operate with "flat meanings" (or meaning representations). This is a case in which much of the explanatory richness of the meaning of a word is not utilized, and we operate in fact only with the m-factor specified in most general terms, and some elements of the s-factor, with all else left as taken for granted in the sense that we assume there is a way of filling these out, but in the context of communication these are not relevant. For example, in some contexts we use 'rain' with such semantic content. We realize that it is something spatiotemporal, but then concentrate only on a few typical distinguishing marks, such as wet stuff, colorless, coming "down" in drops. This will hardly do in explanatory contexts, but in some cases the speaker–audience relationship restricts relevance to a few observational features, with all else taken for granted–questions affecting the rest of the meaning are irrelevant to the communication. However, sudden changes in tasks faced, cooperation needed, can create contexts in which the full explanatory force of 'rain' is relevant. We need to know what raindrops are made of, that it is really rain and not some other similar looking but poisonous stuff coming down, or that the source is indeed nature and not some human-made disaster, etc.

Certain uses-in-context of artifacts names exhibit the same semantic behavior. In many everyday contexts we use 'refrigerator' with such a flattened meaning. We know that it is concrete, and we distinguish it from other concrete things in terms of some of its salient functional characteristics. We take for granted that in that context anything answering that much of the meaning of 'refrigerator' will also fit the other more sophisticated and complex requirements. Of course, the refrigerator can, and occasionally does, break down, and at that point the full explanatory force of the meaning of 'refrigerator' comes into play as efforts are being made to find ways of repairing it.

Why should we not allow for a large number of shallow meanings, and separately more complex meanings for descriptive terms? For one, this would proliferate meanings, and one should use Ockham's razor on polysemy. But, more importantly, such a move would not do justice to our cognitive life. *Any* term at any time can have applications that make the denotata problematic! The distinction between "flat" and full utilization is a matter of degree, and it cuts across the distinction between scientific and everyday uses. In a laboratory, under highly controlled circumstances we can utilize "flat" concepts for reporting observations. Not all of scientific discourse used in research requires full theoretical understanding. Likewise, in everyday discourse we can find contexts for minimal needs of semantic understanding; we assume that the fruit trees in our gardens have not changed their nature dramatically, and are not sick. Then again, suddenly the picture can change, and we need to rely on the explanatory force of meanings in order to make something problematical (new phenomena, old phenomena in new configurations, etc.) once more intelligible.

There are a variety of ways in which what we took for granted can become problematic. For example, at certain historical stages people took the adequacy of explanation in terms of origin for granted. For example, "Achilles is a superhero because his mom was a goddess". But at some point a person in a mood of wonderment might ask: "What is it about being born with such-and-such a person as one's mother that enables one to have certain characteristics?" At that point people might look at analyses in terms of constituency with some "transfer mechanism" posited. Eventually they might treat origin as useless in that context, and develop further analysis by constituency ("people who have as parts x, y, z, are likely to be superheroes").

Thus within our theory we look at the meaning complexes as abstracted, under idealization, assuming the full use of the meaning is required. We can then, derivatively, also specify "flat" or partial uses, and the ongoing processes of information processing and communication. In real life these processes go on in many cases simultaneously, with the information flow being embedded in the explanatory frameworks and at the same time influencing these, while the "information" coming in is already conceptualized in accordance with the explanatory structures that our language provides at any given time.

IV. THE COGNITIVE LIFE AND LEXICAL STRUCTURES

The hypothesis that humans are basically explanation-seeking and-forming creatures and that information processing is embedded in this set of holistic systems has been presented in the past sections. But from this the nature of the AFT representation of lexical meaning does not follow. An alternative scheme could accept the embeddedness of information in explanatory schemes but construe the elements of such schemes as consisting of types of abstract structures not resembling the aitiational frames. The argument of this essay goes as follows. The AFT representations of lexical meaning stand on their own as the most plausible structures to account for salient properties of human semantic competence. In addition, however, there are interesting interrelations between this lexical theory and the cognitive life as we sketched it.

Let us go back to the point made earlier that concepts are indefinitely divisible, and dense entities in the sense that there may be an infinite number of ways in which conceptual parts can be cross-classified. We see this in the case of physics. The alleged fundamental ingredients of "matter" are divided further and further into still more "fundamental" elements. This physical division is mirrored on the conceptual plane, with no general argument showing that this process cannot go on indefinitely.

But we can see the same phenomenon in connection with notions like freedom, justice, or utility. Hence at any historical stage the concept is always more than the sum of the parts into which it has been articulated at any time.

This phenomenon is mirrored in AFT and qualia structures. As we saw, a general notion such as captured in the meaning of 'emergency' can be used to generate an indefinite set of denotation ranges, with no apriori limit on the kinds and number of these. Furthermore, there is no one way of dividing up emergencies into kinds. Enormous number of cross-classifications are possible within any concept. For example, sciences can be seen as a priori versus empirical, or applied versus pure. Either of these dichotomies opens up indefinite ways of further specifications.

We can compare the meanings of 'science', 'emergency', and so on to the meanings of what linguists call underspecified verbs such as 'use'. From the specific point of view adopted here, underspecification is a matter of degrees, and under our analysis it infects all of the descriptive vocabulary of a natural language.

Hence concepts in general and meanings of lexical items, both mirror on a smaller scale the nature of explanatory schemes that we posited as the key blocks of human cognition.

We must not confuse in these structures the several hierarchies posited. As we move in AFT from levels 1 and 2 to level 3, we might not move to meanings that contain less explanatory power. If anything, at that level the explanation schemes posited on the higher ones are filled in more. So level 3 should not be confused with the "observational" level of empiricist theories of semantics and epistemology.

For some the indefinite ways in which concepts and meanings can grow and differentiate might be reminiscent of the idea that instead of meanings all we have is a variety of "routines" associated with lexical items. But the resemblance is only superficial. The higher levels (1 and 2) give unity to lexical meanings, even if not sufficient application conditions. Principles of individuation and persistence are specified on level 1, and these are inherited by the lower levels. Similar points can be made about the f-factor. Understanding the key functional specifications is vital for the understanding of 'house'. No amount of routines and observations can substitute for a general description. A further example should make this clear. In some contexts 'she is a patient' is interpreted simply as the person in question having the right papers on her bed and wearing the right identification tags. But sooner or later there will be a need to understand various instructions the justification of which is "because she is a patient" (e.g., taking blood samples regularly, taking temperature, x-rays, etc.). Our analysis allows for a wide variety of interpretations and responses, without destroying the unity of lexical meanings.

Our cognitive life includes the development of new concepts and explanations. This too is mirrored on the lexical level, since changing key elements in the AFT structure constitutes meaning change. These changes can be sudden, by stipulation, or gradual, just as in our cognitive life in general conceptual changes can be gradual or in discrete chunks.

Whether in terms of meaning change, or just differentiation and cross-classification, the potential for these processes remains in lexical meanings at any given stage, at all levels.

The notion of idealization keeps coming up in this work. We need to separate three types of idealization. First, there is a normative sense of idealization, when we sketch a possible state of affairs that we regard as a target to be reached or at least approximated. For example, in some ethical theories the notion of an ideal observer plays an important role. This ideal observer is not a mere abstraction from actual cases. Rather, it is the kind of observer that we–in our rational moods?–deem to be appropriate for the judging of moral issues. The same holds for philosophers' notions of an ideal city or community.

Another type of idealization places a phenomenon such as gasses into an artificially simplified environment such as a vacuum or laboratory experiment. The theory that emerges and is applied to these idealization, or deliberate oversimplifications, needs to be supplemented by a set of variables that lead us from the theoretic to the actual cases.

There is a third type of case in which we study something under the hypothetical conditions that certain limitations of the subject are taken away; thus we get an abstract characterization of phenomena. The notion of a competent speaker-hearer falls into this category, considered apart from limitations on memory and attention span. Similarly, we might want to characterize rational choice under the idealization of full information, or omniscience.

At times, these different types are not distinguished. This may or may not cause harm. A normative conception of a competent speaker-hearer leads only to people wanting to increase their memory or attention span–hardly catastrophic tendencies. More serious difficulties arise if we take the notion of the Rational Economic Man, as used in some parts of economics, as a normative ideal for the kind of human we should try to be, in any contexts. In our current context, the distinction between audience-relative and not-audience-relative explanations and the accompanying idealizations are not meant to be normative. We clearly need in human interactions both types of explanation and identification or reference.

Let us now invoke another nonnormative idealization in order to bring out sharply the difference between understanding and mere gathering of information. Let us imagine an ideal book that contains all of the true singular statements that describe the world. We called it before a complete description, or the Book of Simple Truths. Let us add to it also all of the true nonlawlike generalizations. It is clear that even with all of this information we would not have understanding, or a complete explanation of the universe. We would know what is the case; we would not know why, or what the basic ingredients are.

The account of explanation sketched is meant to apply across both scientific and commonsense reasoning. Much of the latter has been discussed in the recent literature under the heading of "folk psychology." Let us turn to how this account of explanation deals with folk psychology. First, we should note that the problem can hardly be unique. If there is such a thing as folk psychology, then there is also folk physics, folk geometry, and so on. Second, we should not construe folk psychology, or folk anything, in a monolithic way. Some of it may be parts of an innate human conceptual mechanism that serves us well in getting thinking in humans going. Some of it may be as has been suggested, a set of concepts that can be made precise and then used for scientific purposes. For example, the move from the commonsense notion of choice to the technical sense of preference. Still other parts may belong to what we called above strong common sense, and thus unavoidable as starting points, though not as necessary ingredients in the sciences. It is also misleading to think of folk psychology as a theory. It is more plausible to think of it as a series of theory fragments, and concepts only loosely connected. This helps to explain why we can think of the totality of beliefs of a human at any given time as most likely making up an inconsistent set, and nevertheless not concluding that we cannot use common sense. Humans can live with an inconsistent set of beliefs as long as they use at any time in any contexts only consistent parts of this set.

Explanatory patterns cut across the science–common sense distinction. We leave it an open question how much overlap there is or can be between the vocabularies of science and common sense, and how much of earlier science becomes the common sense of a subsequent period, except that the ingredients of strong common sense, for example, 'I', 'agent', 'decision' and so on. do not have that origin and remain parts of the permanent framework for the human condition.

V. REFERENCE AND BELIEF; QUO VADIS?

The earlier chapters have shown the differences between a project aiming at representing relations between parts of language and reality, and another that aims at a general characterization of human linguistic competence. Both projects view their subject matter under idealizations, but these are–as one would expect–different. For the first project one would want to abstract away from ambiguities, pragmatic factors, and syntax not motivated by semantic considerations. For the second those syntactic structures are important that play key roles in allowing the human mind to use language for a variety of purposes through historical periods, regardless of whether these structures are semantically motivated or not. One would also view as central features of language that facilitate human communication, regardless of whether this involves pure designative relations between language and reality.

The same dichotomy helps us in placing notions like reference and belief into proper perspective within the theory developed in this book. The term 'reference' has been used in a variety of ways. I shall use it to contrast with 'denotation' so as to isolate cases of speaker–audience relative singular identifications. In this sense it is certainly true that referring is something we do, not words. We use for such purposes a variety of types of locutions; for example, "that guy did it" or "I am missing the screwdriver". This use of language is characterized by a number of interesting conditions. First, as was pointed out by many philosophers, mistakes of use in language are possible, without endangering the success of the identification. For example, in a crowded room a speaker might successfully identify someone to a friend with the locution "the man with the wine in his glass", even if the man identified has champagne in his glass. Second, the success does not depend on objective truth but only on intersubjective agreement and coordination. Speakers in a linguistic community can identify for each other successfully certain putative entities even if after centuries those entities turn out not to exist. Finally, truth is less relevant to identificational success than what J. O. Urmson called aptness of reference.[12] In some contexts successful identification requires that I refer to the person to be identified as your brother rather than as "the banker in town" or with any number of other true marks that I know the hearer not to be aware of.

All of this suggests that this phenomenon belongs to what Chomsky has recently called "variety of performance systems", and Carnap, in earlier vocabulary, pragmatics. Still, it is a part of linguistic competence that we know of this possibility of language use, and know also of the types of expressions available to us for utilization.

There are also other types of singular reference; for example, "the smallest even number". In this case global uniqueness is necessary for success of reference, and this uniqueness is provided by the configuration of the meanings of the elements of the reference, without pragmatic and sociological factors.

This second type of reference depends on the meaning and what I will call here the denotation of the words involved. Furthermore, our primary assessment will be in terms of truth, not just what is needed in a variety of contexts for successful communications.

12. J. O. Urmson, "Criteria of Intentionally," *Proceedings of the Aristotelian Society* 42 (1968): 108–122.

The terms 'reference' and 'denotation' have been used in the literature in a variety of ways. I am using 'reference' to cover singling out one entity with the appropriate singular term or complex expression, and 'denotation' to cover the class of entities to which general term or complex expression can apply. Thus what Russell covered under "On Denoting" is treated here as a matter of reference, and some of what Strawson treats as a matter of referring is treated here as denotation, since it involves general terms and the domain of entities to which these can apply.

Within my view denotation is a matter of linguistic competence, while matters of reference involving nonsystematic names is a matter of what Chomsky now calls concerns for performance systems.

The denotation of a word or larger descriptive complex is the set of entities to which the linguistic expression truly applies. We cannot use just any expression we feel like and correctly describe a given collection of entities. Just as meaning is prescribed by the rules of the language, so too is denotation. Hence within my theory "people refer, but words denote". In more traditional semantic theories meanings directly determine denotation. In the lexical theory we have been developing, the determination of denotation is a three-level process. The first level constrains the parameters within which denotation has to be fixed and provides guidelines for the specification of the denotation-determining contexts. The second level is the set of such contexts, and on the third level we find the actual denotation relations.

The relation between linguistic expressions of the appropriate types and the denotata is that of language versus reality. But this "reality" includes what some might describe as elements "tainted" by human interest, perspective, and utilization. Hence on the first level meanings specify not complete propositions, but only partial ones.[13] Together with the creation of contexts on level 2, what the meaning specifies is propositional potential as well, since we saw how the lexicon can generate an indefinite number of new complexes. The elements denoted by expressions in contexts carry their own principles of individuation and persistence and other permanent qualitative structures the grasp of which is a part of linguistic competence. The fact that the reality we denote with the appropriate expressions is colored by human interest in some parts is not a reason to regard this aspect of language use as part of pragmatics or mere performance systems.

Thus truth and denotation do constitute a part of the structures that specify the objects of linguistic competence. At the same time the key semantic component of linguistic competence is the ability of form, change, and relate the set

13. I am indebted to suggestions by Scott Soames.

of concepts containing qualitative specifications and forming the explanatory schemes that within our account are what meanings yield.

So far we have talked about semantic and pragmatic notions. We now turn to their cognitive counterpart, namely belief. What is belief? Is it mere expectation, or only expectation with some form of self-reflection or awareness, or does human belief require the capacity to represent in one's mind logically and syntactically complex states of affairs? We have a wide range of options here, some making belief ascriptions applicable to certain types of animals as well, others restricting it to human cognition. From the linguistic point of view the syntactic S-node is important in the generation of structure for declarative sentences. It is assumed, then, in some cases, that whatever these declarative sentences express is the kind of abstract object that humans can understand and assess from the point of view of veracity (true, false, probable, etc.). This characterization differs sharply from purely psychological ones. Even these vary. According to some the concept of belief is invoked to explain behavior. According to others, it is a psychological state of which we can be aware introspectively.

In view of this diversity, it makes little sense to ask, in general: "Are there beliefs? Can the concept of belief ever be eliminated from an adequate theory of human cognition?"[14] From the agential point of view, the idea that belief is just a theoretical term to explain parts of behavior seems ludicrous. A human agent plans, and plans require the conceptualization of alternatives and the weighing of alternatives in a decision from the points of view of probability and desirability. This conceptualization of alternatives and their assessments is what I call in a minimal sense belief. In this sense we can hardly avoid positing beliefs as parts of our conceptual framework, whether we favor or oppose behaviorism, introspectionism, and so on. For my purposes this commitment to belief is all I need. As I said earlier, my theory discourages philosophers (or anyone else) from making predictions about empirical matters "for eternity." I tend to reduce such stances as close to zero as possible.

Our theory also assumes that beliefs become of theoretical interest primarily in those contexts in which the person articulating the belief and the one to whom it is communicated are not via the senses in touch with whatever state of affairs corresponds to the belief. As the story goes, humans started developing rationality and complex communicational procedures only after they got into tall grass and thus could see neither the object of belief nor the communicant.

14. E.g. S. Stich, From *Folk Psychology to Cognitive Science* (Cambridge, MA: MIT Press, 1983), and N. Chomsky, "Language and Nature," *Mind* 104, (1995), pp. 1–61.

Given then at least this richness and variation in beliefs, in what ways does our theory commit us to the existence of beliefs? Within this theory meanings are explanatory schemes, and these have beliefs as some of their elements. Some acceptance or rejection of what certain declarative S's express is required in order to make the notion of an explanatory scheme intelligible.

But as we saw, our beliefs are functions of the explanatory schemes within which they are embedded. Thus we cannot regard them as the basic building blocks of our cognitive life. I see trees out of my window. This experience leads me to form a number of beliefs. These beliefs are couched within a system of accepted explanatory patterns, having to do with causality, botanical phenomena and their origin as well as persistence, the explanatory power of some individuating principle over others, and so forth. Beliefs rest on concepts, and AFT is a further development of a claim made by others, that our beliefs and judgments of similarity rest on prior categorizations, and not the other way around.[15]

The status of beliefs in this theory can be summed up in the following. Are there beliefs in reality? Yes and no. On the one hand, there is no proof that an adequate conceptual system accounting for cognition and linguistic competence could not be built in which beliefs are not basic primitives. On the other hand, neither do we have arguments showing the possibility of such a theory. Then again, beliefs in our theory are not the basic building blocks of cognitive life and language use and understanding. These entities are elements in the basic specification of human thought and language interpretation, but are embedded in what we called explanatory schemes, holistic structures both semantically and cognitively in the sense that the whole is greater than the sum of parts. Finally, as we saw within current representations of cognition and linguistic competence, certain key phenomena centering on judgment, decision, planning, communication, are fundamental in the sense that any adequate theory of cognition and linguistic competence must account for these, whether the concept of belief is fundamental in these theories or not. The situation is analogous to geometry and physics. Certain universal human experiences of space, time, and persistence of concrete objects are fundamental, and theories of physics and geometry must account for these even if their primitives do not correspond to commonsense notions of time, space, and material object.

This completes then our outline of a conception of *Homo sapiens* as *Homo*

15. L. Rips, "Similarity, Typicality, and in Categorization," *Similarity and Analogical Reasoning* S. Vasniadou and A. Ortony, eds., (Cambridge, MA: MIT Press, 1989), pp. 21–57 and "Similarity and the Structure of Categories," *Bridges Between Psychology and Linguistics* in D. Napol and J. Keyl, (Erlbaum, 1991), pp. 35–53.

explanans. Within it explanation-seeking and forming guides our cognitive life, informing both how we form and revise beliefs as well as the basic structures of lexical meanings. We have seen that a viable conception of explanation and understanding can be sketched that consists of more than mere beliefs and logic; it has room for holistic insights as well. I also presented arguments why these structures are fundamental both for cognition and for semantics.

We have seen as well that certain facts point to the productive or generative nature of lexical meaning, and correspondingly on the psychological plane, to a kind of creativity additional to what Chomsky described in his earlier writings. Word and phrase meanings contain propositional potential; with an indefinite set of complexes to be formed, new concepts and links between these–hence new propositions–arise constantly in our uses of words and sentences. We should not think of this merely as continuing further specifications, but also as cross-classifications. For example, what is a walk for a baby is not a walk for an adult. Hence there are in many cases no denotations "out there," what is or is not in the denotation of types of 'walk' differs and can conflict with each other. Hence no simple denotational assignments can do justice to the complexity of lexical semantics.

If someone steeped in modern analytic philosophical traditions were to ask, How then, does language relate to reality?, our answer would be that there is no uniform way. My theory agrees with Wittgenstein's later writings and Chomsky's recent suggestions on this point. There are a variety of different ways in which parts of language are related to various parts and aspects to reality. Practical use, decision and planning, and mere curiosity enable us to place parts of language and reality in different relations, some "tainted" by pragmatic considerations some less so, some centering on truth, some more on insight.

This picture should also have important consequences for artificial intelligence and so-called knowledge representation models. If my theory is more or less correct, then knowledge should not be represented as a static web of concepts with various paths crisscrossing between the nodes, but rather, a set of nodes related via explanatory links, and with the constant potential to create further concepts by differentiations and cross-classifications. Spelling this out in detail is a project for the future.

Much was said in this chapter about understanding. How well can we explain human understanding? How well can we understand it? The final chapter takes up these questions.

CHAPTER 6

IS THE HUMAN MIND PARTIALLY INSCRUTABLE?

In the preceding three chapters I spelled out the generative and creative aspects of lexical meaning and its cognitive processing, and linked them to the conception of humans as primarily explanation-seeking and -forming creatures. In this chapter we shall lift out certain salient aspects of the analysis given so far, and on the basis of these present an argument supporting the thesis that the human understanding of human understanding must at any given time be only partial. But first we shall place this conception into the context of various other approaches showing limitations on human knowledge. These other approaches propose limitations on *what* can be known, but do not show that we cannot know or understand certain modes or aspects of human understanding.

I. LIMITATIONS ON HUMAN KNOWLEDGE

There are some obvious ways in which human knowledge is limited. We cannot know at any given time everything that is to be known. We cannot know now what all the things are that are or can be known today, and we have no ways of knowing what all the things are that will be known in the future. These limitations, however, do not prevent us from knowing what knowledge is—the acceptance of something true and having complete justification for this acceptance. The domain of what we can know is a set of true propositions. What should count as complete justification may vary from one area, such as mathematics, to another, such as physics, and there may be disagreements on what the natures of various kinds of completeness are. But these factors do not prevent us from having a general conception, in outline, of what knowledge is.

One important way in which we can have complete justification is when we have a proof for what we accept as true. Thus one would hope that in arithmetic, we could prove every proposition that is true. There is, however, an important result by Kurt Gödel that shows such a dream to be illusory. Nagel and Newman describe the situation aptly.

> it was assumed that each sector of mathematical thought can be supplied with a set of axioms sufficient for developing systematically the endless totality of true propositions about the given area of inquiry.
>
> Gödel showed that this was impossible to do. The "axiomatic method" has its limitations... which rule out the possibility that even the ordinary arithmetic of the integers can ever be fully axiomatized. There will be some true proposition not provable.[1]

This "incompleteness" is certainly not a trivial limitation on human knowledge. Its discovery is one of the great feats of the logic of the twentieth-century. But while it is a limitation on what we can know, it still leaves us with the general conception sketched above of what knowledge is. As we go on, we shall see that there are reasons to suppose that in the case of understanding and explanation we may never have a complete grasp of the nature of these units, semantic and cognitive. In short, this result places limitations on the domain of what we can know but leaves intact the question of whether we can characterize understanding and explanation in terms of essential features.

Another claim of limitations on what we can know and understand is the positing of intentionality, as a fundamental and indefinable part of human cognitive processing. Thus such activities as worshipping, hoping, seeking, respecting, are interpreted as intentional. Many philosophers have claimed that we can explain intentional notions only with reference to one another, and that we can never break out of this circle.

One response to this claim is to accept it but then turn it back on itself. If the intentional notions form a circle, why not construe the extensional notions also as forming a circle?[2] Within each circle the items can be explained only in terms of other members of the respective circle, and the two circles can be ex-

1. E. Nagel, and J. Newman, *Gödel's Proof* (New York: New York University Press, 1960), p. 6.
2. J. Moravcsik, *Thought and Language* (Routledge: London, 1990), pp. 132–138.

plained fully only in contrast with each other. Analyticity, intension, synonymy, and so on form one circle, denotation, extension, coextensiveness another.

Why should the fact that what we know falls into these two classes be a limitation on human knowledge? Our general characterization of what knowledge is still holds. We divide what we know into different areas in any case, such as the apriori and the empirical. Why should this not be still another basic dichotomy?

Empiricists think that unless we can reduce items to the extensional and physical, the terms are not well understood. They also claim that the intensional can never be within the reach of scientific understanding. But, as we saw earlier, these are arbitrary assumptions. We have no a priori argument showing that it is impossible for physics to someday regard one of its domains as constituting an intentional system.

If there are these two circles, this places some limitation on human knowledge in terms of how uniform the domain is, but it does not show that we cannot characterize in general terms what knowledge is.

There is also the problem of how to characterize intentionality in semantic terms. Lack of existential import? (if John worships x it does not follow that there is an x). Lack of substitutivity in the description of the object? (If John worships Aphrodite, and she is the most temperamental goddess, it does not follow that John worships the most temperamental goddess.) As J. O. Urmson has shown, none of the characterizations given in recent times is adequate.[3] The considerations presented above, however, do not depend on any particular technical delineation of the intentional.

Another possible source of limitations on human knowledge might be self-referentiality. Can we know knowledge? Here we need to distinguish the phenomenon of self-referentiality in general from specific species of it. There is nothing problematic about some cases of self-referentiality. For instance, the word 'short' is short, and in some languages the word corresponding to 'difficult' is difficult to pronounce. There are, however, cases falling under a certain species that do cause problems. One such sentence is, notoriously, "This sentence is false."

There is a treatment within the semantics of formal languages developed by Tarski that shows ways of dissolving the resulting paradox by relativizing truth and falsehood to languages, and developing a hierarchy of languages.[4] In

---

3. J. Urmson, "Criteria of Intentionality," *Proceedings of the Aristotelian Society* suppl. Vol. 42 (1968): 108–22.

4. A. Tarski, "The Concept of Truth in Formalized Languages." Reprinted in *Logic, Semantics, and Meta-mathematics.*

short, the problem is not with self-referentiality in general but with sentences assessing their own semantic value.

The problem does not arise only within the framework of formal languages. The sentence just quoted as an illustration is a part of a natural language. Some remedy has to be developed in any systematic semantics dealing with either formal or natural languages. But though the type of sentence may be a limitation on what we can know, once more, it is not a limitation on understanding knowledge in general.

Still another alleged source of limitation is provided by the fact that in any system of concepts arranged according to definability, with a set of primitive indefinables and then derived defined terms, there must be something that is left undefinable. The conclusion is supposed to follow that because these notions are indefinable, we cannot really know them, or know what they are. The structure we are supposed to have in mind is analogous to a set of axioms and then the derived theorems according to rigidly defined rules of inference.

Applying all of this to natural languages we are presented with two conceptions. According to one, the terms in a natural language are interdefinable; so there are no "basic" primitives. What we take as primitive in clarifying the lexical meanings within a given language is a matter of choice. According to another view, there may be some "natural primitives" on the basis of considerations of our cognitive and perceptual structures. So color terms, for example, purely phenomenally interpreted, may be such "natural" primitives. More interesting cases are 'number' in ordinary use, or 'set' in the language of logic.

For our purposes it does not matter which of these alternatives we take. What needs to be challenged is the assumption that knowing what something is must be articulated in terms of having a definition of it. When we look at actual practice, this seems patently false. There are many ways in which we can explain what the nature of a given primitive is. We can contrast it with certain other basic notions. Such is the example sketched earlier, the extensional–intentional (or intensional) contrast. Or we can show how the notion of a set enters into axioms, theorems, how we can use it in different applications, etc. In some cases rational reflection shows that certain notions must be taken as primitive, and also that we can learn what these are. An obvious case in that category is the concept of health. There may be discussions as to how to apply it to various contexts, what are obstacles to it, but the World Health Organization will be discussing *these* issues, and not what health is. At the same time, it is a useful notion, for it plays a vital role in characterizing what medicine and healing are.

Thus I conclude that the fact that we cannot define something within a certain scheme is not a limitation on knowledge. We can know what that notion is, and what the nature of the denotatum is by the use of a variety of procedures other than definition.

If someone insists that unless you can define it, you don't know it, our response is not only that this is an arbitrary restriction, but also that in any reasonable sense we can *explain* such notions and we can bring people to *understand* what these are. So within such a framework the restricted concept of knowledge is overshadowed by the wider notion of explanation and understanding concerning the nature of things. And these two epistemic notions are at the center of our investigation in any case. These considerations affect limitations on what we can know or understood, but do not affect, for example, a general characterization of knowledge as completely justified true belief.

II. FACTORS UNDERLYING THE HYPOTHESIS OF INSCRUTABILITY

This section relies on the analysis of understanding and explanation sketched earlier. To understand what the nature of something is, when the understanding is made explicit, is to be able to give an explanation of it. Likewise, explanations of what something is–if successful–yield understanding. If I understand what 'emergency' means, then I should be able to give an explanation of it in terms of the four-factored scheme that AFT contains.

We shall now review the AFT analysis of 'understand' and 'explain'. Then we shall single out four aspects of these analyses: conceptual density, the productivity and creativity of the lexicon, the holistic nature of understanding and its objects, and the priority of explanatory schemes over mere information processing. We shall discuss each of these, and then show how on their basis the argument for partial inscrutability of the human mind by humans can be articulated.

Let us consider the AFT analysis of 'understand' (in the sense of "understand what") m-factors: time and abstract, hence cross-categorial. I want to bring out of this analysis the following concepts. First, the distinction between granularity and density, then the productive nature of the lexicon, and the holistic nature of understanding, all of which we need for the argument supporting partial inscrutability.

This is because understanding requires an object, and the object must be an abstract complex. (Attempts at nominalism, finitism, even when undertaken by outstanding logicians and mathematics in the first half of this century, have failed.)

s-factor: understanding is a state; hence its representation as taking place within a time interval, represented as a set of points. Unlike 'walk' there are no temporal gaps in the representation. If someone understands and then he does not, we say that he forgot, and then may have later started a new state of understanding.

The principle of individuation specifies that we individuate states of understanding by agent, object, and continuity of state. Two different persons can understand the same thing; still, these are two different psychological states. Likewise, the same person can understand a theorem in mathematics and also a theory in biology; there are two states in this case.

The persistence principle requires persistence of agent, sameness of object, and continuity of state.

The distinguishing factor must separate understanding from mere acceptance, belief, knowledge, having a mere description of the object, and so forth. Hence:

> to articulate to oneself and others in appropriate ways a meaningful complex into an appropriate whole with parts and a structure in which the whole is more than the sum of parts, so that it makes the object intelligible and presents it as an appropriately adequate unit for conceptual use.

Each of these clauses is needed in order to reflect various aspects of understanding, and the insertion of 'appropriate' at key points is crucial; these are the signs that enable us to move within AFT from level 1 to levels 2 and 3.

a-factor: Human or sufficiently humanlike entity (the lexicon stays neutral on such metaphysical questions as to whether only humans can understand or also angels, machines, etc.).

f-factor: The achievement and maintenance of the state results in regarding the previously problematic as nonproblematic, and enables us to use the abstract object as the starting point for interpretations, proofs, and other means of illumination.

For the purposes of illuminating the density, holism, and priority we shall restrict ourselves to considering this, level 1, analysis, since bringing in the other levels is not necessary.

Let us now consider 'explain'.

m-factor: time and abstract, hence cross-categorial
s-factor: activity, and in particular process verb–that is, an activity that has a final culmination point in terms of qualitative specifications of a state obtained.

The principle of individuation is similar to that of 'understand', that is, object, agent, differences, with the exception that the semantics allows here temporal gaps; one can explain and then after a pause continue the same process.

The same considerations apply to the persistence criteria.

The distinguishing criteria have to separate explaining from mere informing, information gathering, predicting, or describing.

Hence, roughly: the activity of articulating a structure that enables us to see what was problematic or unclear as making sense, having appropriate unity, and scope, in terms appropriate to the subject at hand.

a-factor: human or humanlike
f-factor: It functions as a foundation for beliefs, predictions, and further progress in investigations.

Here again, we see the need for the "gaps of appropriateness" that then lead us to the other levels of analysis.

These analyses show us that in both cases (explanation and understanding, or E/U) we are dealing with conceptual articulation, be this the charting of one concept or that of a whole network of these. With this as our background we turn to certain salient features of the concepts to be explained and understood.

We need the contrast between conceptual granularity and density, because the fact that concepts are dense is needed in the argument to follow. The denotation of 'human' is granular. We understand what it is to be a human when we know how to count, under ideal circumstances, humans as distinct entities. The same holds for abstract collections such as numbers (especially positive integers). But now let us consider dividing concepts themselves. In how many ways can we divide the concept of art, or of number? There are infinite ways, as Plato already suggested in his work on so-called divisions. Arts can be intellectual or not, productive or not, concerned with human welfare or not; divisions can be dichotomous, or having ten parts and so forth. Thus there are infinite ways of articulating a concept. Furthermore, there are no absolute minimal parts. What is an absolutely minimal basic unit of art? Drawing distinction can, in theory go on, forever. Numbers can be divided "naturally" into odd and even, but with a little imagination we can find an indefinitely large number of alternate ways–clearly not all equally illuminating–to anticipate the argument to come. In this respect concepts are like pictures, as I will show. This distinction is crucial because we can specify the nature of granular collections in certain ways that do not apply to the conceptually dense units.

CONCEPTUAL DENSITY AND GRANULARITY

The collection of positive integers is a granular collection. It is made up of so many distinct elements. Sound, time, weight, and so on are dense. We need to introduce units and then in terms of these, measurement in order to end up with a granular collection. The distinction cuts across the spatiotemporal abstract dichotomy. There is also conceptual density. For example, what are the "basic parts" of a painting? We can articulate a painting in an infinite and indefinite number of ways, depending on the aesthetic viewpoint from which the interpretation is presented. As mentioned earlier, when we consider a concept like health, nation, or walking we encounter the same situation. It is not only the matter of there being no minimal parts to some overall analysis of health. (The minimal parts are always relative to a given analysis). It is also the case that one can divide kinds of health from so many points of view. Furthermore, the articulations crisscross each other. What is one unit in one analysis may be divided in another analysis into three parts and be absorbed by three other units. Another good example of conceptual density is the metaphysical notion of a particular. This is any entity that has spatiotemporal nonrecurrent position. From this it follows that there is no well-formed answer to the question: "How many particulars are there in this room?" Depending on how we "cut up" the space inside the room, we get different and equally good answers. At times linguists mark this kind of distinction with the contrast "mass versus count term". But my point here is not syntactical. It is purely ontological. For example, 'particular' as a noun pluralizes but, as we saw, this is purely a linguistic convention. In fact the collection of particulars is no more granular than the water parts in a cup of water.

We use concepts in a variety of ways, and require stability for such uses. In some context we deal only with naval emergencies, while in others with intellectual emergencies in a science. But such investigation-relative demarcations should not blind us to the essential density of most concepts, everyday or scientific. Thus concepts as such must be treated as dense. This has implications for how to delineate the articulations that yield something explanatory and intelligible. We are presumably looking for a function that will separate the explanatory articulations from those that lack this quality. We encounter difficulties in this. Ideally we are looking for a function and associated algorithm, such as we find in the case of positive integers. We have an infinite collection, but we can generate the members to any degree of magnitude with the help of the well-defined successor function. In the same way we can generate the appropriate units of a given measurement system for length, for example. We impose the units on the nongranular mass that we find. The question we will have to face in the next section is whether we can have a function that separates in all conceptual analyses the intelligible and explanatory from those infinite ones that do not yield illumination. The key problem facing us is that concepts can be divided and hence articulated in infinitely many ways. Furthermore, many concepts do not have minimal parts. For example, knowledge does not have minimal parts. Any division into kinds of knowledge can be followed by further divisions. Of course, not all of these will be yielding understanding. Likewise, the concept of "concept" has no minimal parts. "The concepts we have" is always relative to a certain level of analysis. This analysis of "concept" cannot be carried to further parts and is senseless if taken in an absolute sense.

LEXICAL PRODUCTIVITY AND OPENNESS

Chapter 3 gave evidence for what we call the productivity of the lexicon. Lexical items have very general meaning specifications that provide guidelines for specifying denotation-fixing contexts. Let us consider now various ways of construing productivity. The clearest example is the generation of positive integers. We have an infinite domain that is generated by a function with the algorithm linked to the notion of a successor. One might think of the meanings of general terms as algorithms specifying a function that sorts out reality into the class of items that fall under the term, and the complement class. Our three-level analysis shows that this is an oversimplified conception. Furthermore, we have no way of making the "sense" or "meaning" of an expression into what is actually and formally an algorithm. We think in this context of a rule or set of instructions that is analogous to the formal notion of an algorithm.

We should contrast now the algorithm associated with "even" with the instructions one might give in connection with the word 'use'. In the first case we have a decision procedure: take all of the positive integers; if divisible by 2, they are even, if not they are odd.

In the second case, we have nothing as rigorous as that. Using something requires an agent and an object in the broadest sense, treated as a means to some end. The underspecified nature of this notion entails that with different additions, completions, the resulting complex verb phrases will have different entailments.

Our semantic investigations showed that this is true also with verbs that are not treated syntactically as underspecified, such as 'walk' or 'read'. The meaning specification will provide general instructions in terms of achievement, temporal anatomy, criteria of success, means used, kind of agent required. Within the frame set, different contexts, linguistically marked or not, will then demarcate denotation ranges and instructions on how to separate what falls under the term in that context and what does not. As Pustejovsky showed, in many cases the context is marked linguistically. "She used the car", the hammer, her head. In others it is not–for example, ethical disagreements: "He is using me". What counts in any given context as use?

So there is the productivity in mathematics that we can characterize as providing an algorithm to generate members of an infinite set. There are instructions or alleged criteria that philosophers and linguists used to associate with general terms. Then there are the guidelines in AFT. What is of special interest to us is that in the case of 'understand', the guidelines, such as they are, resemble algorithms even less than in the other types of cases listed.

As the AFT analysis given shows, understanding is a cognitive state in which we can articulate a variety of complexes into parts as well as a holistic structure that makes them more than the mere sum of parts. This is quite clear within AFT in the case of understanding lexical meanings. The meaning can never be the mere sum of denotation-fixing contexts and related denotata at any given time. There is the potential in the meaning to provide the background for new and still newer denotation-fixing contexts. This is what gives meanings a holistic nature and thus the corresponding cognitive state of understanding the analogous form. There are, however, many other things besides lexical meanings that we understand. We understand theorems, proofs, empirical theories, ethical justifications, biographies. Thus the domain over which we would have to extend the function picking out the cases if understanding is not clearly delineated. In the case of 'use', as long as humans are participants in means–end structured activities, there is the possibility of delineating what using amounts to. But how do we give an analogous characterization for contexts for understanding? Understanding involves articulating complexes into parts. But the nature of these complexes, and thus also of the parts is quite indeterminate. It can change not only at any time from one cognitive challenge to another, but also through history. What counts as understanding at one stage does not count as understanding at another. This by itself would not be very significant. For example, what counts as using technology in one case does not count as such in a later one. But in the case of understanding the differences are not matters of progress. The differences involve different structural configurations that seem explanatory in one framework and not in a subsequent one. For instance, at an early stage it was deemed explanatory if we can analyze physical constituents into basic masses. Subsequently, a pioneer like Democritus proposed–successfully–that the alleged basic masses were the explananda, and that we needed very special kinds of countables as underlying the masses. Why did this seem so illuminating? Why was it accepted by so many thinkers? If we had the right "function" sorting out the intelligible from the nonexplanatory, we would have the answer. I shall use this point in the construction of our "limitation argument".

HOLISM

The notion of holism is easier to illustrate than to define. There are different notions of holism. Some philosophers think of a science like physics as being tested against experience only in its entirety. Others have metaphysical views according to which there are wholes that are ontologically prior to their constituents. We need for our purposes only the notion of a whole that cannot be reduced to a mere sum of its parts. The most obvious examples come from biology and technology. An animal is a holistic unit, or as it is called at times, an "organic unit." This means that a mere enumeration of the parts will not suffice as specification of the whole. In the nonholistic cases it does. Thus, if we took the time and energy to label and enumerate all of the parts of a certain size of a pile of sugar, then we would have specified the unit: "all the sugar on this table." In biology we need to understand how the various parts work together before we can understand an animal or an organ. The same holds for political units. A country cannot be reduced to the sum of its population and land. A country declares war, not the sum of the population.

The same phenomenon surfaces in connection with artifacts. A car is a holistically functioning unit. The mechanic must understand how the parts work together in order to understand the functioning of the whole unit.

There are various holistic units on the abstract plane. Perhaps the most perspicuous kind is a set. We define identity conditions on sets in terms of sameness of membership. Two sets are identical if and only if they have the same members. But this does not mean that the set and the sum of its members are the same entity. For example, Napoleon and the unit-set whose only member is Napoleon are not the same entity.

We move to even stronger holistic units when we consider properties and their instantiations. Two properties are not identical just because their instantiations coincide. The set of creatures with kidneys and the set of creatures with heart, are presumably the same set, but the property of being a creature with kidneys and the property of being a creature with heart are not the same.

Theories, proofs, and so on can be interpreted as made up either of sets alone, or of sets and properties; in any case, holistically.

The lexical theory we considered raises the specter of a unit defined intensionally, but corresponding to which there is nothing like an algorithm. Let us take again a scientific theory. Suppose that you want to define an explanatory theory as one with a certain deductive-nomological structure. The theory would still be a whole to be understood, but the holism would be weak. And we would be able to assign to "explanatory theory" a function and something analogous to an algorithm. The function would pick out all of those logical combinations of sentences that have the right domain and the appropriate logical structure.

I have argued there is no logical structure that by itself defines what is explanatory. So we need to specify an additional factor. It seems that we can do this only in terms of its results. But we do not seem to have anything vaguely resembling an algorithm for this "additional factor". As K. Manders's beautiful work shows, we can cite and analyze examples in which there are two ways of explaining geometrical phenomena, equal in terms of covering the "data", and neither better in some purely logical sense than the other. Still, everyone among the experts agrees which gives the more insightful account.[5] The nature of the elements of the explanatory complexes change. These can be propositions, or models, or analogies, etc. We do not have an adequate way of characterizing for all times and contexts what the elements of something explanatory must be.

Thus we see that the notions of understanding and explanation bring with them not only holism, but special problems attached in these cases to these structures.

PRIORITY

The priority claim places a great burden on the objectivity claim for understanding and explanation. For let us suppose that the priority claim is true, and explanation and understanding are merely subjective phenomena, subject to

5. K. Manders, "Logical and Conceptual Relationships in Mathematics," *Logic Colloquium '85* (Amsterdam: Elseviere), pp. 193–211.

fashions, extrascientific considerations, and the like. If that is so, and the explanatory frameworks underlie information processing, then the whole edifice is open to the charge of subjectivism and relativism. This is a price most researchers will not want to pay unless absolutely necessary. Note that mere change in technology and economic conditions only constrain the choice of models, scientific tools, and so on. This by itself does not show that understanding and the explanatory are subjective or relative.

The priority claim places information processing into proper perspective. It no longer serves as what is basic to human rationality and knowledge representation. To be sure, it remains a necessary ingredient. We cannot have explanations, and there will be no objects for understanding if we lack altogether information. But information processing is now seen as selecting information and structuring it according to predesigned schemata. These in general form are likely to be innate, with specifications or new variations emerging from interaction with the environment.

To the suggestion that positing the four factors of AFT gives a criterion for intelligibility, the answer is that if correct, the AFT scheme may be a necessary condition, but it is not a sufficient one. Democritus and his predecessors both followed–implicitly–the AFT structure, but within that Democritus's model seemed at that time and context more explanatory than the "mass explanations". What is it in humans the application of which renders in a certain conceptual context one structure as explanatory, and in another its opposite? Density becomes relevant in this discussion. We cannot specify a set of distinct elements as what is relevant to physical explanations across history. The options are also unlimited because of nongranularity. Hence, while we may be able to provide a historical explanation for a specific change in what seemed illuminating, it is difficult to see how we can attain the abstract general level at which we can generalize.

III. THE ARGUMENT FOR PARTIAL INSCRUTABILITY

In preparation for the argument, I tried to forge a concept of understanding, we argued for the density of concepts in general, and have shown the productivity of the lexicon. To set the problem of understanding understanding let us review in outline Chomsky's characterization of grammar and then see the obstacles in the way of trying to give an analogous characterization of human understanding.

Let us consider in a language the set of minimal syntactic units, and consider the set made up of all of the possible combinations of these units, and the building of larger units.

Now let us construct a function that will divide this set into the part that contains all and only the well-formed complexes, and the other part that contains the ill-formed ones. (Since we are dealing with sets with infinite membership, recursive devices are needed for this operation.) This function gives you what grammaticality achieves. The algorithm for computing this function can be seen as the grammar of the language at a certain stage. (See Figure 1.)

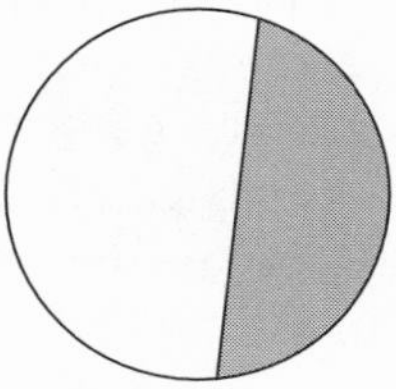

FIGURE 1

In this figure the whole circled area represents the class of all possible combinations of minimal syntactic units. The shaded area represents the well-formed complex expressions. The line separating off the shaded area is the function, the calculation, computation, or specification of which is the task of the grammar.

In order to talk about the grammar of a natural language within stages in which the syntax remained reasonably stable, we must consider the set as projected over time, and the function to separate out the subclasses within each temporal part. (See Figure 2.)

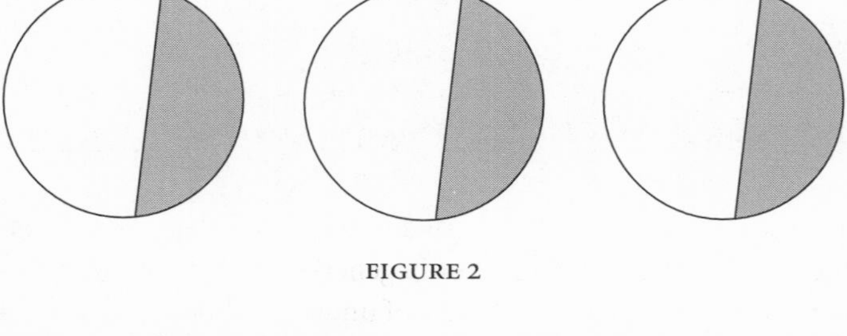

FIGURE 2

If we want to characterize grammars over different languages, we need to take what we have so far and extend it over the different collections made up of parts of the different languages. Universal grammar will be the common elements we discover as we draw our "line" across different languages, and consider successful modes of constructions.

The analogue to algorithm will be the mode of computation. We then attempt to find indirect evidence for (1) which modes are likely to correspond to how humans do this interpretation, and (2) in which ways the common element and the others help delineate what the humanly possible grammars are in contrast with all sorts of merely logical sorts of grammars.

Herewith three remarks about this pattern of characterization. First the basic collection is granular; the minimal well-formed elements are discrete. Second, we are dealing with functions that connect formally characterizable structures, and there are fairly reliable tests for success. Testing for grammaticality is not a simple task, but a combination of factors help to establish reasonable hypotheses. The lines may or may not be very rigid; "in between" cases do not affect the main issues with which we deal here. Third, the intensions underlying the function that we seek, the ones the human organism uses are also subject to indirect testing of a variety of sorts developed by psycholinguists.

Let us try to construct now an analogous characterization for human understanding. We consider now a given concept and its possible articulations. Since concepts are "dense," this will be an infinite class. We now construct a function that is supposed to pick out those articulations that are explanatory and give us insight in contrast with those that do not. An example is classifying biological species in theoretically interesting ways in contrast with ways culled from the diaries of famous naturalists, merely describing habitats. (See Figure 3.)

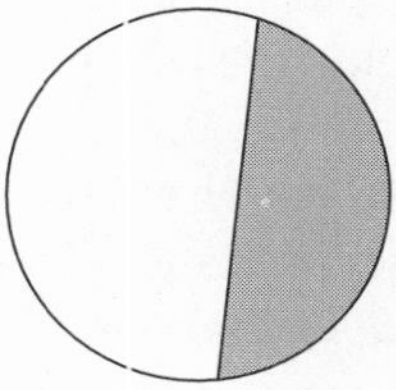

FIGURE 3

In this figure the circled area represents the indefinite collection of conceptual parts and ways of relating them. The shaded area represents the relations, or conceptualizations that are explanatory or illuminating. The line separating off the shaded area is the function sorting out the explanatory from the nonexplanatory. If we knew the procedure that specifies this function, then we would know what–at least in this restricted context–illumination and insight is.

At any given time we have a set of concepts and complexes of concepts related within theories and explanations in general. For sake of simplicity we represent all of these entities, complex in a context or not, as a collection of sets, and draw lines across them that jointly demarcate the articulations that yield understanding from the domain of those that do not. (See Figure 4.)

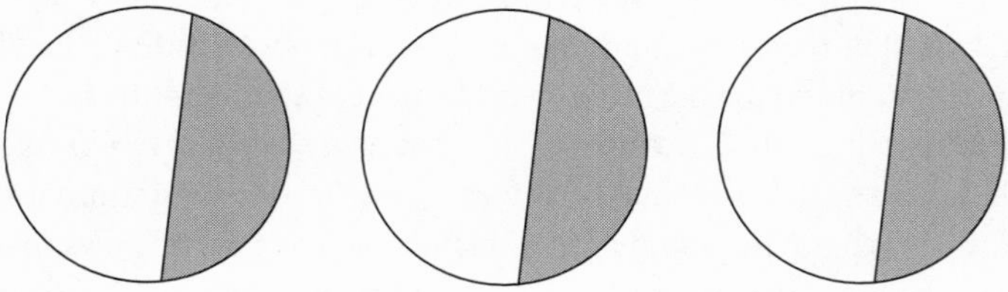

FIGURE 4

I made three remarks about the representation of explaining grammar. What can we say about this representation of human understanding? First, in contrast with the case of grammar, the collection of basic elements is not granular but dense. This makes the gathering of the set of all articulations even in any one concept at any one historical stage a purely idealized theoretical process, which humans could not carry out.

Second, let us consider the elusive intensional nature of what is to be "computed." At bottom level we have an indefinite number of conceptual "parts." A way of linking these is a conceptualization. Given the density of the basic level, and the lack of rules for conceptualizations in general, we have an indefinite collection of conceptualizations. Then we need to separate the explanatory and illuminating conceptualizations. Presumably we do this by a specifying what properties the explanatory must have. But given the indefiniteness of the basic elements and of the conceptualizations, the task of specifying the properties that all explanatory conceptualizations must have seems daunting. Our current conceptual armory does not provide the tools that would be needed for constructing the rule (rules) of the explanatory under these circumstances.

What conclusions can we draw from this comparison? Let us distinguish a number of different claims one might test.

C1. There is no computable function that would sort out in general the humanly intelligible, illuminating, and explanatory from other articulations.

C2. There may or may not be such a function; we can never know whether it exists or not.

C3. Even if there is such a function, at any given stage in history, humans would never be capable of understanding fully what it is.

If C1 is true, what follows? We can say then that the set of all humanly explanatory and illuminating structures is not recursively enumerable. It is possible, after all, that the explanatory is like etiquette. There is no common core, but at the same time, at any given context there is intersubjective agreement on what "goes" and what does not. If this is so, then given the priority claim advanced earlier, this limits the richness of rationality that we can invoke to characterize the whole human cognitive enterprise.

But what is the evidence for C1? All of the considerations so far are epistemological. We don't know how to "compute the function," we don't have the right evidence, or rigorous ways of characterizing the domain over which the function is to range. None of these contradict the ontological claim that C1 denies. For all we know, there may be such a function but it will remain unknown to humans. Even here the caveat is needed: "for all we know *now*"; these informal considerations do not provide sufficient evidence to *prove* that we in principle can or cannot know the truth of C1.

This leads us to C2. C1 makes an ontological claim, C2 an epistemological one. But the problems about conceptual density, the productivity of concepts and meanings, and the holistic nature of understanding and its objects merely provide formidable obstacles in the path of proving or refuting C2; by themselves these obstacles do not amount to a proof.

Let us turn, then, to C3. The following considerations render this claim likely to be true. What is it for humans at any stage *within* the stream of explanations and states of understanding to form an illuminating conception of the whole? It is to consider—if data is available—the whole variety of possible cases of human illumination, and find this illuminating from the necessarily limited vantage point of understanding at which the researchers in question find themselves. Might there not be structures that are illuminating in one conceptual context, but the illuminatory force of which is not conceivable within another conceptual context with its own positive and negative characterizations of what is illuminating? At this point, one can only speculate. For example in earlier chapters we considered the possibility that in physics some parts of the subatomic realm will be interpreted as intentional systems. Can we really understand why and how this would be illuminating? And yet a negative answer to this question does not show that such a state of affairs is not possible.

We are told that in some parts of physics the notion of an event splitting into two spatially distinct parts but retaining its identity is not only conceivable but has explanatory value. Can we conceive of a situation in which this is also true of what we call material objects?

Pondering c3 helps us in understanding not only the limitations of our own understanding but also the limitations on what the pondering of such human limitations can and cannot indicate.

The following is an informal argument leading to partial inscrutability. The argument assumes that unlike logical modalities (on some accounts), epistemic modalities do not collapse when iterated. Thus "necessarily necessarily p" can be interpreted as amounting to "necessarily p", and the same has been claimed about possibility. But this does not work for knowledge and understanding. We can know that a certain mathematical statement is true without knowing that we know that. Also, we can understand a certain theory without having an understanding of that understanding.

Let us now consider a function that demarcates at a given time what we understand from what we do not understand. Let us also assume that—under idealization—we know what that function is. In order to understand this function we need to have a grasp of all of the cases of understanding that are parts of our conceptual framework at a temporal/historical point. But what we said about the productivity of the lexicon shows that at one point we will encounter complexes of concepts that are illuminating but were not considered by us so far. For there are no recursive devices to capture all of the productive potentials of combinations of linguistic items. Hence there is no guarantee that there will not be new modes of understanding needed to cope with new conceptual combinations. So now we have a new mode of understanding added to the ones we considered. We can represent this as u1 + u2 + u3 + u4 + ... + un and u*, the last representing the understanding of the new combination. We can bracket all of this and represent our understanding of understanding as U(...). But this is now a modified notion of the understanding that we had when we considered only u1 + u2 + ... + un. So when we added u*, we called also for a new understanding of human understanding that includes this case also. Hence we have U2(U1 + u! + ...). But now we need—in order to understand human understanding—a new mode of understanding, U3. It is easy to see how this argument will force us to come up with new modes of understanding, not regarded as intelligible before. Some philosophers have said that some items are "conceivably becoming conceivable." But my point is that most likely there are items that are not conceivable to becoming conceivable, and nevertheless, they will become conceivable. At any given time we have only a partial understanding of the modes of human understanding. This argument could be strengthened if we add a historical dimension to our representation. The argument then shows that there are modes of understanding and patterns of explanation that at a previous point in time and conceptual context we would not have regarded as intelligible and yielding insight. But the density and lexical productivity claims show that this is also true of a reflection on all of the explanatory patterns and modes of understanding that we possess now. Partial diachronic intellectual blindness is preceded by partial synchronic intellectual blindness.

Universal grammar within the conception sketched is not a full grammar for any particular language but a partial structure and constraints within which local rules are formulated for specific languages. Likewise, the conception of understanding considered here would have a universal and local levels, with the latter filled in in various ways for different contexts.

The following survey should facilitate the comprehension of the complexity of the functions involved in this analysis.

Level 1. The articulations of one concept for one individual.
Level 2. The articulations of all concepts for one individual.
Level 3. The articulation of all concepts for one intellectual generation.
Level 4. The articulation of all concepts for generations across history.
Level 5. The understanding of the structures on level 4.

The key point of the argument sketched in this chapter is that there is no recursive way for us to generate all of the explanation demanding contexts and related explanatory structures for levels 3 and 4, and hence also not for 5.

The difficulties of formalizing the basic notions in terms of which we analyze understanding is their multiply intensional status. The formalizations in mathematical logic, so successful in this century, are always extensional. It is difficult to conceive of equally rigorous ways of capturing the intensional.

The speculations mentioned concern empirical matters, even if on a large scale. This brings us to the problem of testing. As Patrick Suppes remarked in lectures, many of our key cognitive processes (consciousness, illumination, etc.) take place without our having direct access to them. There are, of course, good reasons having to do with adaptation for this. If our cognitive processes of calculating, understanding, explaining, reasoning would be always open to introspection, then all of these processes would slow down to the point that the rational activities needed for survival and improvement of life would never get done at the required speeds. Be that as it may, this fact makes testing and gathering information about how these things take place in our mind very challenging.

These ruminations should not lead to nihilism, subjectivism, relativism. Nothing in these speculations about partial inscrutability force us to give up the claim of objectivity, either for our general explanatory frames, or the assessment of what is insightful and illuminating, or for the embedded information processing. Statements of the following sort: "creatures with such-and-such cognitive equipment and such-and-such environmental living space can realize their cognitive potentialities in optimal ways by the embodiment of such-and-such patterns" can be argued for rationally, and justified in objective ways. Limitations on understanding the cognitive equipment do not dictate losing faith in that equipment.

Much work remains to be done. We need many more examples of case studies of understanding working in the sciences, such as we find in the papers of K. Manders already mentioned. Instead of worrying too much about how other extrinsic factors influence the development of rational understanding, we should abstract from intervening factors as much as possible, and try to understand why and how different structures in different fields seem to the qualified human as illuminating.

What density and productivity, as explained in this book, suggest is that human concepts always have the potential for further articulation, reconceptualization, and refinement. This is not just an independent remark about human history, but a consequence of what lexical semantic structures are and what the human cognitive apparatus is that uses these structures. This follows from our three-level analysis, and the posits of creative cognitive structures that we need to posit in order to characterize lexical understanding. In philosophy it is traditional to analyze the diachronic in terms of a set of synchronic stages. This misses, somehow, the dynamic potential that on our analysis the fundamental cognitive structures of explanation, understanding, and use of lexical items possess. Finding the right rigorous framework for capturing this important human cognitive capacity is unfortunately beyond the scope of this essay.

This book opened with the picture of people in the tall grass making noises at each other. We saw some of the intricate structures that emerge and are necessary so that the noises can culminate in mathematics, science, philosophy, and poetry. Our appreciation of this need not be lessened by the plausibility of the hypothesis that we will most likely never understand completely either the nature of these structures or our cognitive processes that utilize them.

REFERENCES

Armstrong, S., L. Gleitman, H., Gleitman. 1983. "What Some Concepts Might Not Be" *Cognition.* 263–308. L. Gleitman, H. Gleitman, C. Miller, and R. Ostrin. 1996. "SIMILAR and similar Concepts" *Cognition* 55: 321–76.

Austin, J. 1961. *Philosophical Papers.* Ed. J. O. Urmson, and G. Warnock. Oxford: Oxford University Press.

Barwise, J., and J. Perry. 1983. *Situations and Attitudes.* Cambridge: MIT Press.

Bridgman, P. W. 1952. *The Nature of Some of Our Physical Concepts.* New York.

Bromberger, S. 1992. *On What We Know We Don't Know.* Chicago: University of Chicago Press.

Carlson, G. 1978. *Reference to Kinds in English.* New York: Garland.

Carnap, R. 1956. *Meaning and Necessity.* Chicago: University of Chicago Press.

Cartwright, R. 1962. "Propositions." In *Analytical Philosophy* Oxford: Blackwell, pp. 81-103.

Chomsky, N. 1965. *Aspects of the Theory of Syntax.* Cambridge: MIT Press.

———. 1992. "Explaining Language Use." *Philosophical Topics* 20: 205–231.

———. 1995. "Language and Nature." *Mind* 104: 1–61.

Churchland, P. 1988. *Matter and Consciousness,* rev. ed. Cambridge: MIT Press.

Davidson, D. 1967. "Truth and Meaning" *Synthese* 17: 304–323.

Feferman, S. 1991. "Working foundations–'91." In G. Corsi et al., eds., *Bridging the Gap: Philosophy, Mathematics and Physics.* Boston Studies in the Philosophy of Science 140, Kluwer, Dordrecht, 1993, pp. 99–124.

Frege, Gottlob. 1892. *Philosophical Writings.* Ed. M. Black and P. Geach. New York, Humanities Press, 1952, esp. pp. 56 ff.

———. 1923. "Compound Thoughts." Reprinted in E. Klemke, ed., *Essays on Frege.* Urbana: University of Illinois Press, 1968.

Gabbay, D., and J. Moravcsik. 1974. "Branching Quantifiers." *Theoretical Linguistics* 1: 139–157.

Gabbay, D., and J. Moravcsik. 1980. "Verbs, Events, and the Flow of Time." In C. Rohrer, ed., *Time, Tense, and Quantifiers.* Tübingen: Niemeyer, pp. 59–83.

Goodman, N. 1954. *Fact, Fiction, Forecast.* Cambridge: Harvard University Press.

Grice, H. P. 1957. "Meaning." *Philosophical Review* 66, and Schiffer, S. 1972. *Meaning.* Oxford: Clarendon Press.

Hacking, I. 1981. "Do We See through a Microscope?" *Philosophical Quarterly* 62: 305-322.

Hempel, C. 1950. "Problems and Changes in the Empiricist Criterion of Meaning." *Revue Internationale de Philosophie* 11.

Johnson-Laird P., and B. Bara. 1984. "Logical Expertise as Cause of Error: A Reply to Boolos." *Cognition* 17: 183–184.

Kitcher P. 1989. "Explanatory Unification and the causal Structure of the World." *Minnesota Studies in the Philosophy of Science* 13: 459–507.

Kluckhohn, C. 1985. *Mirror for Man.* Tucson: University of Arizona Press.

Kreisel, G. 1967. "Informal Rigour and Completeness Proofs." In *Problems in the Philosophy of Mathematics.* I. Lakatos, ed. Amsterdam: North Holland: 138–157.

Manders, K. 1987. "Logical and Conceptual Relationships in Mathematics." *Logic Colloquium '85.* Amsterdam: Elsevier, pp. 193–211.

———. 1994. "Diagram Contents and Representational Granularity." Mimeographed paper.

Montague, R. 1974. "English as a Formal Language." In R. Thomason, ed., *Formal Philosophy.* New Haven, CT: Yale University Press, pp. 188–221.

———. 1979. "The Proper Treatment of Mass Terms in English." In F. Pelletier, ed., *Mass Terms: Some Philosophical Problems.* Dordrecht: Reidel, pp. 173–178.

Moravcsik, J. 1965. "Strawson and Ontological Priority." In R. Butler, ed., *Analytical Philosophy,* Second Series. Oxford: Blackwell, pp. 106–119.

———. 1973. "Mass Terms in English." In J. Hintikka, J. Moravcsik, and P. Suppes, eds., *Approaches to Natural Language.* Dordrecht, Reidel, pp. 263–285, 301–308.

———. 1974. *Logic and Philosophy for Linguistics.* The Hague: Mouton.

———. 1975. *Understanding Language.* The Hague: Mouton.

———. 1979. "Understanding." *Dialectica* 33: 201–216.

———. 1981. "La Radicale Rottura di Chomsky nei Confronti della Tradizione Moderna." In N. Chomsky, ed., *Regole e Rappresentazioni.* Milano il Saggiatore, pp. 233–237.

———. 1981. "Frege and Chomsky on Thought and Language." *Midwest Studies in Philosophy*: 105–123.

———. 1987. "Conceptions of the Self and the Study of Cognition." In *Logic, Philosophy of Science, and Epistemology,* Vienna: Hölder, Pichler, and Tempsky, pp. 294–302.

———. 1990. *Thought and Language.* London: Routledge.

———. 1992. *Plato and Platonism.* Oxford: Blackwell, ch. 6.

———. 1994. "Is Snow White?" In P. Humphries, ed. *Patrick Suppes: Scientific Philosopher.* Amsterdam: Kluwer, pp. 71–87.

———. 1994. "Genericity and Linguistic Competence." *Theorie des Lexicons, Arbeiten des Sonderforschungsbereich 282* no. 54, Wuppertal.

Moravcsik, M. 1987. *Musical Sounds.* New York: Paragon House.

Nagel, E. and J. Newman. 1960. *Gödel's Proof.* New York: New York University Press.

Nunberg, G., I. Sag, and T. Wasow. 1994. "Idioms." *Language* 70: 491–537.

Pustejovsky, J. 1995. *The Generative Lexicon.* Cambridge: MIT Press.

Putnam, H. 1955. "The Meaning of 'Meaning.'" Reprinted in *Mind, Language, Reality* 2. Cambridge: Cambridge University Press, 1975, pp. 215–271.

Quine, W. V. O. 1953. "Two Dogmas of Empiricism," *From a Logical Point of View* Cambridge. MA: Harvard University Press, pp. 20–46.

———. 1960. *Word and Object.* New York: John Wiley, pp. 91–95.

———. 1970. *Philosophy of Logic.* Englewood Cliff, NJ: Prentice-Hall, p. 65.

Richard, M. 1993. "Reference and Competence: Moravcsik's *Thought and Language.*" *Dialogue* 32: 555–563.

Rips, L. 1989. "Similarity, Typicality, and Categorization." In S. Vasniadou and A. Ortony, eds. *Similarity and Analogical Reasoning.* Cambridge: MIT Press, pp. 21–57.

———. 1991. "Similarity and the Structure of Categories." In D. Napol and J. Keyl, eds., *Bridges between Psychology and Linguistice.* Hillsdale, NJ: Erlbaum, pp. 35–53.

Rosch, E. 1978. "Principles of Categorization." In E. Rosch and B. B. Lloyd, eds., *Cognition and Categorization.* Hillsdale, NJ: Erlbaum, pp. 27–48.

Russell, B. 1918. *The Philosophy of Logical Atomism.* Minneapolis: Department of Philosophy of the University of Minnesota.

Salmon, W. 1989. "Four Decades of Scientific Explanation." *Minnesota Studies in the Philosophy of Science* 13: Minneapolis: 3–196.

Sen, A. 1986. "The Standard of Living." *Tanner Lectures on Human Values* 7. Utah: University of Utah Press, pp. 1–54.

Simons, P. 1987. *Parts. A Study in Ontology.* Oxford: Clarendon Press.

Stich, S. 1983. *From Folk Psychology to Cognitive Science.* Cambridge: MIT Press.

Strawson, P. F. 1949. "Truth." *Analysis* 9, no. 6.

———. 1950. "On Referring." *Mind* 59: 320–344.

———. 1963. *Introduction to Logical Theory.* London: Methuen.

Stroll, A. 1988. *Surfaces.* Minneapolis: University of Minnesota Press.

Tarski, A. 1936. "The Concept of Truth in Formalized Languages." Reprinted in *Logic, Semantics, and Meta-mathematics.* Oxford: Oxford University Press, 1956, 152–278.

Taylor, C. "Rationality." In *Philosophical Papers,* 1956, 2 ch. 5.

Urmson, J. 1968. "Criteria of Intentionality." *Proceedings of the Aristotelian Society,* suppl. vol. 42: 108–122.

Wittgenstein, L. 1922. *Tractatus Logico-Philosophicus.* London: Routledge & Kegan Paul.

INDEX